THE BLESSING AND THE CURSE

ALSO BY ADAM KIRSCH

Who Wants to Be a Jewish Writer?
And Other Essays

The Global Novel:
Writing the World in the 21st Century

The People and the Books:
18 Classics of Jewish Literature

Emblems of the Passing World:
Poems After Photographs by August Sander

Rocket and Lightship:
Essays on Literature and Ideas

Why Trilling Matters

Benjamin Disraeli

Invasions: Poems

The Modern Element:
Essays on Contemporary Poetry

The Wounded Surgeon:
Confession and Transformation in Six American Poets

The Thousand Wells: Poems

THE
BLESSING
AND THE
CURSE

*The Jewish People and Their Books
in the Twentieth Century*

ADAM KIRSCH

W. W. NORTON & COMPANY
Independent Publishers Since 1923

For information about permission to reproduce selections from this book, write to
Permissions, W. W. Norton & Company, Inc., 500 Fifth Avenue, New York, NY 10110

For information about special discounts for bulk purchases, please contact
W. W. Norton Special Sales at specialsales@wwnorton.com or 800-233-4830

Manufacturing by LSC Communications Harrisonburg
Book design by Lovedog Studio
Production manager: Julia Druskin

Library of Congress Cataloging-in-Publication Data

Names: Kirsch, Adam, 1976– author.
Title: The blessing and the curse : the Jewish people and their books in the
twentieth century / Adam Kirsch.
Description: First edition. | New York : W. W. Norton & Company, [2020] |
Includes bibliographical references and index.
Identifiers: LCCN 2020013974 | ISBN 9780393652406 (hardcover) |
ISBN 9780393652413 (epub)
Subjects: LCSH: Jewish literature—20th century—History and criticism. |
Judaism—20th century.
Classification: LCC PN842 .K468 2020 | DDC 809/.9335299240904—dc23
LC record available at https://lccn.loc.gov/2020013974

W. W. Norton & Company, Inc., 500 Fifth Avenue, New York, N.Y. 10110
www.wwnorton.com

W. W. Norton & Company Ltd., 15 Carlisle Street, London W1D 3BS

1 2 3 4 5 6 7 8 9 0

CONTENTS

III. ISRAEL: LIFE IN A DREAM

IV. MAKING JUDAISM MODERN

INTRODUCTION

N EAR THE END OF THE BOOK OF DEUTERONOMY, Moses charges the Israelites to keep the laws that God has given them, setting out two possible futures for the Jewish people. If they follow God's laws, they will be blessed with prosperity and power in their Promised Land: "And the Lord will make thee overabundant for good, in the fruit of thy body, and in the fruit of thy cattle, and in the fruit of thy land, in the land which the Lord swore unto thy fathers to give thee." But if they forsake God, they will be cursed with pestilence and famine, defeated in war and left powerless before their enemies: "The Lord will bring a nation against thee from far, from the end of the earth, as the vulture swoopeth down; a nation whose tongue thou shalt not understand; a nation of fierce countenance, that shall not regard the person of the old, nor show favor to the young."

Moses promises the Israelites that their fate lies in their own hands, that God will deal with them as they deserve: "I have set before thee life and death, the blessing and the curse; therefore choose life, that thou mayest live." Strangely, however, Moses's words also suggest that both parts of the prophecy, the blessing and the curse, are destined to come true: "And it shall come to pass, when all these things are come upon thee, the blessing and the curse, which I have set before thee." It is as if he could foresee that, over the next three thousand years, the Jewish people would experience both blessing and curse, not just once but over and over again, with eras of glory and security giving way to eras of dispossession and terror. But in no epoch did the Jews experience the blessing and the curse in more extreme forms than in the twentieth century. In the span of a single lifetime, things that Jews had long thought impossible, because they were too precious to dream about or too horrifying to imagine, came to pass.

✧ ✧ ✧ ✧

IN THE YEAR 1900, some seven million Jews lived in Eastern and Central Europe, about two-thirds of the world's Jewish population. The primacy of this Ashkenazi heartland had, in fact, already begun to erode. Starting in the 1880s, a vast emigration, ultimately numbering two million people, had begun to carry Jews out of Eastern Europe to a new life in the United States. Around the same time, a much smaller group of Jews, numbering in the tens of thousands, began to settle in Palestine under the inspiration of Zionist ideals. These movements created the nucleus of the two communities that now make up most of world Jewry: today, America and Israel are each home to about 5.5 million Jews. These emigrations also turned out to be lifeboats sent out at the last moment, for between 1939 and 1945, Eastern European Jewry was largely annihilated in the Holocaust, which killed six million Jews. As a result, the world's Jewish population is barely higher today than it was in 1900, even as the world's total population grew sevenfold.

Each of these three histories—the fate of the Jews in Europe, America, and Israel—was in its own way unprecedented. The Holocaust did not completely eradicate Jewish life in Europe—today, there are some 1.5 million Jews on the continent, now mostly in the west rather than the east—but it did destroy a Jewish civilization that had endured, despite persecutions and expulsions, for a thousand years. In the decades before the Holocaust, many European Jews had tried to join gentile civilization, many others had remained committed to traditional ways, and an intrepid few had tried to unite both worlds. But the Nazis were indiscriminate, killing every Jew they could find—and thereby falsifying every answer to the question of how the Jews could live in Europe. The extremity of the evil called into question the central assumptions of both traditional Judaism and Western civilization, and perhaps neither has fully recovered since.

Ironically, at the very same time that Europe was proving itself unimaginably hostile, America was proving itself unprecedentedly welcoming. In the United States, particularly after World War II, Jews found a more open and liberal environment than perhaps anywhere they had lived in the Diaspora. Previous Jewish golden ages— Islamic Spain, Enlightenment Germany—had offered limited cultural and political opportunities to an elite, at best; America offered security and openness to almost everyone. Indeed, for much of the twentieth century, the chief worry of American Judaism was that it might disappear in the warm embrace of assimilation and intermarriage— rather than in gas chambers, as was happening in Europe.

Meanwhile, Jews in Israel were fulfilling a dream even older than the dream of safety. In the year 70, after a Jewish revolt against Roman power, a Roman army destroyed the Temple in Jerusalem; in 135, after a second revolt, the Romans exiled the Jews from Judea and erased it from the map, renaming the province Syria Palestina (the origin of the modern name Palestine). For the next eighteen hundred years, no matter where they lived, Jews considered themselves to be in *galut*, exile. The idea that they would one day return to the Land of Israel was central to Judaism, if not to the actual daily lives of most Jews; but that return was conceived of in miraculous terms, as a deliverance that would come in the messianic age. But in 1948, after half a century of effort by Zionists and against violent opposition, the State of Israel was born, and Jewish sovereignty was restored in the very place where it had disappeared two millennia earlier.

Perhaps the best way to think of these twentieth-century destinies is as the liquidation of the Jewish concept of exile. In Europe, it was terminated by the death of six million Jews, which seemed to show that exile was no longer a possible way of life but only an avenue to death. In America, exile came to seem like a false description of Jewish life, as Jews began to see themselves as part of the new narrative of American immigration, rather than the ancient story of Jewish wandering. And in Israel, exile was directly refuted by Zionism, whose goal was the creation of a country where Jews could finally be at home, rather than unwanted guests. After all these transformations—and the enormous, universal transformation wrought by modern secularism and rationalism—how could Jews in the twentieth century continue to believe the same things in the same way that their ancestors did? But if they didn't—if most modern Jews no longer believed in Jewish doctrines or obeyed Jewish laws—then what did it mean to call themselves Jews?

In one way, at least, Jews met these revolutionary times with a traditional response: they wrote books. Judaism is a religion founded on texts—the Bible and the Talmud—and textual study had always been the hallmark of Jewish education; in rabbinic Judaism, mastery of textual interpretation was the highest religious as well as intellectual achievement. Over the centuries of exile, while Jews were largely unable to create physical monuments or exert political power, they channeled their creative energy into the production of books.

But in literary terms, too, the twentieth century marked a departure. In post-biblical Jewish writing, the most prestigious texts were not what we would now call imaginative literature. They were, rather, books of legal analysis, philosophy, mystical speculation, biblical interpretation, liturgical poetry, or moral instruction. Jewish literature was literature about Judaism in all its aspects. Not until the nineteenth century did this begin to change, as Jews made contact with secular European culture and began to produce autonomously literary writing. And not until the twentieth century does it become possible to gain an unprecedentedly rich and intimate understanding of Jewish experience by reading novels, poems, plays, and memoirs by Jewish writers—in Yiddish and Hebrew, as well as in English, Russian, German, and the other languages Jews began to speak in large numbers.

The Blessing and the Curse is divided into four sections, one for each of these themes in twentieth-century Jewish history: Europe, America, Israel, and the attempt to formulate Judaism as a modern faith. Each section offers a chronological survey of major books, drawing mainly on fiction and memoir in the first three sections, and on theology and philosophy in the fourth. The purpose of this arrangement is twofold—to introduce readers to some of the most significant and compelling Jewish books of the twentieth century, and to use these books to explore central aspects of Jewish experience.

In Europe, literature documents how it felt for Jews to see their future disappear, as the dark intuitions of the first decades of the century—given fictional form by writers like Franz Kafka, Isaac Babel, and Isaac Bashevis Singer—gave way to the even darker actualities witnessed by Victor Klemperer, Anne Frank, and Primo Levi. In America, literature shows how the New World made it possible for Jews to shed most of what had long defined Jewishness, only to leave them wondering what, if anything, made Jewish identity still meaningful. This quandary, which appears already in the earliest American Jewish fiction, by writers like Abraham Cahan and Anzia Yezierska, would take on moral, metaphysical, and political dimensions in the work of Saul Bellow, Philip Roth, Bernard Malamud, and Cynthia Ozick.

In Israel, literature occupied a particularly challenging role, as it carved out a space for individual imagination and experience in a place defined by collective effort and historical myth. Even before the State of Israel was created, this tension between Zionist dream and Israeli reality was a great theme for S. Y. Agnon, who first came to Palestine in the 1900s—just as it would be for writers like Amos Oz, David Grossman, and Yehuda Amichai. Finally, the last section, "Making Judaism Modern," examines the work of religious thinkers who tried to reconcile tradition with twentieth-century needs and realities, offering different strategies for synthesis and renewal—from the cultural Zionism of Martin Buber to the existential engagement of Abraham Joshua Heschel to the feminist reinventions of Judith Plaskow.

As this outline shows, the scope of the book is limited in important ways. It focuses primarily on Ashkenazi experience—that is, on Jews from Central and Eastern Europe and their descendants—

at the expense of Sephardic and Mizrahi experience. It focuses on secular and modern genres, which means that it takes little account of the writing that continued to be produced in traditional religious genres. And it discusses only books that are available in English translation. Clearly, this means *The Blessing and the Curse* cannot be a comprehensive history of twentieth-century Jewish writing, nor a canon of the best books by Jewish writers—though I believe most of the books discussed here would find a place in such a canon. Rather, my hope in writing this book is more modest: to use literature to illuminate the extreme contrasts of modern Jewish experience, while introducing the reader to some of the richness of twentieth-century Jewish writing.

I

EUROPE: THE FUTURE DISAPPEARS

The Road into the Open by Arthur Schnitzler and The Trial by Franz Kafka

VIENNA IN THE YEARS BEFORE WORLD WAR I WAS ONE of the golden ages of Jewish history. Over the preceding half-century, Jews from Austria's Polish and Ukrainian territories, freed from old residential restrictions, flocked to the capital's economic opportunities. In the 1850s, there were only 2,500 Jews in Vienna; by 1900, there were 150,000, almost 10 percent of the city's population. And while most of them were poor or working class, the Jewish bourgeoisie was prosperous and open minded enough to serve as the main patrons of the city's cultural and intellectual life. According to the writer Stefan Zweig, looking back on this period in his memoir *The World of Yesterday*, "the part played by the Jewish bourgeoisie in Viennese culture, through the aid and patronage it offered, was immeasurable. They were the real public, they filled seats at the theater and in concert halls, they bought books and pictures, visited exhibitions, championed and encouraged new trends everywhere with minds that were more flexible, less weighed down by tradition."

Jewish artists and thinkers, too, were central to the city's ferment. An inhabitant of Vienna in these years could have made an appointment with Sigmund Freud for psychoanalysis in the afternoon, heard Gustav Mahler conduct one of his new symphonies in the evening, and then stayed up late at a café listening to the arguments of writers like Zweig and Karl Kraus. Among their subjects would likely have been Zionism, the movement founded by the Viennese journalist Theodor Herzl in 1897.

Yet all of this activity did not endear the Jews of Vienna to their gentile neighbors. On the contrary, as the Jewish population of the city grew, so did popular anti-Semitism. From 1897 to 1910, the mayor of Vienna was Karl Lueger, an anti-Semitic politician who railed against the presence and influence of the Jews. Many Jews didn't take Lueger's hatred very seriously, but many of his gentile listeners did—including Adolf Hitler, who contracted his own case of virulent anti-Semitism while living in Vienna before World War I. The city that was a showcase of Jewish life also served as a testing ground for the Jew-hatred that was to culminate in the Holocaust.

During these years, Arthur Schnitzler was one of Vienna's most prominent Jewish writers. Trained as a doctor, he had given up medicine to pursue a career in literature—a choice that made perfect sense in a city that made a religion of the arts. Schnitzler became famous thanks to his 1903 play *Reigen* (better known by its French title, *La Ronde*)—an unsparing look at the city's erotic life, framed as a series of sexual encounters between partners from every social class, from prostitutes to noblemen. The play was too risqué to be performed publicly, but it became a best seller—and the source of much moralistic criticism, often framed in anti-Semitic terms.

In 1908, Schnitzler continued his investigation into Vienna's sexual malaise with the novel *The Road into the Open*. At the center of the novel is a gentile character—indeed, an aristocrat, Georg von Wergenthin, who embarks on an affair with a young Catholic girl named Anna Rosner. Georg is a study in indecision, refusing to make serious commitments either to his musical career, which he engages in only amateurishly, or to Anna, whom he gets pregnant but refuses to marry.

But what gives *The Road into the Open* its enduring interest is not Schnitzler's portrait of the sexual mores and spiritual drift of Viennese intellectuals. It is, rather, the novel's sympathetic portraits of Georg's Jewish friends, who are trying in various ways to come to terms with their anomalous place in an increasingly anti-Semitic society. For an aristocrat like Georg to have so many Jewish friends is a sign that, on an elite level at least, the barriers to social intercourse were declining. In these circles, a baron like Georg can socialize on equal terms with Jews like Else Ehrenberg—a music aficionado who cherishes a silent, unrequited love for him—or Heinrich Bermann, a writer who proposes to collaborate with him on an opera.

For most of the Jewish characters in *The Road into the Open*, Jewishness is no longer a religious identity or even a cultural one. In all visible respects, they share the same values and lead the same life-style as their gentile neighbors. Yet this only makes the anti-Semitism they face harder to deal with, since no conceivable adaptation on their part can defuse it. The result is that relationships between Jews and gentiles, even when they approach intimacy, are never without self-consciousness. They may be able to dissimulate some of the time, Schnitzler suggests, but at bottom every Jew mistrusts every Christian, and every Christian has contempt for every Jew. As Heinrich Bermann demands of Georg, "Do you think there's a single Christian in the world, even taking the noblest, straightest and truest one you like, one single Christian who has not in some moment or other of spite, temper or rage, made at any rate mentally some contemptuous allusion to the Jewishness of even his best friend, his mistress or his wife, if they were Jews or of Jewish descent?"

To Georg, on the other hand, it seems that Jews are simply too quick to take offense, too obsessed with their own Jewishness. "Why do they always begin to talk about it themselves? Wherever he went, he only met Jews who were ashamed of being Jews, or the type who were proud of it and were frightened of people thinking they were ashamed of it," Georg reflects. He can't understand why Jews lack the instinctive ease and self-confidence he enjoys as a titled aristocrat; as we might say today, he is blinded by his own privilege. Indeed, the very terms of his complaint show that Jews are in an impossible situation. Neither shame nor pride is the "right" reaction to their condition, but what is the alternative?

Through Georg's eyes, we witness the agonizing attempts of Vienna's young Jews to make sense of their place in a country that both is and is not their home. One of his acquaintances, the musician Leo Golowski, attends a Zionist Congress and is impressed by the serious purpose of the Jews who have embraced Zionism: "With these people, whom he saw at close quarters for the first time, the yearning for Palestine, he knew it for a fact, was no artificial pose. A genuine feeling was at work within them, a feeling that had never become extinguished and was now flaming up afresh under the stress of necessity." Leo, who is persecuted by an anti-Semitic army officer, ends up challenging the man to a duel and killing him—evidence, perhaps, of the self-respect that Zionism tried to imbue in Europe's Jews.

Leo's sister Therese, on the other hand, opts for the other great political movement of the age, socialism. She becomes a Social Democratic deputy to Parliament and spends time in jail for insulting the emperor. But no one in the novel takes her quite seriously—partly because she is an elegant young woman, partly because the idea of a future socialist revolution seemed incredible, at least in 1908. Meanwhile, Dr. Stauber, another young Jewish politician, has to resign his seat in the face of the unrelenting anti-Semitic abuse that is showered on him every time he gets up to speak in Parliament. Party politics, Schnitzler suggests, is no cure for the Jewish problem.

Then there is Oskar Ehrenberg, who believes he can force his way into Austrian society by aping the aristocracy and pretending not to be Jewish at all. This strategy ends in disaster when he demonstratively takes off his hat in front of the door of a church—a gesture of respect that is meant to help him pass as a Catholic—only to be seen by his father, who is infuriated at this Jewish betrayal and publicly boxes Oskar on the ears. The episode becomes the talk of the town, Oskar is disgraced, and he even tries to commit suicide; but he fails to aim properly and ends up losing an eye. His friends debate whether his fate is tragic or, as Therese says, "enough to make one laugh till one cried." For Jews in an anti-Semitic society, even suffering lacks dignity, since it is so bound up with feelings of shame and self-loathing.

In the end, it is left to Heinrich, Georg's closest Jewish friend, to express the true hopelessness of the situation. Heinrich rejects Zionism because he rejects any form of group identity: "He felt himself akin with no one, no, not with anyone in the whole world." For

Judaism, as for all religions, he has only contempt: "What does the faith of your father mean to you? A collection of customs which you have now ceased to observe and some of which seem as ridiculous and in as bad taste to you, as they do to me," he tells Leo. Yet while he rejects positive forms of solidarity, Heinrich identifies completely with the Jews when it comes to feeling shame and embarrassment. "We have been egged on from our youth to look upon Jewish peculiarities as particularly grotesque or repulsive," he explains to Georg. "I will not disguise it—if a Jew shows bad form in my presence, or behaves in a ridiculous manner, I have often so painful a sensation that I should like to sink into the earth."

But this revulsion does not delude Heinrich into thinking that he could ever become a true Austrian, either. In Austria, he says to Georg's shock, Jews are "in a foreign country, or . . . in an enemy's country." That is precisely why Jews are such good students of Austrian culture and society: after all, "the primary essential is to get to know one's enemies as well as possible—both their good qualities and their bad." Finally, Heinrich throws up his hands and declares that the problems of anti-Semitism and Jewish self-hatred will take at least a thousand years to solve:

> In our time there won't be any solution, that's absolutely positive. No universal solution at any rate. It will rather be a case of a million different solutions. For it's just a question which for the time being everyone has got to settle for himself as best he can. Everyone must manage to find an escape for himself out of his vexation or out of his despair or out of his loathing, to some place or other where he can breathe again in freedom . . . Everyone's life simply depends on whether or not he finds his mental way out.

As it turned out, the Jews of Vienna didn't have a thousand years to wait; they had exactly thirty. In 1938, Nazi Germany would annex Austria, amid a fierce outburst of popular anti-Semitism. Over the next year, about two-thirds of the city's Jewish population of 200,000 fled. The "mental way out" that Heinrich looked for was not nearly enough: of the Jews who remained in the city, all but 2,000 were exterminated in the Holocaust. By 1945, the Jewish population of Vienna had returned to the level of the 1850s; Jewish Vienna, it turned out, had lasted a little less than a century. The art and literature created in that brief span have made it an object of fascination and nostalgia ever since. But *The Road into the Open* is melancholy proof that even at their peak of wealth and achievement, the Jews of Central Europe sensed they were living a life without a future.

The hopelessness that Schnitzler diagnosed in *The Road into the Open* was not confined to Jews alone. Georg von Wergenthin himself suffers from a disease of the will that makes it impossible for him to commit to any course of action—whether it is his dream of becoming a great composer or his guilty sense that he is morally obligated to marry the mother of his child. For him, too, it seems impossible to chart a path to the future; he is a perpetual youth, "frivolous and a little unconscientious," as Heinrich describes him, who is never quite ready to take up the responsibilities of adulthood.

Georg, however, doesn't suffer from his condition, the way the novel's Jewish characters do. If he is living a dream, at least it is a pleasant dream, full of music and romance. It's not hard to see in this character Schnitzler's fond yet critical portrait of the Austro-Hungarian Empire itself, a country that used the arts as a narcotic to distract itself from the impending collapse everyone could see coming. Indeed, the empire would disappear in 1918, destroyed by the First World War and carved up by the nationalist ambitions of Czechs, Hungarians, and Slavs. Schnitzler's novel of imperial Vienna would lose its salience, and today it is read mainly by students of Austro-Hungarian literature and Jewish history.

But in August 1914, just days after the outbreak of World War I, another Jewish writer in the Austro-Hungarian Empire began a novel that would have a very different fate. Franz Kafka was thirty-one years old when he started *The Trial*, a writer with a modest local reputation who lived with his parents and spent his days working for an insurance company. But by night, he had recently begun to produce the strange, ambiguous, menacing stories that would turn his name into an adjective. Kafka worked on *The Trial* for about six months before setting the manuscript aside, and when he died—of tuberculosis, in 1924, at the age of just forty—it was still incomplete, just like his other two novels, *Amerika* and *The Castle*.

Kafka left instructions for his friend and literary executor, Max Brod, to destroy all of his unpublished work. But Brod, convinced of Kafka's genius, refused to carry out his wishes. Instead, he edited *The Trial*, which Kafka had left as a set of freestanding chapters, into something like a coherent sequence and arranged for it to be published. The first edition came out in 1925 and attracted little attention, but in the 1930s Kafka's reputation began to grow, and in the post–World War II era *The Trial* became one of the twentieth century's emblematic stories.

That story is so simple it can be summarized in a few sentences, yet so mysterious that countless pages have been devoted to analyzing it. Joseph K., an ordinary middle-class office worker, wakes up one morning to find that two men are waiting to arrest him. But they are not officers of any recognized court, and they never inform him what he is supposed to have done. All he is told is that he is now on trial, and the bulk of the novel consists of his encounters with various representatives of the unofficial legal system that has taken over his life—magistrates, guards, lawyers, even a chaplain. The more he finds out about the court, the clearer it becomes that its tentacles are everywhere, and it inspires genuine dread in the people Joseph K. meets. Yet at the same time, it is a ludicrous institution, whose officials wear shabby clothes and operate out of tenement attics, when they are not lecherously accosting women.

At first Joseph K. is indignant at the idea that this collection of charlatans could threaten him, and he makes self-righteous speeches about how he rejects the court's authority. But as time goes on—the novel takes place over the course of exactly one year—the anxiety of his situation preys on him and he becomes unable to think about anything except his trial, which he nurses like a serious illness. The worst part is that no one seems to be able to explain the laws under which he is being tried, which are infinitely complex.

All he can glean is that acquittal is seemingly impossible: "I know of no actual acquittals," the painter Titorelli tells Joseph K. "Of course it's possible that in the cases I'm familiar with no one was ever innocent. But doesn't that seem unlikely? In all those cases not one innocent person?" To which Joseph K. bitterly replies: "A single hangman could replace the entire court." Indeed, that proves to be the case with his own ordeal: at the end of the book, in an abrupt and terrifying scene, Joseph K. is seized by a pair of court-appointed executioners and slaughtered with knives—"like a dog," as he exclaims with his dying breath.

The Trial is deliberately stripped of the kind of realistic local references that tether Schnitzler's novel so closely to its time and place. While Kafka lived in Prague—one of the leading cities of the Austro-Hungarian Empire, and later the capital of the new state of Czechoslovakia—the city where Joseph K. lives contains no Prague place names or landmarks. The settings where the story unfolds are generically urban: a boardinghouse, a bank office, a church. Similarly, Joseph K. himself is deprived of a complete name, which might give us a clear sense of his nationality. He seems to be less a unique individual than a representative everyman.

This same vagueness extends to the most fundamental questions raised by the story, which are all left unanswered. Who is behind the unofficial court system that puts Joseph K. on trial? Where does its authority come from? What crime is he actually being accused of? How can such an elaborate organization, with offices throughout the city, go unnoticed by almost everyone? All such questions, which we might expect to be addressed in a realistic novel, simply fade into the background of *The Trial*. Kafka's story takes place in a very ordinary world, and this very ordinariness is part of its horror. The court does not stand above the world, judging it from a position of legitimate authority, but springs out suddenly from the world's holes and corners, where it lies in wait for the unsuspecting.

It is because ordinary narrative logic fails to apply in Kafka's story that it practically demands to be read as an allegory. One common way of understanding *The Trial* is as a prophecy of totalitarianism, which was just over the historical horizon when Kafka wrote in 1914. It's no coincidence that *The Trial* consolidated its reputation as a masterpiece just as totalitarian movements like fascism and Communism were taking root in Europe. For many readers then and since, the story of Joseph K. made intuitive sense as a parable of life under such regimes. His fate prefigures that of millions of victims of Soviet and Nazi persecution, who were put to death by arbitrary legal systems that turned their very existence into a crime.

To the poet and playwright Bertolt Brecht, Kafka's work was a prophecy of "the future concentration camps, the future instability of the law." Indeed, Kafka himself avoided being killed in the Holocaust only because he died so young; if he had lived until the 1940s, he would surely have ended up in Auschwitz, as many of his family members did. But even to later readers who did not experience these extremes of totalitarian violence, Kafka's depiction of the court's bureaucracy, with all its pettiness and inertia, can seem like a familiar description of the workings of any modern state.

At the same time, *The Trial* has also been read as a philosophical parable. The notion that human beings are born guilty, that they must struggle to achieve any kind of freedom, and that the world itself is irrational and absurd, were all central to the existentialist thought that became influential in the post–World War II years. Joseph K. can be seen as the original existentialist hero—an ordinary man thrown into a world he did not create and must struggle to understand before he succumbs to an inevitable death sentence.

How did Kafka become a prophet of experiences that, not long after he died, were to become so universal? The key, as his first readers were quick to understand, lay in his Jewishness. The word "Jew" never appears in *The Trial*, and it is entirely possible to read it without knowing or suspecting that Kafka was Jewish. Yet Kafka was not far removed in time or space from the Jews of Schnitzler's novel. Like them, he spent his whole life in a Jewish community frequently beset by popular anti-Semitism; and like them, he was not religiously observant. Kafka's upbringing in an assimilated family left him with ambivalent feelings about Judaism, as he explained in a long letter to his father:

> [Your Judaism] was too little to be handed on to the child; it all dribbled away while you were passing it on. In part, it was youthful memories that could not be passed on to others; in part, it was your dreaded personality. It was also impossible to make a child, over-acutely observant from sheer nervousness, understand that the few flimsy gestures you performed in the name of Judaism, and with an indifference in keeping with their flimsiness, could have any higher meaning.

Despite this legacy, as an adult Kafka took a serious interest in Jewish subjects, including Yiddish theater and Zionism. Toward the end of his life, he even began to study Hebrew in preparation for a possible emigration to Palestine. If figures like Schnitzler's Heinrich Bermann were painfully aware of their Jewishness in every moment, how could it not have been equally important to Kafka, who resembles them in so many ways—above all, in his extreme self-consciousness?

Indeed, one way to read *The Trial* is as an oblique fable about the same Jewish condition that Schnitzler treated in a direct, realistic mode. "Someone must have slandered Joseph K.," says the book's first sentence, "for one morning, without having done anything wrong, he was arrested." Is this not the very condition in which the assimilated Jews of Europe found themselves—the targets of hatred and suspicion that they could not dispel because it was not based on their actual character or actions, but on myth and prejudice? These Jews were constantly on trial in the court of gentile opinion, and like Joseph K. they were doomed to lose their case, because they faced hostile judges who operated according to indefinable rules.

At first, Joseph K. believes that he can rise above this hostility, the way that many assimilated Jews believed that anti-Semitism was a mere nuisance, not to be taken too seriously. In an early scene, he makes a long, self-righteous speech to the crowd at his first court hearing: "I'm completely detached from this whole affair, so I can judge it calmly," he assures them. He claims to be interested only in abstract fairness: "What has happened to me is merely a single case and as such of no particular consequence, but it is typical of the proceedings brought against many people. I speak for them, not for myself." But this lofty rhetoric only annoys the crowd, and makes the magistrates still more biased against him.

The kind of hostility Joseph K. is dealing with, he learns over the course of the novel, cannot be sidestepped or dismissed. It is serious, irrational, and in the end, lethal. Nothing Joseph K. does to prove his innocence will be of any use; he is on trial not for something he has done, but simply because he has been singled out. In all these ways, his situation exactly matches that of a Jew trying to fit into an anti-Semitic society. (The same dynamic can be identified in several of Kafka's short stories, particularly "Report to an Academy," in which an ape reports on his painful attempts to assimilate to life among human beings.)

And the ending of *The Trial* can be read as a foreboding of the fate of Europe's Jews, who in a shockingly short time went from respectable citizens to pariahs to victims of slaughter. In the novel's last scene, what strikes Joseph K. as he faces death at the hands of the court's executioners is the nearness and indifference of bystanders. He spies a person leaning out of a window and asks: "Who was it? A friend? A good person? Someone who cared? Someone who wanted to help? Was it just one person? Was it everyone?" These are exactly the questions that, less than thirty years after Kafka wrote *The Trial*, his own friends and family members might have asked about the gentile neighbors who watched as they were deported to Auschwitz.

The key to the unsettling power of *The Trial*, however, and to its global readership and influence, is that unlike Schnitzler, Kafka did not write about these experiences as Jewish experiences. Rather, he allowed the Jewishness of *The Trial*, and of much of his other work, to remain a kind of optical illusion, visible only to those readers who were equipped to recognize it. Part of what creates the atmosphere we have come to call Kafkaesque is precisely this sense that there are reasons and motives at work in his writing that he does not explain.

It would thus be wrong to say that *The Trial* is "really" about anti-Semitism, as if the work's many other theological and political dimensions were illusory. But it was surely his experience of being a modern European Jew at a time of profound Jewish crisis that gave Kafka such an intimate knowledge of the alienation and isolation, the helplessness and guilt, that would be shared by so many people in the twentieth century. Jewishness, he suggests, is not a unique fate but an extreme one, which equips the writer—at least, when the writer is Kafka—to see truths too terrible for most people to recognize until it is too late.

Red Cavalry
by Isaac Babel

THE DEVASTATION OF WORLD WAR I WAS ESPECIALLY intense in the heartland of Eastern European Jewry. The territories of Poland and Ukraine lay on the border between the enemy empires—Russia on the east, Germany and Austria on the west—and some of the worst fighting of the war passed repeatedly through the area. In 1915, the Russian government, suspicious of the loyalties of a long-mistreated Jewish population, expelled more than half a million Jews from the border zone, resulting in some 60,000 civilian deaths from exposure, disease, and hunger. Jews also fought and died in large numbers in the opposing armies: 100,000 Jewish soldiers were killed on the Russian side and 40,000 on the Austrian. By the end of the war, Jewish Eastern Europe lay in ruins. Poverty, hunger, and dislocation were widespread, and only charity efforts from abroad, especially the United States, prevented even worse suffering.

Nor did the formal conclusion of the World War mean an end to the ordeal. The Russian Revolution of 1917 gave rise to a series of further regional wars, as the Bolshevik government fought against counter-revolutionary White armies. After the German surrender in 1918, nationalist movements in Ukraine and Poland fought for independence against the Red Army, which sought to reincorporate them into the Soviet empire. These wars unleashed terrible anti-Semitic passions, as national and religious hatreds took on a new ideological dimension.

Only a small percentage of Jews had ever been Communists,

and Communism in power proved to be a deadly enemy of traditional Jewish religion and culture. But in czarist Russia, Communism attracted a following among Jews who believed it was the only chance for a better future, free of ethnic and religious hatred. Jews were overrepresented among the leadership of the new Soviet Communist Party, including most notably Leon Trotsky, the commander of the Red Army. After 1918, Jews in Ukraine and Poland often welcomed Soviet forces as a bulwark against local anti-Semitism.

The result was that among many Poles and Ukrainians, anti-Russian, anti-Communist, and anti-Jewish feeling merged, with catastrophic results. In 1919–20, some 100,000 Jews were murdered in pogroms in Poland and Ukraine, vastly more than the number killed during the well-publicized pogroms of the prewar period. Though these atrocities are often forgotten today, in light of the genocide to come in World War II, the postwar slaughter was at the time the worst mass killing of Jews since the seventeenth century.

Isaac Babel witnessed this traumatic chapter in Jewish history from an unusual vantage point. Babel was born in 1894 in Odessa, the Ukrainian city on the Black Sea that was a center of Jewish intellectual and literary life. He combined a traditional Jewish education with modern, Russian-language schooling, and during World War I he moved to St. Petersburg to launch his literary career. Under the influence of the revolutionary writer Maxim Gorky, Babel moved into the Communist orbit, and he worked for several government agencies after the Bolshevik Revolution.

In 1920, during the Polish-Soviet War, Babel was a correspondent for the Soviet state news agency, assigned to the First Cavalry Army—a formation of Cossack horsemen under the command of Semyon Budyonny, a future marshal of the Soviet Union. The Cossacks were seen by Jews as their historic persecutors, their name a byword for barbarous violence. In the seventeenth century, Cossacks under the command of the Ukrainian leader Bogdan Chmielnicki had slaughtered some 100,000 Jews in one of the bloodiest episodes in all of Jewish history.

Babel's position, then, was full of contradictions. As a Jew, the

Cossacks were his enemies; but these were Soviet Cossacks, fighting in support of the Communist regime that promised to abolish anti-Semitism. The Soviets saw themselves as representatives of the enlightened, secular future, fighting against Polish priests and landlords; yet they retained much of their traditional anti-Jewish feeling. Personally, too, Babel was an odd man out in the army—a civilian and intellectual rather than a horseman or soldier.

Writing at the intersection of Jew and Cossack, intellectual and warrior, Babel produced a series of short stories about his wartime experiences that were published in 1926 as *Red Cavalry*. In many ways, *Red Cavalry* was an unlikely book to become a classic of Soviet literature. For one thing, it was the chronicle of a defeat: after initial successes, the Russian armies were pushed out of Poland and finally had to sue for peace, with Russia giving up territory to the new Polish state.

For another, Babel did little in these tales to idealize the Soviet soldier and worker, in the way that would be required by socialist realism in the Stalinist period. He portrayed his fellow soldiers as brave and loyal, but also unbelievably brutal, ignorant, and violent. Their stories become even more lurid thanks to Babel's unique prose style, which is full of startling images and surprising, artificial metaphors. He took full advantage of the climate of artistic experimentation that followed the Russian Revolution, when it seemed that a new society would encourage new ways of writing and seeing.

Babel's insistence on writing about people as they actually are, rather than as ideology wants them to be, receives a covert defense in the story "Pan Apolek." Apolek is an itinerant church painter who gets in trouble with the Polish Catholic authorities because his portraits of biblical figures are based on recognizable local people—and not only the prominent or respectable; his Mary Magdalene is based on a neighborhood prostitute. Shocked by this apparent blasphemy, the priests try to have Apolek's murals painted over. "He has installed you among the saints in your own lifetimes," a bishop complains. But that is exactly why the common people love the paintings and insist on keeping them. Daringly, Babel uses Apolek's religious art to advance a radically democratic aesthetic. After all, the promise of Communism is that the lowest members of society—workers, peasants, even prostitutes and criminals—will be redeemed; and wasn't this Jesus's promise as well?

It is in this spirit of realism that Babel portrays the murders, rapes, and thefts committed by the Cossacks of Budyonny's army. In "Salt," a woman boards a train full of soldiers who are at first solicitous of her, because she claims to be carrying an infant. When it turns out that her bundle is actually a bag of salt, which she plans to sell on the black market, the soldiers turn in a flash from defenders into righteous avengers: she is betraying both motherhood and the revolution, and they immediately throw her off the train and shoot her. "We will deal mercilessly with all traitors," brags the killer, a soldier called Balmashov.

In their barbaric grandeur, Babel's soldiers sometimes resemble the heroes of the *Iliad*, not least in their easily inflamed sense of honor. In "The Story of a Horse," a Cossack named Khlebnikov tearfully quits the Communist Party after a superior officer confiscates his white stallion. "The Communist Party was founded, I believe, for happiness and unwavering justice without limit," he writes in his letter of resignation. So how can a Communist officer be so unjust as to steal a Cossack's horse, which is his pride and joy?

This story offers a bathetic treatment of what turns out to be a central theme of *Red Cavalry*: the glaring disjunction between the high ethical claims of the Communist army and its actual behavior. Some of the men we meet in Babel's stories demonstrate extraordinary ideological commitment. In "Treason," the same Balmashov who killed the woman on the train rages against a conspiracy, as he sees it, to keep him in the hospital, away from the front, even though he is badly wounded. In some cases, the soldiers' simplicity is almost a species of holiness—as with the soldier nicknamed Sashka Christ, "because of his meekness."

Yet Babel leaves the reader poised between admiration for the soldiers' courage and horror at their brutality. Often in these stories death takes place casually, as in "Beresteczko," where the narrator remarks in passing that "under my window, several Cossacks were shooting an old Jew with a silvery beard for espionage." Babel can never quite manage to close his eyes to this violence, even though he knows that pity is a betrayal of both revolutionary sternness and soldierly stoicism. And as a Jew himself, he is unusually alert to the tragedy of the mainly Jewish civilians caught in the crossfire between Soviets and Poles.

In the first story in the book, "Crossing the Zbrucz," the Babel-like narrator is billeted in the house of a poor Jewish family, where he finds the corpse of an old man murdered by the Poles. At first, the narrator affects a stern indifference; but the last word in the story goes to the dead man's daughter, who recounts how he was killed and demands, "with terrible force," "where else in all the world would you find a father like my father . . ." In the face of mass violence committed in the name of the state, this Jewish woman insists on preserving the unique identity of the victim.

Officially, so to speak, Babel's narrator sneers at such innocence, seeing it as mere sentimentality that has no place in revolutionary times. In one of the best-known stories in *Red Cavalry*, "Gedali," the narrator encounters an old Jewish man who complains that while he believes in the Bolshevik Revolution, he can't accept the injustices that come with it. "Good deeds are done by good men. But good men do not kill. That means the revolution is being made by bad men," Gedali reasons. In Babel's telling, this ethical simplicity is closely linked to Gedali's role as a representative of the Jewish past— a religion and culture that is in the process of being destroyed by war and revolution.

But the narrator, as a committed revolutionary, has no choice but to look down on Gedali's naïveté. When Gedali complains, "The International, *panie* comrade, one doesn't know what to eat it with," the narrator replies with bravado: "One eats it with gunpowder, and seasons it with the finest blood." Yet in the story's last paragraphs, the narrator turns out to long for a very different kind of food: he asks Gedali for "a Jewish shortcake, a Jewish glass of tea," the familiar flavors of his own childhood. In this way, Babel delicately suggests that he himself is torn between the stern Communist vision of the future and the gentle Jewish spirit of the past.

That self-division is one of the central themes of Red Cavalry, and Babel makes clear that it is a product of the narrator's anomalous position as a Jew among Russian soldiers. The Cossack ideal of manhood—tough, brutal, passionate—has a great allure for him; he thrills, for instance, to the exotic sight of a commander combing his horse's mane with his pistol. And he longs to prove to his comrades that he can be just as bloodthirsty as they are. In "My First Goose," the narrator is initially an outcast in his army unit, simply because his glasses mark him as a reader, an intellectual, and perhaps by implication a Jew. It is only when he proves his toughness by roughly confiscating and slaughtering an old woman's goose that he begins to find acceptance. This is the gratification of his dearest wish—and yet the story ends with the narrator suffering from bad dreams, in which "my heart, stained crimson with murder, squeaked and overflowed." The role of Cossack remains foreign to his nature, which is more akin to Gedali's than he wants to acknowledge.

Despite all the rigors he undergoes over the course of Red Cavalry, Babel's narrator remains an outsider, unable to join wholeheartedly in his comrades' ways. The last story in the book, "Argamak," is another drama revolving around a horse; in this case, the titular stallion is taken away from its owner, Tikhomolov, and assigned to the narrator. But he is not a skilled enough horseman to ride this powerful beast, and Argamak ends up lamed. When Tikhomolov sees what has been done to the horse, he burns with cold fury at the narrator, who has proved himself unworthy of Argamak—and, by implication, unworthy of his place in the army. Only in his dreams does the narrator become a skilled rider, and what is so glorious about these dreams is that none of the Cossacks are paying attention to him: "Their indifference signified that there was nothing special about my manner of sitting in the saddle, I rode the way everyone else did, there was no reason to look at me."

Here is the same Jewish dream that Schnitzler's alienated urban Jews knew—the dream of being inconspicuous, of simply belonging.

For Babel, this is one of the promises of the revolution, and at the very end of "Argamak," he writes that it can come true: eventually, he says, he learned how to ride properly, and "my dream was fulfilled. The Cossacks stopped following me and my horse with their eyes." But this dream does not come true within the confines of *Red Cavalry* itself. It remains a wishful prospect, just as the perfect society promised by the revolution is always still to come.

Babel's most convincing image of the Jewish Communist, rather, comes in the story "The Rebbe's Son," in which the narrator recognizes a dying soldier named Ilya as the son of a Hasidic rebbe—a kind of prince of Judaism, who has given up his birthright to enlist in the Communist forces. When he goes through Ilya's trunk, he finds evidence of a divided spirit: "Portraits of Lenin and Maimonides lay side by side . . . A strand of female hair had been placed in a book of the resolutions of the Sixth Party Congress, and in the margins of communist leaflets swarmed crooked lines of Ancient Hebrew verse."

How can the Jew and the Communist in Ilya be reconciled? Or is his death in combat the only possible solution? At moments in *Red Cavalry*, Babel darkly suggests that perhaps there is no future for the Jews of Poland and Russia. Ostensibly, the Soviet forces are fighting for the abolition of anti-Semitism—after all, Babel, a Jew, is allowed a role in the Red Army that he could never have played in the czar's army. Yet Babel knows that it is not just the reactionary Polish enemy who hates the Jews. "The Jew is guilty before all men, both ours and yours," observes a Russian peasant in the story "Zamosc." When he asks the narrator how many Jews there are in the world, and receives the answer "ten million," he muses that after the war, "There'll be two hundred thousand of them left."

This turned out to be a more accurate prophecy than Babel could have imagined. By the end of World War II, the Jewish population of Poland had been reduced by the Nazis from 3.5 million to about 250,000. By that time, Babel too was dead, but it wasn't Hitler who killed him. Rather, he was murdered in one of Stalin's camps in 1940—a victim of the revolution he tried so hard to praise.

Satan in Goray
by Isaac Bashevis Singer

POLAND EMERGED FROM THE POLISH-SOVIET WAR with expanded borders, controlling large swaths of formerly Russian and Ukrainian territory, along with the people who lived in it. Of the 29 million citizens of Poland, one-third were not ethnically Polish, but Ukrainian, German, Lithuanian, Byelorussian, or Jewish. And the three million Jews of Poland soon found that living in an independent state was not necessarily an improvement over czarist rule. On the contrary, Poland cultivated an identity based on ethnic nationalism and Catholicism, which tended to exclude Jews from full membership in the community.

Jews and other minorities were supposed to be protected by laws and treaties, backed up by the new League of Nations. But these protections quickly proved impossible to enforce in the face of widespread popular hostility. Instead, there was a continually increasing pressure on Poland's Jewish population, which took social, political, and economic forms. Attempts were made to ban kosher slaughter; Jewish students in Polish universities were attacked; the nation's largest political party, the National Democrats, called for the boycott and expulsion of the Jews. Poland was a poor country, but these pressures made the Jews' plight especially difficult. The historian Howard Sachar writes that by 1936, two-thirds of Polish Jews were receiving charity, many from organizations funded by the donations of American Jews. Meanwhile, high birth rates meant that the Jewish population continued to grow, resulting in further economic strain.

Before World War I, increasing poverty and oppression in the czarist empire had motivated millions of Jews to emigrate. But in the
interwar years, and especially once the Depression began in 1929,
many traditional Jewish destinations shut their doors—including
the United States, which severely restricted immigration from Eastern Europe. In Palestine, which had been intended as a Jewish home
under the terms of the Balfour Declaration, the British Mandatory
government accepted a strictly limited number of Jewish immigrants.
Altogether, only some 400,000 Polish Jews managed to emigrate in
the twenty years between the world wars.

One of those emigrants was a young writer named Isaac Singer,
who was known to the readers of the Yiddish press by his pen name
Bashevis—a tribute to his mother, Batsheva. Singer, born in 1902,
was the son of a Hasidic rabbi, and he was educated to become a
rabbi himself. But in the early 1920s, he exchanged Torah and tradition for a modern literary career. In making this break, he was
following in the footsteps of his older brother, Israel Joshua Singer,
who was already well established as a Yiddish writer and journalist.
In 1935, Isaac followed Israel's example once again by emigrating to
New York. Explaining this decision in an interview decades later,
Singer recalled the atmosphere of the time: "The situation of the Jews
in Poland became worse from day to day . . . My only hope was to
come to America. I foresaw that there would be no rest in Poland."

In the following decades, Isaac Bashevis Singer would become
the world's most famous Yiddish writer, eclipsing his older brother
and finally winning the Nobel Prize for Literature in 1978. When
he arrived in New York in 1935, however, there was no sign of this
future glory. At the age of thirty-three, he was the author of just
one book, which appeared in print just after he left Poland. Yet that
novel, *Satan in Goray*, was already the work of a master, marked by
the obsessions that would continue to drive Singer's work for the rest
of his life: sexuality, transgression, the supernatural, and the spiritual
chaos that emerges when traditional religion disappears. Indeed, the
crisis atmosphere that characterized European Jewish literature in
the early twentieth century finds its most acute and grotesque expres-

sion in *Satan in Goray*. Here is a portrait of a Polish Jewish community broken by war and massacre, cut loose from tradition, its faith
in itself and in the future shattered. This was the Jewish world Singer
knew firsthand; he had spent part of his childhood in a shtetl called
Bilgoray, which served as a model for the town of Goray in the novel.

Singer, however, writes about the twentieth-century crisis only
allegorically. It is left to the reader to draw comparisons between
the Polish Jews of 1935 and the Polish Jews of *Satan in Goray*, which
is set in the year 1666. But those similarities are not hard to find.
In 1935, the Jews of Poland were less than twenty years removed
from World War I and the massacres that followed it; likewise, in
1666, the Jews of Ukraine were less than twenty years removed from
the Chmielnicki massacres, which have left the small town of Goray
a depopulated ruin. The terrors of the Chmielnicki period are not
directly narrated, though Singer lists them in a brief catalogue: "They
slaughtered on every hand, flayed men alive, murdered small children, violated women and afterward ripped open their bellies and
sewed cats inside."

These horrors are unbelievable, yet they really happened—a paradox that will haunt the bizarre story Singer tells in *Satan in Goray*.
For in a world where live cats can be sewed into women's bodies, how
can anything be ruled out as incredible or impossible? Is the existence
of ghosts and devils really any harder to believe in than what these
people actually lived through? Certainly, the experiences of the Jews
of Goray seem to have erased their sense of any boundary between
reality and dream. Events that, to the twentieth-century reader, can
only be superstitious or symbolic—demonic possessions, encounters
with devils and dybbuks—are to them very real; and Singer's novel
implicitly asks whether that antique sense of reality might be closer
to the truth than a modern, secular worldview, which has so much
trouble making sense of the forces of evil.

As the novel opens, the scattered survivors of the town of Goray
are beginning to make their way back home, hoping to rebuild their
lives. But they have been permanently scarred by their ordeals, and
the traditional Jewish life of the past, with its strict religious and

social hierarchy, has come undone. Rabbi Benish, once the stern, benevolent ruler of the town, now faces disorder and indifference even within his own family. Eleazar Babad, the richest man in Goray, is now impoverished, and his daughter, Rechele, is half insane, a shut-in who refuses to receive guests, much less consider suitors.

At first, this social breakdown manifests itself in trivial ways: "Time and again Rabbi Benish called a town meeting, only to have the townspeople doze off, or yawn at the walls. They would agree to everything, but carry out nothing." But this apathy and demoralization conceals a tremendous spiritual need. The people of Goray are desperate for someone to explain why their world was destroyed and what they should do next. Rabbi Benish is helpless to provide this guidance; he is a conservative figure, hoping to bring back the way things used to be before the disaster. The people of Goray, however, want to be told something different. They are hungry for a new world and a new Judaism. "In almost every town," Singer writes, "one person ran about testifying that the Jews would all soon be redeemed. Some declared that they could hear the great ram's horn being blown, signifying the end of days."

When news arrives that a messiah has arisen in the Land of Israel, then, many of the Jews of Goray are eager to listen. This was Sabbatai Zevi, a Sephardic Jew from the Ottoman Empire, whose claims to be the promised redeemer caught the imagination of the whole Jewish world in 1665–66. From Amsterdam to Jerusalem, Jewish communities fractured as many people declared themselves followers of Sabbatai Zevi. Some sold all their possessions in expectation of the imminent end of the world. What's more, the Sabbateans, who called themselves "Believers," believed that in the messianic age that was about to begin, most Jewish laws and observances would be abolished, lending a transgressive tone to the movement. Stories circulated that Sabbateans were deliberately engaging in sins, especially sexual sins, to demonstrate that they had been liberated from Jewish law.

The forms that Sabbateanism takes in Singer's Goray are dramatic and grotesque. As soon as the news of Sabbatai Zevi reaches the town, submerged enmities and power struggles begin to surface. Rabbi Benish tries to silence the rumors, while Mordecai Joseph, a man who was previously considered an eccentric loser, emerges as the head of the Sabbatean party. In a disturbing scene, Mordecai leads a mob that beats a man almost to death inside the study house itself, in a parody of the Yom Kippur scapegoat ritual.

Meanwhile, Rechele, who had previously seemed merely unbalanced, now begins to issue Sabbatean prophecies that she says were confided to her by an angel. At her wedding, to a fellow Believer who is himself impotent and half mad, men and women end up dancing together. It is a clear sign of the social and sexual chaos that the new movement is helping to inspire. When Rabbi Benish tries to stop it, he is kept from approaching the wedding by what could be simply a strong winter wind—though the novel suggests, and Benish himself believes, that it is a demonic power. This blurring of nature and the supernatural is one of the ways Singer creates such a powerful sense of disquiet in the novel; as readers, we never know how far we are expected to accept the events described as literally true.

As the book progresses, the supernatural becomes harder and harder to deny. After Rabbi Benish flees Goray, his place is taken by Reb Gedaliah, a slaughterer by trade who becomes the town's spiritual dictator. (For Singer, who was a principled vegetarian, Gedaliah's profession is already a sign that he is on the side of wickedness; the novel is full of disgusting descriptions of bloody meat.) Gedaliah steals the uncanny Rechele from her husband, enacting a public but illicit union with a woman he regards as a direct conduit to the Divine Presence. When Rechele appears at the synagogue, she mesmerizes the congregation: "Calling by name angels and seraphim, she told of the heavenly mansions and the lords ruling in each of them . . . Several individuals fainted."

In keeping with this apocalyptic atmosphere, Gedaliah encourages the people to break Jewish laws, especially the laws relating to sexual purity. There is no reason to worry about punishment for sin, because the people of Goray have ceased to believe in the existence of the future—that is, of any future that resembles the past.

Nothing they do matters any longer, because the Messiah is about to appear and they will all be transported bodily to Jerusalem: "The afflicted would be healed, the ugly made beautiful. Everyone would eat from golden dishes and drink only wine." Singer demonstrates the deep connection between messianism and despair: it is when this world becomes unbearable that the next world starts to seem possible, because it is necessary.

This condition was familiar to many European Jews in the early twentieth century, and it drove some of them to embrace modern forms of messianic hope, from Zionism to Communism. But Singer implies that twentieth-century ideologies of total transformation are as sinister, and finally as hopeless, as Sabbateanism was, since all messiahs turn out to be false messiahs. Indeed, in 1666, the Ottoman sultan offered Sabbatai Zevi the choice of conversion to Islam or death, and the Jewish savior became a Muslim.

In Singer's novel, when this shattering news reaches Goray, some of the Sabbateans lose their faith while others cling to it all the more strongly. For these devoted Believers, Sabbatai Zevi's apostasy conceals a deep theological mystery, inspiring them to commit their own liberating sins, including incest. The demoralization of the Jews is complete, so that even their Christian neighbors are shocked by their behavior. For while the enemies of the Jews can bring physical destruction upon them, Singer suggests, only the Jews themselves can commit spiritual suicide.

It is Rechele, the prophetess of Goray's "Believers," who demonstrates how difficult it is to rid one's soul of the madness of false hope. In a harrowing final chapter written in the style of a medieval Yiddish chronicle, Singer describes the exorcism she undergoes, in an attempt to rid her of the voice within—a voice that now appears demonic rather than divine. This scene is the culmination of the horror-movie element in *Satan in Goray*, a phantasmagoria in which Rechele copulates with Satan, vomits up reptiles, barks like a dog, and exposes her genitals to a crowd of onlookers. Finally, just before she is released by merciful death, a confession is extorted from the dybbuk that is dwelling in her body: "I rebelled at every command of God and incurred his wrath: On the holy Sabbath day I did work and I did eat of the pig and of the other forbidden foods . . . Woe is me for I said in my heart, There is neither Justice nor Judge, and I denied that the Torah is from Heaven."

Notably, this statement could equally well serve as the confession of a demon, the proud declaration of a Sabbatean, or the rationalist credo of a modern atheist. It is Singer's implicit rebuke to the twentieth-century reader who might see these seventeenth-century characters as benighted, superstitious, prey to irrational fears. But if the old-world Jew could observe his descendants, Singer suggests, he would surely see them as dangerous sinners—and he might be right. Perhaps the modern world, which prides itself on liberation from the old Jewish ways and laws, is simply following the same antinomian impulse that led the Sabbateans into destruction, and for the same reason: the despair that is born from living in a world without a future.

The Diary of
Victor Klemperer

S INGER IMAGINED THE DOOM OF THE JEWS IN SCENES
of lurid horror; Kafka, in the working of sinister, oppressive
laws; Babel, in visions of war and extermination. As it turned out,
they would all be proved right. The Nazi Holocaust would take the
lives of six million Jews during World War II, in countless acts of
unimaginable, demonic cruelty. But the first steps were taken in Germany in 1933, when the new chancellor Adolf Hitler began to turn
the country's laws against its half-million Jewish citizens. They must
have felt just as Joseph K. did—that they woke up one morning to
find they had been slandered, accused of a crime they didn't commit.

Certainly, it would have been hard to find a more devoted German
than Victor Klemperer, who in 1933 was a fifty-two-year-old professor at Dresden Technical University. After all, he had served in the
German army in World War I, seeing combat on the Western Front.
He was married to a non-Jewish woman, his beloved wife Eva. As a
professor of French literature, he saw himself as contributing to the
progress of European culture. The fact that he was Jewish by birth—
his father had been the rabbi of a Reform congregation in Berlin—
was hardly relevant to Klemperer's idea of himself, especially after
he chose to be baptized as a Protestant in 1912.

But Klemperer's fellow citizens made clear that his feeling of
belonging to Germany was not mutual. On March 5, 1933, a general
election gave the Nazis a huge electoral victory: they received 42 percent of the vote, beating their closest rivals, the left-wing Social Dem-

ocrats, by ten million votes. What a Nazi government would mean for Germany's Jews was clear to everyone—the party had made extreme anti-Semitism the core of its identity from the beginning—and Hitler didn't wait long before delivering on his promises. On April 1, he declared a one-day national boycott of Jewish-owned businesses. Nazi stormtroopers stood in front of the targeted firms, carrying signs with slogans like "The Jews are our misfortune."

For Klemperer, the idea of himself and his country that he had built up over a lifetime was suddenly shattered. "I have always truly felt a German," he wrote in his diary. "I have always imagined: The twentieth century and *Mitteleuropa* [Central Europe] was different from the fourteenth century and Romania. Mistake." The anxieties that had haunted German-speaking Jewish writers like Schnitzler and Kafka now proved not to be neurotic after all, but prescient. Jew-hatred had not been made obsolete by modernity. On the contrary, it had been enhanced, transformed from a popular mood into a political program of ruthless effectiveness.

Yet in the early days of the Nazi regime, Klemperer could still write, "I feel shame more than fear, shame for Germany." The nation he believed in was failing to live up to its own best self. It was up to Klemperer to maintain the ideal Germany—cultured, humane, democratic—even as the Nazis brought a world war to Europe and destruction to the Jews. Indeed, over the twelve years of the Third Reich, as Klemperer's situation grew steadily worse—moving from ostracism to poverty to virtual house arrest to near starvation and constant risk of murder—the one thing he could cling to was his certainty that he remained a German. As late as May 1942, with Hitler's armies triumphant and the Holocaust under way in Eastern Europe, Klemperer continued to insist, "I am German and am waiting for the Germans to come back; they have gone to ground somewhere."

Until the Germans "came back," there was little that Klemperer could do but write. As a journalist turned professor, writing was both the habit of a lifetime and the best way he had to make sense of the world. At first he continued to work on a history of French literature that he had begun before 1933, even though he knew that books by

Jewish authors could not be published in Nazi Germany. But eventually his right to use the university library for research was revoked, and he had to give up the work. Instead, Klemperer concentrated on keeping his diary—a lifelong project that became, in the Nazi years, both a means of preserving his sanity and a unique contribution to the historical record.

This was an enormous undertaking. When Klemperer's diary was published in English in 1998, under the title *I Will Bear Witness*, it filled two volumes totaling more than a thousand closely printed pages. The sheer bulk of the diary made it hard to conceal, presenting Klemperer with a problem that became increasingly serious as the pace of Gestapo house searches increased. He regularly wondered whether the risk was justified: "Under these circumstances is it at least a courageous act that I keep this diary?" he asked himself. "I am not sure." Once World War II started and Nazi persecution became more intense and deadly, Klemperer grew accustomed to the idea that he could be murdered at any time and would not survive to see his writing published. But he never stopped keeping the diary: "I shall go on writing," he declared to himself. "That is *my* heroism. I will bear witness, precise witness!"

What Klemperer witnessed was a process of degradation and ostracism that sought to remove Jews completely from German life. As early as April 1933, Jewish professors at Klemperer's university were put on leave. As a Great War veteran, he was allowed to continue lecturing, to ever-dwindling audiences, until 1935, when he was forcibly retired. For Klemperer, this was not just an insult but a pressing financial problem. The Klemperers were engaged in building a summerhouse in Dölzschen, just outside of Dresden, and when it was finished they would need a car to get around. Klemperer worried about whether his retirement pension would cover their expenses, or if it would continue to be paid at all. "Every day the money problems get worse," he wrote in January 1935. "Today an exorbitant electricity bill."

These might seem like trivial problems compared to what other Jews in Germany were facing, and what the future held for the Klemperers themselves. But for a cultured bourgeois couple, the erosion of their class position was highly demoralizing. One of the most trying times for Klemperer came in 1943, when he was ordered to perform labor service in a factory that made file folders. He was humiliated to find that the woman who trained him could produce eleven thousand folders in a day, while he struggled to make four thousand.

From 1933 to 1939, the majority of German Jews left the country, including many academics. But Klemperer's few efforts to find a job abroad came to nothing, adding to his sense of self-doubt. (He was embarrassed that even though his field was French literature, he didn't speak the language well enough to lecture in it.) His passivity wasn't shattered until November 9, 1938, when the nationwide pogrom known as Kristallnacht, the "night of broken glass," destroyed synagogues and Jewish-owned properties across Germany. The scale and intensity of the violence—which was accompanied by mass arrests of Jewish men, many of whom were sent to concentration camps—made clear that his situation was desperate, and prompted him to more serious efforts to emigrate.

But while Klemperer had a brother willing to sponsor him for a visa in America, the immigration quotas were vastly oversubscribed. "In Berlin crowds of applicants camping in front of the American consulate from six o'clock in the morning," he reports in the diary. Klemperer was almost sixty years old, with no money and no practical skills; he started taking English lessons, but with little hope that he would ever have the chance to use the language. And when the war began in September 1939, the doors slammed shut. He would have to stay in Germany until either he or the Nazi regime perished.

The war brought Klemperer a new source of hope and dread. Would the Third Reich be destroyed by the Allies, or would victory make it invulnerable? At first, when Hitler's attack on Poland seemed like it might go unanswered by France and England, Klemperer was in despair: "As I lie down to sleep I think: Will they come for me tonight? Will I be shot, will I be put in a concentration camp?" He told Eva, "A morphine injection or something similar was the best thing for us, our life was over." On the other hand, after learning of a successful British air raid on Berlin in September 1940, he wrote hopefully, "Has there been a turn for the better?" The American declaration of war in December 1941 made him speculate that a German defeat was getting closer. "If I hang a heavier weight on a clock, then it runs down more quickly," he reasoned.

But year after year, Klemperer's hopes for an end to the regime were disappointed. And all the time, the Nazis were escalating their efforts to remove the Jews from the social, economic, and political life of Germany. In 1935, the Nuremberg Laws revoked the citizenship of all Jews (defined as those with at least one Jewish grandparent) and prohibited marriages between Jews and "Aryans." Couples like the Klemperers (who had been married since 1906) were allowed to stay together, though Eva, like other non-Jewish spouses of Jews, faced escalating harassment. In May 1942, for instance, Gestapo agents raided the Klemperers' apartment and slapped Eva—who was then sixty years old—while berating her: "You're Aryan? You Jew's whore, why did you marry the Jew?"

In 1938, Jews were compelled to legally add the middle names Israel or Sarah, so that their religion would be immediately clear from their official documents. In 1940, the Klemperers were ordered to vacate their beloved house and move into a so-called "Jews' House," one of the properties where Dresden's remaining Jews were required to live. And on September 1, 1941, all Jews were required to wear a yellow star on their clothing whenever they were in public, a measure the Nazis had already imposed on Jews in conquered territories in Eastern Europe. Because the law was so strictly enforced—a Jew could be arrested if his or her star was accidentally concealed by a coat or lapel—Klemperer began to stay home as much as possible, venturing out only for short walks after dark. This was just as well, since Jews were also banned from using Dresden's main streets or entering parks, and a careless wrong turn could lead to a concentration camp.

To Klemperer's dismay, these measures against the Jews did nothing to dent Hitler's popularity. One of the diary's central concerns, threaded through the news bulletins and accounts of food shortages, is Klemperer's attempt to gauge the country's true feelings about Nazi anti-Semitism. For their part, the Nazis made no secret of wanting the Jews dead; in one case that Klemperer recorded, Gestapo agents searching a Jew's house demanded, "Why do you not all hang yourselves?" Then "they *showed him* how to make a noose." And many Jews Klemperer knew did commit suicide, often after receiving orders to report for deportation, which was increasingly recognized to be a death sentence.

When the deportation of Dresden's Jews began in late 1941, they were told that they were being sent to occupied Poland to perform labor service—a fate that already looked like death for people like the Klemperers, who were in their sixties and unused to hard physical work. But with remarkable speed, rumors about the deportees' real fate began to circulate. The first transport of Jews arrived in Auschwitz in early 1942, and the name of the camp appears in Klemperer's diary that March: "In the last few days I heard Auschwitz (or something like it) . . . mentioned as the most dreadful concentration camp. Work in a mine, death within a few days." The idea that Jews were being sent to Auschwitz specifically to be gassed on arrival was still unimaginable, but the equation of the camp with death was quickly accepted.

Was the Nazis' murderous hatred of Jews widely shared, or did people merely go along with it because they had no choice? In a practical sense, it hardly mattered, since the Nazis' effective power over Jewish lives was unlimited. As the months and years passed, Klemperer recorded a steady stream of house searches, beatings, arrests, suicides, and deportations among his neighbors in the Jews' House. Yet in a moral sense, it mattered very much to Klemperer whether the Nazis represented the real Germany, since if they did, his entire identity was based on a lie. He resisted this conclusion fiercely, writing in May 1942, "I am fighting the hardest battle for my Germanness now. I must hold on to this: I am German, the others are un-German." At the same time, he had doubts: "I can no longer believe in the completely un-German character of National Socialism," he observed the following month. "It is homegrown, a malignant growth out of *German* flesh."

In fact, Klemperer's own dealings with individual Germans seem to have been surprisingly free from any signs of rejection or prejudice. He lived in the Third Reich for more than eight years before he recorded any personal anti-Semitic abuse, and even then it took a mild form: "At Chemnitzer Platz a section of Hitler Youth cubs," he wrote on November 1, 1941. " 'A yid, a yid!' Yelling they run toward the dairy I am entering, I can still hear them shouting and laughing outside." Yet in the same entry, Klemperer balances this anecdote with another, in which a German he meets goes out of his way to tell him, "I just wanted to say: It doesn't matter about the star, we're all human beings, and I know such good Jews."

"But which is the true vox populi?" Klemperer asks himself, and the question continued to torment him. Meanwhile, as his life was increasingly circumscribed by his Jewishness, Klemperer began to take an intellectual interest in Jewish matters for the first time. As a rationalist and an atheist, religion itself held no appeal for him. But he sought out books on Jewish history and politics, which were, ironically, easier for him to obtain, through the Jewish community center, than the European classics he treasured.

Given the circumstances, the subject of Jewishness naturally inspired complicated feelings in Klemperer. Zionism provoked his special fury: "To me the Zionists, who want to go back to the Jewish state of 70 AD . . . are just as offensive as the Nazis," he wrote in June 1934. "With their nosing after blood, their ancient 'cultural roots' . . . they are altogether a match for the National Socialists." Given that the Nazis wanted to exterminate the Jews and the Zionists wanted to save them, this might look like a bizarre equivalency. But what Klemperer perceived is that Zionism, in its own way, also denied the possibility that a Jew like him could really be a German. It had predicted, two generations before the Holocaust, that Jewish existence in Europe was doomed, and it demanded that Jews like Klemperer sacrifice their German identity in the name of a Jewish identity they scorned and feared. But to Klemperer, only a liberal, humane, and accommodating Germanness could be truly modern, while Zionism was just an atavistic nationalism. Indeed, once the war was over, Klemperer remained in East Germany and resumed his teaching and writing. Despite everything, he remained German, while the Nazis who sought to steal his Germanness were vanquished.

Of course, the fact that Victor Klemperer outlived Hitler and the Third Reich—he would die in 1960, at the age of seventy-eight— makes his story extremely anomalous. In 1933, the Jewish population of Germany was about 500,000. Six years later, when World War II began, it had declined to 200,000, as Jews fled to the few destinations that would admit them—including Palestine, which accepted 60,000 German immigrants in those years. By 1945, only 20,000 of those Jews were still alive. The city of Dresden, where Klemperer lived during the entire Nazi period, was home to about 1,300 Jews in 1941; by 1945, he was one of just 198.

How did Klemperer survive? The answer has to do with the irrational and haphazard nature of Nazi law. Two "privileged" categories of German Jews were granted limited exemption from persecution— veterans of World War I and people with Aryan spouses—and Klemperer fell into both classes. Yet this offered no ironclad guarantee of safety—he personally knew plenty of Jewish veterans and Jews married to non-Jews who were deported—and Klemperer's survival must be largely attributed to sheer bureaucratic randomness. This spared him until February 1945, when the Allied firebombing of Dresden provided Victor and Eva with an opportunity to flee the city in the chaos. They survived until the German surrender by moving from one village to another under assumed names, concealing Victor's Jewishness.

The published diary ends in June 1945, with what Klemperer himself refers to as a "fairy-tale turnabout." During the 1930s, one of his chief fears was that the Nazis would confiscate his house outside Dresden. In 1940 he and Eva were ordered to hand over the house to an Aryan family, but thanks to a long series of legal complications (which Kafka would have relished), the Klemperers remained its legal owners. So on June 10, they returned to Dresden—now mostly destroyed, and under Soviet occupation—and made their way home: "In the late afternoon we walked up to Dölzschen," the book concludes. For a man who didn't believe in miracles, it was a miraculous ending—and for that very reason, an unrepresentative one.

The Diary of
Anne Frank

WHEN HITLER CAME TO POWER IN 1933, VICTOR Klemperer realized that his life would soon be in danger. But a number of reasons combined to keep him from taking flight. Among them was the fact that Victor and Eva were childless, which inevitably affected their attitude toward the future. Klemperer's diary is mainly concerned with his own struggle to survive from day to day; the long-term prospects of German Jewry were not his direct concern.

Otto Frank, however, saw the ascent of Hitler as a much more immediate threat. Frank, who turned forty-four in 1933, had some things in common with Klemperer: both were fully assimilated German Jews and World War I veterans. But Frank was married to a Jewish woman, not an Aryan, and he was the father of two young girls, seven-year-old Margot and four-year-old Anne. These facts made lingering in Nazi Germany a much more dangerous prospect for Frank than it was for Klemperer. At the same time, Frank was a businessman rather than an academic, which meant he had contacts and skills that made it easier to find work abroad. Before 1933 was out, Frank had found a job in the Netherlands as manager of a branch of a firm that made pectin, a fruit extract used in jam.

A few months later, Otto's wife Edith and his two daughters joined him in Amsterdam. They were refugees, but not desperate ones. After a few years Otto Frank started his own company dealing in spices, and the family lived the kind of middle-class life that

Klemperer feared he could never re-create abroad. As Klemperer's world shrank, the Franks' expanded: the children learned to speak Dutch and began to think of themselves as being at home in the Netherlands. For Anne, the youngest member of the family, being Dutch was the only national identity she could remember. "My first wish after the war is to become a Dutch citizen," she would write in her diary.

In fact, the Franks remained German citizens until 1941, when Germany revoked the citizenship of émigré Jews, leaving them stateless. By that time, however, Nazi power had caught up to the Franks, as it did to many of the Jews who had fled Germany since 1933. In May 1940, the German army marched into the Netherlands, disregarding its declared neutrality; the small country surrendered in less than a week. For the Franks as for thousands of other Jewish refugees, their haven had turned into a trap.

In July 1942, Margot, who had turned sixteen, received a notice to report for deportation. The Franks may not have known the name of Auschwitz, but it was already clear that the Jews who were sent "to the East" were doomed, and the family decided that she would not answer the summons. Instead, they put into action a plan that Otto Frank had devised: they would go into hiding on the vacant upper floors of the house where his business was located, on a canal in central Amsterdam. They were soon joined there by the three members of the van Pels family—mother, father, and teenage son—and a little later by Fritz Pfeffer, a dentist.

For the next two years, these eight people did not emerge from the house at 263 Prinsengracht. For most of that time, they were confined to the top two floors of the building, as workers did their jobs in the office and warehouse below. They kept the shades drawn at all times to avoid observation by neighbors. Their only connection to the outside world came through the four Dutch Christians, employees of Otto Frank's company, who risked their lives on a daily basis to protect the Jews' secret and keep them supplied with food. Amazingly, this arrangement worked until August 4, 1944, when the Gestapo arrived at the house and seized its eight Jewish inhabitants, along with two of their gentile protectors, Victor Kugler and Johannes Kleiman.

Kugler and Kleiman were sentenced to Dutch prisons, but they survived until their release. The Franks, the van Pels, and Pfeffer, however, were deported to Auschwitz, in the very last transport to depart Amsterdam for the death camp. Edith Frank died there in January 1945; Margot and Anne were transferred from Auschwitz to Bergen-Belsen, where they died in a typhus epidemic in February or March. By the time the war ended, Otto Frank was the only one of the eight still alive. He returned alone to Amsterdam in June 1945, at almost exactly the same time that Victor and Eva Klemperer were arriving back at their house near Dresden.

There he learned that his wife and daughters were dead. But something of Anne's, at least, had survived. From June 1942 until just days before she was deported, she had kept a diary, which another of the Franks' protectors, Miep Gies, found in the house after she was taken away. Gies rescued the document and returned it to Otto Frank, and two years later, in 1947, he had it published in Dutch under the title *Het Achterhuis*, "The Secret Annex." Five years later, it was translated into English under the title *The Diary of a Young Girl*, and became an international sensation. By the end of the 1950s, it had been published around the world and adapted for both stage and film. Today, Anne Frank—who died at the age of fifteen, known to absolutely no one outside her immediate family— is perhaps the best known of the six million Jews who died in the Holocaust.

Clearly, there is something about the diary of Anne Frank that makes it uniquely serviceable as a work of Holocaust testimony. Victor Klemperer's diaries weren't published until 1995, half a century after the events they describe; but even if they had appeared in the immediate aftermath of the war, they could never have achieved the universal popularity or profound moral influence of Frank's. Part of the reason is simply that Klemperer was an adult, with an adult's staleness and frailties, consumed by worries about money and status.

By contrast, the kinds of responses Anne Frank's diary elicits are in part a tribute to her youth. "It seems to me that later on neither I nor anyone else will be interested in the musings of a thirteen-year-old schoolgirl," she writes when she begins the diary, but the miraculous thing about her writing is its directness and honesty, which perhaps only a teenager could achieve. A child would not be capable of Anne's insight and perceptiveness, while an adult would struggle to emulate her unself-consciousness. She is equally accurate and thorough when describing her first menstrual period as she is when diagnosing her mother's failures as a parent, or her burgeoning crush on the van Pels' teenage son. Nor does she spare her own character. She writes often about her moodiness, touchiness, and inability to swallow an insult, which made her a regular participant in the incessant squabbles in the Annex.

Yet for all Anne's self-criticism, the bedrock of her character is a profound self-acceptance. "I'm stuck with the character I was born with, and yet I'm sure I'm not a bad person," she continues. "I was born happy, I love people, I have a trusting nature, and I'd like everyone else to be happy too," she writes in another entry. And Anne's self-trust is what authorizes the reader to trust her: she is so fully herself that we know she will not pretend in the diary. "I have my own opinions, ideas and principles, and though it may sound odd coming from a teenager, I feel I'm more of a person than a child," she declares.

But who exactly is the reader for whom Anne thought she was writing? At first, it seems, she did not anticipate any reader for the diary but her later self. Yet the entries are framed as letters to an imaginary correspondent, "Kitty," which allows Anne to think of herself as writing for an audience, engaging in a rhetorical performance. Similarly, while she uses real names for herself and her family, the other residents of the Annex are given pseudonyms: the van Pels family became the van Daans and Fritz Pfeffer was called Albert Dussel. It is under these names that they are known around the world today; in a sense, they are Anne Frank's creations, characters in her story.

It might seem that eight ordinary people trapped in an attic would offer little scope for storytelling. But in fact the diary is full of dramatic episodes, carefully staged and narrated by Anne. Sometimes she will devote an entry to a comic set piece with a title of its own, depicting the squabbles that were inevitable with so many people packed into a closed space. Thus "The Best Little Table" is an account of Anne's fight with Dussel over who will get to use the table for their work; "A Daily Chore in Our Little Community" relates the quarreling that goes on when it's time to peel potatoes, a staple of the Franks' wartime diet (as it was for the Klemperers too).

The moments of real drama in the diary, however, come when intruders in the house make the inhabitants of the Annex fear they will be discovered. When thieves break into the warehouse on the ground floor of the building in April 1944, for instance, Anne carefully choreographs the reader's suspense: "The clock struck quarter to ten. The color had drained from our faces, but we remained calm, even though we were afraid. Where were the men? What was that bang? Were they fighting with the burglars?" Knowing that she has an exciting story to tell at last, she draws it out like a serial novel, writing "End of Part One" halfway through.

These are all the skills of a novelist, and in a strange way, the Annex turns out to be good training for the writer Anne eventually decides she wants to be. Her ability to write without embarrassment, to say exactly what she thought, felt, and meant, reflects an unusual strength of character. "I face life with an extraordinary amount of courage," she wrote in June 1944, after nearly two full years of house arrest, fearing discovery and death at every waking moment. "I feel so strong and capable of bearing burdens, so young and free! When I first realized this, I was glad, because it means I can more easily withstand the blows life has in store."

It is this tone of hopeful resolve that accounts, more than anything else, for the appeal of Anne Frank's diary. It might seem strange, on its face, that a book by a girl who was essentially imprisoned for two years, before dying a horrible death at the age of fifteen, should be read, in the words of the American paperback's cover, as "a timeless testament to the human spirit." And the truth is that the diary contains many expressions of fear and despair, exactly as one would expect from someone in Anne's situation. "At night in bed I see myself in a dungeon," she writes in November 1943. "Or they come in the middle of the night to take us away and I crawl under my bed in desperation."

Yet it is not the moments of demoralization that readers of Anne Frank's diary tend to remember. Rather, it is the sense the diary gives of youth and life having their way despite every obstacle. Anne happened to be in the Annex at exactly the age of puberty—she describes getting her first period early in the diary, and the later parts are dominated by discussions of her growing sexual and romantic feelings. These experiences are so fundamentally human that they cannot be suppressed: Anne's example shows that every human being, even the most stigmatized and persecuted, has the inalienable right to grow, feel, hope, and love.

Anne's determination to remain positive extends to her assessment of humanity at large—at least, some of the time. Perhaps the most widely quoted line in the diary comes from her entry of July 15, 1944: "I still believe, in spite of everything, that people are truly good at heart." Read in context, however, Anne's avowal sounds almost desperate, something she says not because it's true but because she needs to believe it. "It's utterly impossible for me to build my life on a foundation of chaos, suffering and death," she continues. And she was fully aware of what human beings were proving themselves capable of, every day that she wrote. In February 1944, she described the inhabitants of the Annex discussing matter-of-factly how "millions of peace-loving citizens in Poland and Russia have been murdered and gassed."

Is there something evasive about describing those victims of the Holocaust simply as "citizens," rather than as Jews? Certainly, whenever she is writing about the plight of the Jews, Anne's language tends to become impersonally sententious. Perhaps this was an echo of the way such matters were discussed in the Annex. But it also registers Anne's sense that she had the responsibility to be what she indeed

became—a quasi-official Jewish spokesperson, tasked with demonstrating the innocence and humanity of the Jews to the world at large.

This insistence that Jews are just people, no different from anyone
else, is another reason Anne Frank's diary has been the most universally acceptable work of Holocaust literature. For Anne, Jewishness
is something close to a purely arbitrary label: it defines the way people treat her, but it has nothing to do with her actual thoughts or
experiences. (In this way, it resembles the crime that Joseph K. is supposed to have committed.) Margot Frank evidently took an interest
in Zionism, and hoped to become a nurse in Palestine after the war.
But Anne's outlook was wholly assimilated and secular: she posted
photos of movie stars on her walls and eagerly followed news of the
Dutch royal family. Yet she already had a glimpse of the difficulty
that so many modern Jews found in combining the identities of Jew
and European: "We can never be just Dutch, or just English, or whatever," she writes in the same entry. "We will always be Jews as well."

But what does being a Jew really mean? Wasn't Anne just a human
being, after all? "I sometimes wonder if anyone will ever . . . not
worry about whether or not I'm Jewish and merely see me as a teenager badly in need of some good plain fun," she writes. In this way,
Anne managed to say with disarming simplicity what Jewish writers
from Schnitzler onward had made the subject of elaborate fables. In
modern European societies, Jews just want to be treated like everyone else. Coming from her, it sounds so self-evident and modest a
wish that it is amazing it could have been denied for so long. For
readers of her diary, empathizing with Anne Frank has been a way of
symbolically granting this Jewish claim to full humanity—but only
when it was too late to make a difference.

Because the Gestapo descended on the Secret Annex without
warning, Anne had no idea that the entry of August 1, 1944, would
be her last. The diary simply breaks off, while Anne went on to experience six months of the worst terror imaginable—hunger, torture,
disease, and death. Of course, every reader of Anne's diary knows
how her life ended. But because her story does not end, it is hard
not to think of her as frozen in time, perpetually alive, curious, and

hopeful. This is the final reason why the diary is such a popular work of Holocaust testimony: paradoxically, it spares the reader a confrontation with the full truth of the Holocaust. In our memory, Anne Frank can remain the brave young writer who proclaimed, in March 1944, "A person who has courage and faith will never die in misery!" But she did.

Night by
Elie Wiesel

O N MARCH 31, 1944, ANNE FRANK NOTED A PIECE OF
news she had heard over the radio: "Hungary has been occupied by German troops. There are still a million Jews living there; they too are doomed." Across the continent, Eliezer Wiesel, a Jewish boy just a few months older than her, was listening to the radio in the small Hungarian town of Sighet and heard the same news. Until 1940, Sighet had been part of Romania, but in that year Hungary annexed it with the approval of Hitler, so when Hungary was occupied by German troops Sighet came under Nazi rule. Three days after hearing the news on the radio, Wiesel recalled years later in his book *Night*, German troops appeared on the streets of the town. "Anguish," Wiesel writes. "German soldiers—with their steel helmets and their death's-head emblem."

By the time the Germans came to Sighet, most of Europe was already familiar with those emblems and the anguish they brought. Spring 1944 was almost three years into the Holocaust, which had begun in earnest with the German invasion of the Soviet Union in the summer of 1941. But because Hungary was a member of the Axis—an ally of Germany that had retained its independence—it had previously been able to control its own policy toward the Jews, which was anti-Semitic and oppressive but not murderous. Now the Nazi occupation of the country meant that Hungary's 700,000 Jews, the largest remaining Jewish population in Eastern Europe, were marked for extermination. Over the next year, more than 400,000 were deported, almost all of them to Auschwitz, where 90 percent were killed on arrival.

As the existence of *Night* testifies, Wiesel was one of the handful who survived. The end of the war found him in Buchenwald, a concentration camp in Germany where Auschwitz prisoners had been transferred in January 1945, as the Red Army advanced through Poland. Just sixteen years old, he was one of about 1,000 child survivors sent to a rehabilitation program at a school in France. Very quickly he mastered the French language, and before the age of twenty he had started a career as a writer and journalist.

It was not until 1955, however, that Wiesel, with encouragement from the famous French writer François Mauriac, began to write about his experiences during the war. What he first produced was a 900-page memoir, *And the World Remained Silent*, that was too massive to find a publisher—only an abridged version appeared, from a South American Yiddish press. So Wiesel translated the story into French and worked with his editor to cut it down into the terse, dramatic, carefully shaped book that became *Night*. This was published in 1958, at a time when Anne Frank's diary was becoming known around the world, and *Night* has joined it as one of the best-known works of Holocaust literature.

In fact, Anne Frank and Elie Wiesel were in Auschwitz at the same time. He arrived in May 1944, at the age of fifteen; she was fourteen when she was deported there in August. Both survived the initial selection, which condemned to the gas chambers Jewish prisoners who were considered unfit to work. Months later, as the Red Army made its way into Poland, prisoners from Auschwitz were sent west to camps inside Germany, on punishing marches through the winter cold. Anne arrived in Bergen-Belsen, where she died in a typhus epidemic in February or March 1945, a month or two before the end of the war. As Wiesel writes in *Night*, he survived a similar march from Auschwitz to Buchenwald. The fact that he lived and she died is testimony to the sheer randomness of survival in the Holocaust.

It could easily have happened the other way around, in which case we might now have neither of their books: *Night* would never have been written, while the *Diary* might not have seen the light of day.

While Nazi anti-Semitism saw them both simply as Jews to be annihilated, Anne Frank and Elie Wiesel had very different understandings of what it meant to be Jewish. Indeed, they epitomized the contrast between assimilated Central European Jewry and the traditional Jewish communities of Eastern Europe. The diary makes clear that Anne had almost no familiarity with Jewish practice: she writes of being fascinated by the spectacle of Albert Dussel praying, in terms that suggest she had seldom seen it before. For her, religion was not tradition or doctrine but something more like conscience.

Wiesel, by contrast, received the same kind of education a Jewish boy might have had a hundred years earlier. He seems to have experienced none of the anguish about belonging to a foreign country and culture that tormented so many Central European Jews. Instead, he describes himself at the beginning of *Night* as "deeply observant. By day I studied Talmud and by night I would run to the synagogue to weep over the destruction of the Temple." When he records the events of spring 1944, he does so with reference to the Jewish calendar: the town's leading Jewish citizens are arrested on the seventh day of Passover, the order of deportation arrives two weeks before Shavuot. No wonder the story he tells in *Night* is centrally concerned with the theological implications of the Holocaust. How, he begins to wonder, can Jews worship a God who allowed Auschwitz to exist? Wiesel referred to *Night* as a work of testimony, and it is God who is on trial, alongside the human race he created.

Looking back at his community in the spring of 1944, what Wiesel feels most of all seems to be anger at their unwillingness to face reality. When the Germans first arrived in Sighet, Wiesel says bitterly, the Jews were totally unprepared for what was about to happen. Unlike Victor Klemperer in Dresden, they had never heard of Auschwitz; the first time they learned the name, he writes, is when they saw it on the sign at the camp's train station. For the first few days after the German troops came, the Jews of Sighet were even able to tell themselves that rumors of German cruelty had been exaggerated.

But he makes clear that this was willful ignorance. It is to underscore this point that *Night* begins with a description of Moishe the Beadle, a friend of Wiesel's who taught him to study the *Zohar*, the central book of Kabbalah, the Jewish mystical tradition. Moishe had been deported early in the war, and when he returned he told unbelievable stories. He had been part of a group of Jews forced by the Gestapo to dig their own graves, then shot; "infants were tossed into the air and used as targets for the machine guns." Somehow, Moishe himself was only wounded and managed to escape, returning to Sighet to warn the Jews of what was coming. "But people not only refused to believe his tales, they refused to listen," Wiesel writes bitterly.

By opening *Night* with this episode, Wiesel invites the reader to see him as another version of Moishe. Wiesel, too, has returned to tell a tale so incredibly monstrous that it is hard to listen to, hard to believe. Implicitly, he challenges the readers of *Night* not to react the way the people of Sighet reacted to Moishe—not to bury our heads in the sand, but to believe and take action. Yet the truth is that Wiesel's anger at his neighbors' passivity only makes sense if the Jews of Hungary had the ability to do something to affect their fate. If Wiesel's neighbors had believed every word Moishe said, what difference would it have made?

For once the Germans' plans for the Jews of Sighet began to unfold, they did so with disorienting speed. First the Germans introduced the kind of bans and curfews familiar to Victor Klemperer and Anne Frank. Then came ghettoization, as the Jews were herded into two small areas of the town. Even now, however, Wiesel writes that the Jews were culpably complacent: "The barbed wire that encircled us like a wall did not fill us with real fear. In fact, we felt this was not a bad thing: we were entirely among ourselves." The human desire for normality and consistency is so strong that even the most oppressive conditions can be accepted, so long as they can be trusted not to change.

But the ghettos turned out to be only holding pens. One night, Wiesel's father Chaim, a prominent citizen, was summoned to a meeting of the Jewish Council, which the Nazis had put in charge of the Jews' affairs. He returned with the news they had dreaded: the ghetto would be emptied and its residents deported. Starting the next morning, the Jews of Sighet were herded into cattle cars bound for an unknown destination. Seeing his friends, neighbors, and teachers— even the town's chief rabbi—marching toward the train station, all Wiesel can think of is that it feels like "a page torn from a book, a historical novel, perhaps, dealing with the captivity in Babylon or the Spanish Inquisition." Much as witnesses of the Twin Towers' fall on 9/11 compared it to a spectacle from a movie, so Wiesel reaches for fiction to explain a reality too monstrous to feel real.

Ordinarily, madness signifies a loss of contact with reality; but in the Holocaust, the reality itself was so insane that the mad prove to be prophets. On the cattle car to Auschwitz, Wiesel writes, a woman lost her mind and kept screaming that she saw fire and flames; as with Moishe, the other Jews dismissed this as nonsense, and resorted to tying her up to keep her quiet. But when the train arrives at the death camp and the woman again screams, "Jews, look! Look at the fire!," this time there really is a fire—the flames rising from the chimney over the crematorium.

Wiesel builds his picture of life in Auschwitz out of a mosaic of short scenes, offering an account that is both personal and representative. What he saw, a million others saw too, though they didn't live to write about it. First the passengers were hurried off the train with shouts and blows, and women and men were separated in an instant. "I didn't know that this was the moment in time and the place where I was leaving my mother and [my sister] Tzipora forever," Wiesel writes. In all likelihood, they were sent directly to the gas chambers and didn't survive the night.

The same fate might have awaited Wiesel and his father if they hadn't received whispered advice from an inmate: instead of their true ages, fifteen and fifty, they should say they were eighteen and forty. This made them sound more fit for work, and ensured that they survived the initial selection—carried out, Wiesel writes, by Josef Mengele, the doctor whose medical experiments on Jewish prisoners made him one of the most notorious monsters of the Holocaust. As the prisoners walked on, Wiesel says, they saw a sight whose horror made it, once again, impossible to understand: a truck unloaded a pile of children's bodies into a burning ditch.

Wiesel interrupts his narrative with a litany of promises not to forget: "Never shall I forget that night, the first night in camp, that turned my life into one long night seven times sealed. Never shall I forget that smoke." This insistence on the sacred duty to remember and bear witness would become perhaps the central theme of Holocaust literature, whether it took the form of memoir or fiction. After being forced into the passivity of victimhood, writing and bearing witness were a way of seizing agency, of striking back at least symbolically against an enemy that had been all-powerful. In a foreword to a new edition of *Night* published in 2006, Wiesel described the book—and his life's work as a teacher and activist—as "that of a witness who believes he has a moral obligation to try to prevent the enemy from enjoying one last victory by allowing his crimes to be erased from human memory."

In *Night*, the sheer magnitude of the horror to be conveyed exerts a pressure on Wiesel's writing, enforcing simplicity and directness. Literary flourishes are rare; more common are short declarative sentences that simply tell the reader what happened next. But *Night* does not just tell us what happened to Wiesel. It also instructs the reader how to think about those events, in ways that seem like the fruit of later reflection rather than first impression. In his description of the Jews' arrival at Auschwitz, for instance, Wiesel is already thinking about the world's failure to prevent the Holocaust, the possibility that the Jews could fight back instead of dying "like cattle in the slaughterhouse," and the imperative to "let the world learn about the existence of Auschwitz." These themes, which would dominate discussion of the Holocaust for decades to come, are presented by Wiesel as if they had been thought or even spoken aloud by prisoners at the very moment of their arrival.

Perhaps it is only in retrospect, too, that Wiesel could have realized how permanently he had been changed by the very first hour he spent in Auschwitz. "The student of Talmud, the child I was, had been consumed by the flames," he writes. The replacement of Wiesel's name by a prisoner's number—A-7713—seems to symbolize this death of the person he had been. For even as he outlines the tortures of life in Auschwitz, Wiesel is also telling the story of his own spiritual ordeal, his loss of faith. This process begins on the first night in the camp, when he hears the Jews around him reciting the Kaddish prayer for the dead. This provokes the same kind of impatience he felt about the Jews' refusal to listen to Moishe the Beadle; in both cases, Wiesel feels, they are evading the truth of their situation. "For the first time, I felt anger rising within me," he writes. "Why should I sanctify His name? The Almighty, the eternal and terrible Master of the Universe, chose to be silent. What was there to thank Him for?"

Wiesel is not exactly announcing that he no longer believes in God, as if atheism would be the logical deduction from Auschwitz. Rather, his fury is directed at a God who is culpable precisely because he does exist, but does not take action to save his people. Yet the anger Wiesel directed against the Jewish God was accompanied by guilt, which took the form of, or was mixed up with, guilt toward his father—a pious man who represented the Jewish tradition Wiesel now rejected. He writes that he clung to his father in the camp and did everything he could to avoid being separated from him. Yet Auschwitz was so brutal that any loyalty to another inmate, even a father, represented a potential liability. On the first evening in the camp, Wiesel recalls, his father made the mistake of asking a guard where the toilet was located; in return he received a blow that knocked him to the ground. Later, he was unable to keep up with the marching and his son tried to give him lessons.

Such experiences bred a guilty resentment of his father that Wiesel tried hard to repress. In January 1945, the remaining prisoners in Auschwitz were evacuated to Germany in the face of the approaching Red Army. This decision reflects the fanatical desire of the Germans to prevent the Jews from being liberated, but also a fear that, taken alive, these inmates would reveal the truth about Auschwitz to the world. (Already in November, the crematoria and gas chambers had been destroyed, to prevent them from falling into enemy hands.)

As Wiesel narrates this march, his story begins to fill up with examples of sons who betray their fathers under the stress of circumstances. Wiesel writes about Rabbi Eliahu, who is separated from his son on the march and goes looking for him. To his own horror, Wiesel begins to wonder if Eliahu's son had deliberately gotten lost to avoid having to bear the burden of helping his aged father. The young Wiesel offers a final prayer to God, asking not to commit the same kind of sin. But when they finally arrive in Buchenwald, his father is so sick that death seems inevitable, and Wiesel, who has been giving him his own rations, wonders if it wouldn't be better to start stealing his father's food instead.

Finally, at the end of *Night*, Wiesel does commit what he feels to be a betrayal, though it takes the most guiltless form possible: he allows himself to go to sleep, knowing that his father is about to die. When Wiesel wakes up, his father is gone. "His last word had been my name," Wiesel reflects, punishing himself with survivor's guilt. "He had called out to me and I had not answered." In other words, Wiesel himself has become like the absent God he once reproached—someone who does not help the people he is supposed to love.

This fact, more than any of his other sufferings, is what destroys his ability to keep feeling and remembering. In the last line of the book, Wiesel looks at himself in the mirror and sees a corpse looking back at him; and it is not just his emaciation he means. The person he was, with all his assumptions about God, religion, the world, and himself, has died in Auschwitz. If there is one thing that *Night* wants to communicate about the Holocaust, it is that afterward—for those who experienced it and those who did not—the world can never be the same.

Survival in Auschwitz
by Primo Levi

W HEN THE EVACUATION OF AUSCHWITZ WAS announced in January 1945, Elie Wiesel was a patient in the camp hospital, but he decided that it was too dangerous to remain behind. In all likelihood, he thought, the departing guards would simply massacre the sick in their beds. Instead, he joined his father on a march that was itself a massacre, as 60,000 malnourished, under-dressed prisoners were forced to walk for miles through bitter cold and snow. Wiesel lived, but some 15,000 people died on the march, many of them shot by guards when they couldn't keep up.

Most of the 800 prisoners in the Auschwitz infirmary, however, were too weak to march. Among them was Primo Levi, a twenty-five-year-old Italian Jew who had been captured as part of a parti-san band and handed over to the Germans. He arrived in Auschwitz in February 1944, three months before Wiesel, and both men were employed in the same subcamp of Auschwitz—the one known offi-cially as Monowitz, but referred to by the prisoners as Buna, after the synthetic rubber compound they were supposed to be manufacturing there. (In reality, the factory never became operational and no rubber was produced.) Wiesel and Levi didn't know each other in the camp, but it's entirely possible they glimpsed one another—never imagining that both would survive, much less that they would become the most important witnesses to the Holocaust.

During the evacuation of Auschwitz Levi was suffering from scarlet fever, and he was among those left behind to face his fate. As it turned out, the Germans did not massacre the sick, but left them to die of exposure and starvation. Levi survived, but many other patients died, some of them after the Russians liberated the camp. In Auschwitz, there was no certain strategy for survival, no clear right or wrong choices. Any survivor of the camp was the beneficiary of countless moments of chance.

One such moment came on October 13, 1944, when the SS carried out a "selection" of prisoners for the gas chamber. Wiesel and Levi both write about this experience in very similar terms: the confinement of the prisoners to their barracks, the agony of waiting for the SS to arrive, and the parody of a medical examination that followed. One by one, the prisoners ran at top speed in front of a doctor, who observed them from a distance for a few seconds at most, then placed their ID cards in one of two piles—life or death.

The prisoners believed that appearing healthy was the only way they could influence the decision: "Try to move your limbs, give yourself some color. Don't walk slowly, run!" advises the leader of Wiesel's barracks, the *Blockälteste* or "block elder." In his barrack, Levi employed the same strategies: "Like everyone, I passed by with a brisk and elastic step, trying to hold my head high, my chest forward and my muscles contracted and conspicuous." Yet the actual "selection" was carried out with horrifying carelessness, and Levi speculates that he only survived because his card was mixed up with that of the man who came after him.

When Levi began to write about his experiences, after he returned home to Italy, he was obsessed with the question of what it took—or what it cost—to get out of Auschwitz alive. It makes perfect sense that the English translation of his memoir was titled *Survival in Auschwitz*, since that is its plot and theme. But the actual Italian title of Levi's book, which was first published in 1947, translates as *If This Is a Man*, which gives a more accurate sense of its concerns. If Wiesel asked how it was possible to believe in Judaism's God after the Holocaust, Levi wondered whether the Holocaust made it impossible to believe in man. If human beings could treat one another the way they did in Auschwitz, how is it possible to ever trust or admire humanity again?

Levi's account of daily life in Auschwitz parallels Wiesel's in many details, but his perspective on the experience is very different. *Night* is a book that wants to record and provoke, while *Survival in Auschwitz* is more interested in observing and understanding. No matter the subject, Levi is a precise and unsentimental observer, telling exactly how things worked, even disgusting and vicious things. For instance, he explains that because the prisoners' diet consisted mainly of soup, it was necessary to get up many times during the night to urinate. When the bucket the prisoners used instead of a toilet was full, the last person to use it was responsible for carrying it outside and emptying it, and some of the contents would always spill onto his feet. Since prisoners slept two to a bunk, turned head to foot, this meant that if one's bunkmate ended up carrying the bucket, one would have to sleep with sewage-covered feet in his face: thus "it is always preferable that we, and not our neighbor, be ordered to do it."

This ordeal might seem minor next to the scenes of horror that filled the camp. But such practical details fascinate Levi because he is such a keen student of the way things work. Auschwitz was a place devoted to death and murder, but while the prisoners lived, they could not help creating a kind of society, complete with its own habits, mechanisms, and even status hierarchies. Levi notes, for instance, that prisoners with lower numbers tattooed on their arms, indicating they had arrived in the camp earlier, looked down on those with higher numbers.

There was also, he shows, an economic system built into the design of the camp. Because no one got enough food to eat or clothing to wear, there was constant pilfering and bartering, often involving useful items stolen from a work site and brought back to the barracks. This economy had its own values and exchange rates: a spoon was required by every prisoner in order to eat the soup, but spoons were not provided to them, so they would steal iron or tin and make clumsy utensils to sell. Even the official institutions of the camp were supplied in this manner: Levi recalls that he pilfered graph paper and sold it to the infirmary for use as a temperature chart.

Such stratagems were necessary for survival, but they raised ethical dilemmas. "Let everybody judge," he writes, "how much of our ordinary moral world could survive on this side of the barbed wire." Indeed, Levi understood Auschwitz as "a gigantic biological and social experiment," a Darwinian contest in which "the struggle to survive is without respite, because everyone is desperately and ferociously alone." Wiesel, too, had been deeply troubled by this enforced selfishness, which he saw tearing apart even the bond between fathers and sons.

For Levi, what emerges from that experiment is not the conclusion that man is "fundamentally brutal, egoistic and stupid": after all, the camps do not show humanity in its pure state, but under extreme duress. Under such conditions, however, two categories of human beings tend to emerge, which Levi calls "the saved and the drowned." The former are willing to do whatever it takes to survive, while the latter become what the camp slang called "*musselmen*," "men in decay," who "die and disappear without leaving a trace in anyone's memory."

Clearly, these categories do not correspond to moral divisions such as "the good and the bad, the wise and the foolish." To survive in Auschwitz at all, Levi suggests, required jettisoning such distinctions. Yet Levi shows that he himself was saved not by ruthless selfishness, of the kind adopted by many prisoners around him, but by cultivating human relationships. Crucially, he was befriended by an Italian at the camp—not a Jewish prisoner but a civilian conscript laborer, who was given much better rations and would save a portion of his soup for Levi. This man, Lorenzo, did more than sustain Levi physically; he "constantly reminded me by his presence, by his natural and plain manner of being good, that there still existed a just world outside our own . . . for which it was worth surviving." For Lorenzo, Levi reserves his highest term of praise: "Lorenzo was a man."

The most important and dramatic episodes in *Survival in Auschwitz* turn on the question of whether such human relationships can exist in the camp. Levi witnessed and suffered the most atrocious kinds of violence, but the episodes that linger in his memory are those in which dehumanization was most insidious. One such episode involved Alex, a German "Kapo"—that is, a prisoner who had been placed in charge of other prisoners. On one occasion, Alex cleaned his greasy hand by wiping it on Levi's shoulder, and this casual treatment of a person as a thing—a gesture that would have been unimaginable in ordinary life—contains for Levi something of the essence of Auschwitz.

Such dehumanization was especially stark when Levi was assigned to the "Chemical Kommando," a unit of prisoners charged with working in the laboratory at Buna. Being assigned to this unit saved his life, he believed, since it spared him from the punishing physical labor most prisoners had to perform outdoors in the winter cold. To get a place there, Levi had to take an examination in chemistry; in other words, he had to demonstrate that he was a skilled professional, a man and not a thing. But this only made it more noticeable that, even in the lab, he was treated as a being from a lower species. Levi was particularly struck by the way the director of the lab looked at him: "If I had known how completely to explain the nature of that look, which came as if across the glass window of an aquarium between two beings who live in different worlds, I would also have explained the essence of the great insanity of the third Germany."

With every power in Auschwitz—terror, exhaustion, hunger, sickness, cruelty—arrayed against the prisoner's humanity, was it possible to remain a man in the elevated sense Levi assigned to the word? His story suggests that it was, but only occasionally, in partial and symbolic ways. The thematic center of *Survival in Auschwitz* comes in the chapter called "The Canto of Ulysses," in which Levi recounts a more or less ordinary day, when he was part of a work detail assigned to clean the inside of a fuel tank. At mealtime, Levi and another prisoner, a Frenchman named Jean, were assigned to pick up a pot of soup from the kitchen and bring it to the work site. This was a difficult task—the full pot weighed one hundred pounds—but an enviable one, since it meant a break from work and a chance to scavenge food in the kitchens.

On this day, Jean asked to be taught some Italian words, and for some reason, it occurred to Levi to recite to him the famous twenty-sixth canto of Dante's *Inferno*, which tells the story of how Ulysses sailed beyond the Mediterranean, past the end of the known world, in search of new lands. Ulysses's speech, in which he convinces his crew to take the risk of tackling the unknown, is a classic statement of faith and pride in the human spirit:

Think of your breed; for brutish ignorance
Your mettle was not made; you were made men,
To follow after knowledge and excellence.

The irony of recalling this scene in Auschwitz, where brutality reigned and humanity was denied, could not be more poignant. Levi cannot fully remember the lines—he stumbles through them, leaving many words out—but he urgently feels the need to communicate the spirit of the poem to Jean, and even his partial recollection of the poem gives him the greatest gift possible in Auschwitz: "For a moment I forget who I am and where I am."

The canto is fitting for another reason, as well: it ends with Ulysses and his crew being drowned, their ship wrecked by a whirlwind. Human reason and daring, Dante suggests, do not always prevail; perhaps they are at their noblest and most necessary precisely when they are doomed. Nobility of mind cannot sustain a human being in Auschwitz, and the "Canto of Ulysses" episode remains just that, an episode, a momentary respite from overwhelming suffering. But it is a crucial part of the story Levi wants to tell, since he believes that the dignity of humanity can and must be asserted in the face of Auschwitz.

That Levi's inspirational text is classically Italian and European, not biblical or Jewish, is central to his humanistic vision. At one moment in his story, Levi writes that he was assigned to latrine detail along with a man named Wachsmann, a Polish Jew whose "comrades tell me he is a rabbi, in fact a Melamed, a person learned in the Torah." But Levi acknowledges that there is no way for the two of them to communicate: "We have no language in common," he writes, and this goes for more than spoken language. One of the ironies of Levi's story—as of Anne Frank's and Victor Klemperer's—is that they were persecuted as Jews even though being Jewish contributed little to their understanding of themselves or their world.

This was not the case for most of the Holocaust's victims. If it is the stories of Western and secular Jews that dominate the canon of Holocaust literature, that is partly a reflection of the way these stories speak to modern, secular readers the world over: such readers find it easier to understand a Western teenager like Anne Frank than they would a young Hasid, or for that matter a young Soviet Communist.

But it also has to do with structural features of the Holocaust. It is no coincidence that Frank, Wiesel, and Levi all remained free until 1944, late in the war—Levi and Wiesel because their countries only then came under German rule, Frank because she was able to hide for two years. By then, the Nazis were losing the war and they were more interested in extracting labor from Jewish prisoners than they had been earlier, when extermination was the focus. Prisoners who might once have been gassed on arrival now were used for slave labor instead. A person deported to Auschwitz in 1944 had a very slim chance of surviving: there were 650 Jews in Primo Levi's train to Auschwitz, of whom only 20 survived the war.

But a Jew captured by the Germans in Poland in 1942 had virtually no chance. Between July 1942 and October 1943, some 900,000 Jews were gassed at the extermination camp Treblinka near Warsaw; only 67 survived. And two million Jews were killed in the so-called "Holocaust by bullets"—shot by German soldiers and their collaborators and buried in scattered mass graves like Babi Yar, the ravine near Kiev where more than 30,000 Jews died over two days in September 1941. Since the beginning of the twentieth century, Jewish writers in Central and Eastern Europe had expressed an intuition that the life they were leading could not continue in the same way for long—that their future was disappearing in front of them. That proved to be true in a sense and on a scale that even the most hopeless would hardly have dared to imagine.

Eichmann in Jerusalem
by Hannah Arendt

IT WAS NOT JUST THE DEMOGRAPHICS OF JUDAISM THAT were permanently altered by the Holocaust. Today, the memory of the Holocaust is at the very core of Jewish identity in America and Israel, shaping the way most Jews think about both religion and politics. As the events recede in time, the flood of books, movies, memorials, and museums devoted to them only increases. In 2016, a reporter observed that "out of the 100 titles on Amazon's list of best-selling Jewish history books, no fewer than 92 are related to the Shoah."

The centrality of the Holocaust to modern Jewish life did not begin in 1945, however. Indeed, for the first decade and more after the liberation of the concentration camps revealed to the world the full scope of the Nazis' crimes, the death of six million Jews remained an unprocessed trauma. How could such a loss be integrated into the evolving self-understandings of both American and Israeli Jews, who were now the only surviving heirs to the European Jewish civilization they each, in different ways, defined themselves against?

The first book to inspire a reckoning with the Holocaust on a large, public scale was Hannah Arendt's *Eichmann in Jerusalem*, published in 1963. It's a gauge of the book's importance, and of the intense feelings it unleashed, that it has continued to provoke bitter criticism since the moment it first appeared as a series of articles in *The New Yorker*. Much of that criticism focused on Arendt personally, in terms that had less to do with the quality of her analysis than with her character and capacity for empathy. In his review of the book, for instance, the critic Norman Podhoretz wrote that Arendt displayed "the intellectual perversity that can result from the pursuit of brilliance by a mind infatuated with its own agility." The scholar Gershom Scholem, who had been a friend of Arendt's for decades, ended that friendship when he publicly denounced Arendt for lacking *ahavat Yisrael*, love of the Jewish people. Even now, there are historians who devote whole volumes to refuting the interpretation of the Holocaust that Arendt advanced in *Eichmann in Jerusalem*.

Yet that interpretation—especially the idea proposed in the book's subtitle, *A Report on the Banality of Evil*—remains central to the way we understand the Holocaust's perpetrators. The genocide of the Jews was one of the worst crimes ever committed by human beings, Arendt writes, but this does not mean that the people who carried it out were exceptional. Rather, she identifies a paradox: it was precisely the ordinariness of the perpetrators that makes their crime so terrifying, since it suggests that average men and women—not just in Nazi Germany but, by implication, in every time and place—are capable of atrocities. This is what Arendt calls "the greatest moral and even legal challenge" of the Holocaust: the idea that a " 'normal' person, neither feeble-minded nor indoctrinated nor cynical, could be perfectly incapable of telling right from wrong."

The test case for Arendt's theory about the "the fearsome, word-and-thought defying banality of evil" is Adolf Eichmann, an SS bureaucrat who played a leading role in carrying out the "Final Solution," the Nazi euphemism for the extermination of the Jews. Eichmann was in charge of organizing the transportation of Jews from across Europe to the death camps in Poland, including Auschwitz. While his name was often mentioned at the postwar Nuremberg Trials of Nazi war criminals, he was not a defendant there; after the end of World War II he had managed to go into hiding in Germany, and in 1950 he moved to Argentina, where he joined a number of other ex-Nazi fugitives. Ten years later, in 1960, Israeli secret agents tracked Eichmann down in Buenos Aires, where he was living under the name Richard Klement, and kidnapped him, bringing him back to Jerusalem to stand trial for his crimes.

The capture and trial of Eichmann were sensational events that received worldwide coverage. For Jews in Israel and beyond, they were enormously cathartic, dramatizing the reversal of the Jews' political plight brought about by the creation of a Jewish state. No longer helpless victims, Jews now appeared on the world stage as potent and resourceful avengers. More, the trial gave Israel an opportunity to put the true story of the Holocaust on record before the eyes of the world. In a sense, the evolution of the Holocaust into a central pillar of modern Jewish identity began with the Eichmann trial.

For Arendt, reporting on the trial was a challenge for which her whole life and work had prepared her. Born to an assimilated Jewish family in Germany in 1906, Arendt studied philosophy under some of the country's leading thinkers—most notably Martin Heidegger, who was also her lover, and who would go on to become a prominent Nazi supporter. When Hitler seized power in 1933, Arendt was arrested on account of her work for a Zionist organization; released after a few days, she escaped to Paris, where she continued her Zionist activism until the outbreak of World War II. Imprisoned again, this time as a German national in France, she managed to escape after the fall of France and made it to America, where she would spend the second half of her life, producing a number of classic books of political philosophy.

The trial of Adolf Eichmann was an opportunity to put her abstract thinking about politics and morality to the test. Here was a man reputed to be one of the worst Nazi criminals, personally responsible for countless Jewish deaths. One Nuremberg defendant testified that Eichmann had said he would "leap laughing into the grave because the feeling that he had five million people on his conscience would be for him a source of extraordinary satisfaction." How did Eichmann become such a monster, and what might his story reveal about the nature of totalitarianism and anti-Semitism?

Eichmann in Jerusalem became a scandalous book because Arendt's answers to these questions were far from what Jewish readers, in particular, were expecting. Eichmann, she communicates both explicitly and by her ironic tone, was no evil genius. Although the prosecution claimed that he was a mastermind of the Holocaust, Arendt argues that he was merely a dull-witted bureaucrat, faithfully carrying out the orders he was given. That these orders happened to involve mass murder made no real difference to him. "Everybody could see that this man was not a 'monster,'" she concludes, "but it was difficult indeed not to suspect that he was a clown."

This understanding of Eichmann, which has been challenged by later historians, made sense to Arendt because it expressed one of her central philosophical claims: that the key to acting morally is the ability to think independently. For Eichmann—as, Arendt implies, for most of us—morality was a matter of following the rules prescribed by society at large. Ordinarily those rules forbid murder, but in Nazi Germany things were reversed: "Just as the law in civilized countries assumes that the voice of conscience tells everybody 'Thou shalt not kill' . . . so the law of Hitler's land demanded that the voice of conscience tell everybody: 'Thou shalt kill,'" Arendt writes. And Eichmann followed that commandment rigorously because he was, in his own eyes, not a criminal but an "idealist," someone who acts out of strict adherence to principle. Arendt notes that near the end of the war, when corruption reigned and many of his superiors began to accept bribes to spare Jewish lives, Eichmann was indignant, since this was a violation of the "morality" of Nazism.

The implications of this way of understanding Eichmann are more frightening than if he had been a psychopath or ideological fanatic. After all, most people aren't crazy or fanatical, and so we might assume that they wouldn't be capable of becoming mass murderers. But Arendt's argument implies that ordinary people are largely incapable of resistance when the society they live in decides to change the terms of morality, turning evil into good. She drives the point home with an example from Eichmann's case history. In the fall of 1941, German soldiers were murdering hundreds of thousands of Jews in the territories Germany had conquered from the Soviet Union, but the Jews of occupied Poland were still living in ghettos, since the extermination camps that would finally kill almost all of them had not yet begun to function.

That September, Arendt writes, Eichmann received an order to ship 20,000 German Jews out of the country, as part of Hitler's drive to make Germany *Judenrein*, "free from Jews." Instead of sending these Jews to occupied Russia, where they would be shot immediately, Eichmann chose to send them to the ghetto in Lodz, Poland. "Here for the first and last time I had a choice," Eichmann testified at his trial, and it was supposed to be to his credit that he chose the less murderous option. (In fact, the Jews of the Lodz ghetto were almost all murdered in death camps, starting in 1942.) However, Eichmann got into trouble with the governor of Lodz for sending him more Jews; so the next month, when another transport of 50,000 German Jews was being organized, he duly sent them to the Russian zone, where they were shot to death. Arendt concludes that this story proves "the accused had a conscience . . . and his conscience functioned in the expected way for almost four weeks, whereupon it began to function the other way around."

Arendt's sarcasm is palpable, but the somber conclusion of *Eichmann in Jerusalem* is that most people's consciences would adapt to murder just as rapidly as Eichmann's did. After all, Eichmann did not carry out the Holocaust alone; he had countless accomplices, from the soldiers who killed Jews on the Eastern Front, to the engineers who drove the trains to Auschwitz, to the ordinary citizens who saw their Jewish neighbors disappear and said nothing. "The trouble with Eichmann," Arendt writes in the epilogue, "was precisely that so many were like him, and that the many were neither perverted nor sadistic, that they were, and still are, terribly and terrifying normal." This idea was and remains controversial, because it seems to minimize Eichmann's evil motives. Could it be true that Eichmann helped to kill five million people without harboring any murderous feelings, or even any strongly anti-Semitic ones? If so, then evil is not a matter of emotion but of cognition—the ability to think about one's actions, to assess them according to an independent moral standard, and to ponder their consequences for other people. Eichmann, Arendt concludes, "to put the matter colloquially, never realized what he was doing."

This doesn't mean that he didn't know his actions would result in the death of millions; rather, Arendt suggests that he didn't realize that participating in murder on such a scale is irredeemably evil. In part, Eichmann and other Nazis were shielded from this knowledge by their use of euphemism, or what they called "language rules": instead of speaking of killing people, they used terms like "evacuation" and "special handling." The purpose of such euphemisms, Arendt writes, "was not to keep these people ignorant of what they were doing, but to prevent them from equating it with their old, 'normal' knowledge of murder and lies." This lesson, too, is not specific to Nazi Germany but applies to all modern governments that make use of euphemisms to disguise the real meaning of their actions.

Arendt's theory is open to objection on factual grounds—later scholars have argued that Eichmann was, in fact, a convinced anti-Semite, who merely downplayed his hatred for the benefit of the Israeli court. But its real explosiveness lies in the challenge it poses to our usual understanding of criminal responsibility and justice. Ordinarily, to be guilty of a crime a defendant must demonstrate *mens rea*—a guilty mind, the intent to do wrong. But if Arendt's analysis is correct, then the worst crime of all, the Holocaust, was committed without any consciousness of guilt on the part of the perpetrators. How, then, could Eichmann be found guilty and executed by the Israeli court—as it was clear from the first day that he would be?

Arendt's disapproval of the way Eichmann was prosecuted is unconcealed in *Eichmann in Jerusalem*. She believed that the state prosecutor, Gideon Hausner—acting at the direction of the prime minister, David Ben-Gurion—had stage-managed a show trial, in which the Eichmann case was used to publicize the suffering of the Jews of Europe. Hundreds of survivors were called to testify about their experiences in the Holocaust, even when these had nothing to do with Eichmann personally, so that the trial dragged on for many months. The goal was not only to appeal to the conscience of the world, but also to teach young Israelis a Zionist interpretation of the Holocaust that emphasized the helplessness of Jews in the Diaspora. Cruelly, in Arendt's view, Hausner asked survivors why Jews in the concentration camps hadn't rebelled against their Nazi captors—even though, she pointed out, "no non-Jewish group or people behaved differently."

Yet Arendt's own views on the subject of Jewish resistance and collaboration were also ambivalent. Even as she seems to minimize the conscious guilt of Eichmann, she writes bitterly about the Jewish community leaders who served on the *Judenrate*, the Jewish Councils established by the Nazis to manage Jewish affairs, who were often responsible for drawing up lists of individuals to be deported to the death camps. "To a Jew," Arendt writes, "this role of the Jewish leaders in the destruction of their own people is undoubtedly the darkest chapter of the whole dark story." If the Jews had been totally leaderless and disorganized, she argues, far fewer people would have fallen into the Nazis' hands.

This line of argument provoked some of the strongest criticism of *Eichmann in Jerusalem*, partly because Arendt seems to display more indignation about the behavior of the Jewish victims than she does about Eichmann himself, whom she dismisses with mockery. But if Arendt is angry at the Jewish leadership in Europe, it is exactly because she has higher expectations for her fellow Jews than she does for the Germans. Arendt was critical of Israel in *Eichmann in Jerusalem* and elsewhere, but it was not for nothing that she spent almost a decade working for Youth Aliyah, an organization that trained young European Jews for emigration to Palestine. Her critique of Diaspora passivity and complicity stems from a Zionist political consciousness: she believes the Jewish leadership should have been quicker to identify the Nazis as deadly enemies who had to be resisted, even though such resistance would have been effectively hopeless.

Zionist, too, is Arendt's conclusion about the legitimacy of the trial itself. The proceedings were open to serious legal objections, ranging from the way the Israelis had captured Eichmann, to the competence of an Israeli court to sit in judgment on a German defendant, to the problem—which had also been raised at the Nuremberg

Trials—that the Nazis' crimes had not violated existing German law. In her epilogue, however, Arendt makes clear that she believes the Israelis had every right to put Eichmann on trial, because she accepts the fundamental Zionist principle that Israel is the state of the Jewish people. Just as Poland, Czechoslovakia, France, and other countries had the right to try Nazi war criminals for crimes committed against their citizens, so Israel had jurisdiction over crimes against Jews. That the Holocaust did not take place on Israeli territory was insignificant, Arendt argues, because "territory" should not be considered to refer only to a piece of land. It is equally a matter of "relationships, based on a common language, religion, a common history, customs, and laws."

Still, this doesn't mean Arendt believes that the trial did full justice to Eichmann's crimes. In the Israelis' view, Eichmann was on trial as an enemy of the Jewish people—one of the worst and most effective Jew-haters of all time, but nevertheless a familiar historical type. To Arendt, this is to miss what was distinctively new about the Holocaust, which was not a crime against the Jews—"the most horrible pogrom in Jewish history," as she puts it—but a crime against humanity. In her provocative formula, "these modern, state-employed mass murderers must be prosecuted because they violated the order of mankind, and not because they killed millions of people." For genocide is something more than the killing of many individuals; it is the deprivation of the human race of one of its parts, and so it harms not just the people it targets, but humanity as a whole. Just as, in an ordinary murder trial, the prosecution does not represent the victim but the state, so in trying Eichmann, Arendt believes, the prosecution must not represent the Jewish people but the human race, whose moral order Nazism violated. The Holocaust was "a crime against humanity, perpetrated upon the body of the Jewish people."

Here Arendt ultimately diverges from the Zionist interpretation of the Holocaust and its lessons. The creation of a Jewish state may help the Jews to fight back against their enemies, but it can't ensure that no future criminal regime will commit genocide against another people—as indeed has happened several times in the years since

Arendt wrote. She believes that only international law, collectively enforced by the nations of the world, can prevent a recurrence of Eichmann's crimes. For the most terrifying thing about what happened to the Jews of Europe, Arendt concludes, is that "the unprecedented, once it has appeared, may become a precedent for the future." In this sense, the Holocaust represented a turning point in the destiny not just of the Jews, but of humanity itself.

II

AMERICA: AT HOME IN EXILE

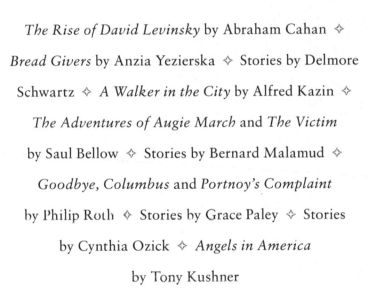

The Rise of David Levinsky by Abraham Cahan ✧

Bread Givers by Anzia Yezierska ✧ Stories by Delmore

Schwartz ✧ *A Walker in the City* by Alfred Kazin ✧

The Adventures of Augie March and *The Victim*

by Saul Bellow ✧ Stories by Bernard Malamud ✧

Goodbye, Columbus and *Portnoy's Complaint*

by Philip Roth ✧ Stories by Grace Paley ✧ Stories

by Cynthia Ozick ✧ *Angels in America*

by Tony Kushner

The Rise of David Levinsky by Abraham Cahan

I N MARCH 1881, CZAR ALEXANDER II OF RUSSIA WAS assassinated by members of a revolutionary terrorist group called People's Will. Although only one of the assassins was Jewish, the official government response to the murder was to foment popular anti-Semitism, and over the next three years a wave of more than two hundred pogroms broke out across the Russian Empire. Pressure increased with the May Laws, promulgated in 1882, which restricted where Jews could live and buy land. Combined with a rising birthrate, these new barriers meant that most Jews living under czarist rule were condemned to a life of desperation. Their response was flight. Between 1881 and 1924, when new, restrictive immigration laws went into effect, some two million Jews emigrated from Eastern Europe to the United States, utterly transforming a Jewish community that had previously numbered just 250,000, mainly descendants of German immigrants.

Abraham Cahan was one of the earliest members of this tidal wave. Born in the Russian Empire in 1861, a descendant of rabbis, Cahan had been educated to become a rabbi himself until he conceived a passion for secular learning and the Russian language—classic experiences of the modernizing Jews of his generation. As a student in Vilna he became involved in subversive political activity, and he was sufficiently well known to the police to have his apartment searched in the wave of repression that followed the czar's death. Rather than risk further persecution, Cahan chose to leave Russia for America.

He arrived in 1882 and settled on the Lower East Side of New York, which was already emerging as the capital of Jewish life in the United States: by 1910, almost 400,000 people lived in its one square mile. No wonder that when the novelist Henry James visited the area in 1905, it struck him as powerfully foreign: "There is no swarming like that of Israel when once Israel has got a start, and the scene here bristled, at every step, with the signs and sounds, immitigable, unmistakable, of a Jewry that had burst all bounds."

But though it may have been invisible to an observer like James, Americanization was already in full swing among New York's Jews. Cahan was both an example of this process and one of its leading facilitators, in his role as editor of the *Forward*, a Yiddish daily newspaper that he took over in 1903 and would continue to run for the next forty-three years. Under his leadership, the *Forward* grew into one of the biggest newspapers in America, selling 300,000 copies daily at its peak. Like Joseph Pulitzer and other turn-of-the-century press barons, Cahan gave his public an accessibly written paper full of human interest stories. He also hewed to a socialist political line, strongly supporting the unionization efforts of Jewish garment workers.

But while Cahan's journalism kept him firmly anchored in Yiddish-speaking New York, he also developed literary ambitions in his third language, English, which he learned soon after arriving in America. Cahan's early fiction, consisting of realistic portraits of Jewish life on the Lower East Side, attracted the support of William Dean Howells, America's leading man of letters. Editing the *Forward* and his many other activities left little time for Cahan to write fiction. But in 1913, Cahan was asked by *McClure's* magazine to produce a series of sketches about the life of an immigrant Jewish businessman. He chose to tell the story of a garment manufacturer, since it was in the clothing trade that Eastern European Jews had made their biggest mark. By 1917, he had developed these sketches into a full-length novel, which is now regarded as the first major work of American Jewish fiction: *The Rise of David Levinsky*.

Cahan's novel covers territory he knew at first hand—the journey of a Jewish immigrant from obscurity and poverty to worldly success—but it is by no means autobiographical. Instead of a left-wing activist, David Levinsky is a conservative businessman, who, as he informs us on the novel's first page, has amassed a fortune of "two million dollars and [is] recognized as one of the two or three leading men in the cloak-and-suit trade in the United States." Cahan spent his life fighting for unions; Levinsky's success is built on union-busting and the exploitation of Jewish workers. Cahan was an intellectual, while the great regret of Levinsky's life is that he gives up intellectual pursuits for a career in business.

In writing about David Levinsky, then, Cahan was creating a portrait of his opposite, even his enemy. But he wrote with sympathy and insight, above all when it came to the sense that the achievements of a Jewish immigrant in America were somehow extraneous, not a part of his true identity. David Levinsky, and by implication the millions of Jews who shared his journey, remains two people: the pious boy who grew up in a Jewish town in Eastern Europe, and the secular man who remade himself in the image of American business success. It may be a cliché to say that immigration is a kind of rebirth, but Cahan embraces the metaphor. More important, he writes that immigrants themselves instinctively embraced it. "The day of an immigrant's arrival in his new home is like a birthday to him," Cahan writes. "Indeed, it is more apt to claim his attention and to warm his heart than his real birthday. Some of our immigrants do not even know their birthday. But they all know the day they came to America."

The image of rebirth may seem to be a joyful one, but in this story it turns out to be much more ambiguous. For Levinsky, at least, it does not mean becoming a new person, but splitting into two people who have nothing to do with one another. On the novel's very first page, Levinsky reflects that his adult American life is divorced from his true identity, which "impresses me as being precisely the same as it was thirty or forty years ago. My present station, power, the amount of worldly happiness at my command, and the rest of it, seem to be devoid of significance." The difficulty of integrating the

Jewish past with the American future would become a central theme of American Jewish literature, but few writers have treated it as pessimistically as Cahan did at the dawn of the genre.

The question at the heart of *The Rise of David Levinsky* is whether we are to take its title literally or ironically. By all tangible measures, Levinsky does rise in the world: he arrives in America "with four cents in my pocket" in 1885, and thirty years later he is a millionaire. Yet the way Cahan writes about this rise makes it feel almost accidental; it is not the fulfillment of Levinsky's destiny, but a betrayal of it. Indeed, Levinsky attributes all his success to a literal accident. One day, early in his American life, he is working as a manual laborer in the Manheimer Brothers cloak factory when he spills a bottle of milk onto some silk coats. The owner of the factory explodes with anger, insulting Levinsky and demanding that he pay for the ruined goods out of his salary. Furious and humiliated, Levinsky conceives his plan of revenge: he will start a manufacturing business of his own, hire away Manheimer's chief designer, and become "a fatal competitor of theirs."

Revenge and pride, then, are the fuel for Levinsky's rise. It is an unflattering view of the psychology of capitalism offered by a veteran socialist, and Cahan pulls no punches when it comes to revealing the ugly secrets of Levinsky's success. Levinsky brags that he and his fellow Jewish immigrants have provided a great boon to the American consumer: their innovations in the manufacturing and distribution of women's clothing have made the American woman "easily the best-dressed average woman in the world." Yet Cahan allows the reader to see through this sales pitch, by showing how Levinsky's prosperity is built on underhanded business practices such as colluding with textile manufacturers and pirating popular designs.

Above all, Levinsky prospers through his exploitation of the Jewish working class. The fact that he started out as a member of that class does not make him more sympathetic to the workers' cause. Even when he was slaving away in a garment factory, he was hostile to the idea of socialism. "Do you think it right that millions of people should toil and live in misery so that a number of idlers might roll in luxury?" demands one of his coworkers, in language he might have picked up from Cahan's *Forward*. To which Levinsky replies coldly, "I haven't made the world, nor can I mend it."

Once he has his own company, Levinsky figures out that he can make the growing unionization of the garment industry work to his advantage: he claims to pay union wages, but then forces his workers to hand back some of their salary. All the while, he convinces himself that he is a benevolent boss, because he hires immigrants from his old hometown and allows them to work Sundays instead of Saturdays, the Jewish sabbath. But his paternalism only barely conceals Levinsky's contempt for his workers, which finds a philosophical justification in social Darwinism, a popular doctrine of the late nineteenth century. After reading the Darwinist writer Herbert Spencer, Levinsky is converted to the idea that competition is the rule of life, and that the rich and successful are the fittest to survive. "A workingman, and everyone else who was poor, was an object of contempt to me—a misfit, a weakling, a failure, one of the ruck," Levinsky says.

Yet somehow Levinsky is never truly gratified by his victory in the struggle for survival. After all, the purpose of being fit to survive, in Darwinian terms, is to be able to pass on one's genetic material to the next generation. But this he cannot do; the main disappointment of his life is his failure to find a wife or start a family, and the most dramatic episodes in the novel concern three love affairs that all end in disappointment. Notably, Levinsky's inability to get married is not just a Darwinian failure. It is, more primally, a Jewish failure, since the commandment to "be fruitful and multiply" is one of the most important in Jewish tradition. Symbolically, Cahan suggests, Levinsky's way of life is a dead end, not a viable model for future generations. In this way, he raises the question of whether Americanness and Jewishness are incompatible strains, and whether they can be crossbred to create a successful hybrid identity.

In connecting Levinsky's Jewish identity with his sexuality, and in particular with sexual struggle and discontent, Cahan set a precedent that would be followed by many future American Jewish writers. For Cahan, the disturbance of sexuality is a direct result of the shocking encounter between traditional Jewish life, which was puritanical and sheltered, and secular modernity, which sees sex and love as a realm of adventure and self-discovery. Tellingly, this conflict emerges even before Levinsky comes to America; Cahan shows that Eastern Europe was already grappling with the kind of modern problems that immigrants would find in the New World. For it is in his hometown that the teenage David meets and falls desperately in love with Matilda, who will continue to haunt his imagination for the rest of his life.

They are divided not only by class—Matilda is rich, David extremely poor—but by education and lifestyle. David is a pious Talmud student in a yeshiva, where he is taught that sexual desire is inherently sinful and that he must not so much as look at a woman. This lesson sits uneasily alongside the realities of life among the poor, where the young David sleeps in a room with three other families, constantly exposed to sexual behavior. But after his mother is murdered by gentile neighbors—a tragedy that permanently warps his ability to form human connections—the orphan David is brought into a modern, Russified Jewish household. Here he meets Matilda, a divorced young woman who has been initiated into the secrets of sex. She enjoys teasing the shy scholar and flirting with him. But their relationship collapses one night when Matilda visits David's bed and grows annoyed by his failure to make the first move: "Oh, you are a Talmud student after all," she snaps. It takes David many years to realize that she was impatient with his sexual naïveté, and that he failed at the first romantic challenge of his life.

Once in America, David quickly discards his chastity, along with most of the Jewish values he grew up believing in. Indeed, Cahan suggests that most Eastern European Jewish immigrants found it very easy to set aside the rituals and taboos that had defined the lives of their ancestors for countless generations. America is a kind of limbo, a zone of moral weightlessness, where inhibitions seem to vanish of their own accord. For instance, David arrives in New York with a beard and sidelocks, like all pious Jewish men; but when he is advised to get shaved, he submits without protest. "One may go without [sidelocks] and still be a good Jew," he is told, and it is convenient for him to believe it.

In fact, Cahan suggests, assimilation is a steep and slippery slope. Shaving one's beard leads to working on the sabbath, skipping daily prayers, and giving up Talmud study, which was the great joy of young David's life. By the end of the book, Levinsky has become "a good Jew" in the very different sense that defines American Judaism: he is a generous benefactor of Jewish charities and synagogues, a pillar of the community, but he no longer practices Judaism or believes in it. This spiritual loss is connected with what Levinsky diagnoses, at the end of the novel, as "a brooding sense of emptiness and insignificance . . . my lack of anything like a great, deep interest." America has taken away Levinsky's early sense of the meaning and purpose of life, and at first this feels like liberation. But it cannot give him any new beliefs to live by, other than the empty pursuit of money and status.

For David, it is less the metaphysical and moral precepts of Judaism that he misses than the premium it places on intellectual activity. Here again, Cahan established a theme that would continue to resonate in American Jewish literature: the sense that being Jewish has something to do with honoring the mind. David never really misses his belief in God or his lost chastity, but he deeply regrets not becoming "an educated man." As a boy, the realm of his intellectual activity was the Talmud; as an adult in America, he transfers his allegiance to secular subjects like mathematics and literature. But the content of his study matters less than the fact of study itself. He sees his own business career as a fatal distraction from his true calling, which is to go to college and become a doctor or a writer. City College is what Levinsky calls "the synagogue of my new life." In forsaking that faith, he commits an even greater sin against himself than he did in forsaking Judaism.

This sense of having missed his calling is connected with Levinsky's inability to settle down in his new life. His failure to marry, which he regrets so often, is largely self-determined; he is offered many possible matches, but he only falls in love with women he cannot conceivably end up marrying. Once in New York, he is drawn to Dora, the wife of a friend; they become lovers, but eventually they must separate, leaving them both brokenhearted. Later, Levinsky will throw himself into a hopeless passion for the bohemian Anna, a much younger woman who is interested in socialism and art, and who looks down on him as a rich philistine. Cahan does not speak the language of Freudianism, which was becoming popular around the time *The Rise of David Levinsky* was published. But there is a deep psychological insight in his portrait of a man unable to feel love for any woman who might actually love him back.

The reasons for Levinsky's emotional disability are partly personal, having to do with the brutal loss of his mother: "You're an orphan, poor thing," a friend observes when he is already middle aged. The violence and vulnerability of the Jewish past, Cahan observes, continue to leave traces far into the American future. But Levinsky's predicament is also cultural and generational: he is unable to love because he is unable to conceive of a viable future for himself in America. How could he, when, as he observes at the end of the book, "my past and my present do not comport well"?

In a sense, it is precisely Levinsky's prosperity that dooms him. Freed from the urgent daily struggle to survive that consumed most of his fellow first-generation immigrants, he is able to look inside himself; and what he finds there is dislocation and regret. For the immigrant, Cahan shows, striving and achievement can go hand in hand with spiritual confusion and emotional isolation. From the very beginning, American Jewish literature never doubted the possibility that Jews could "rise" in the New World. But it couldn't stop wondering about what gets left behind on the upward journey.

Bread Givers
by Anzia Yezierska

L ATE IN CAHAN'S NOVEL, DAVID LEVINSKY VISITS A
Catskills resort that caters to Jews. The very existence of the
resort testifies to the fact that Jews were excluded from gentile hotels,
as from many mainstream American institutions. Levinsky, for all
his wealth, continues to live in a completely Jewish environment; he
knows only a few Christians through his business, and worries constantly about whether they approve of him. Near the end of the book,
he briefly considers proposing to a middle-aged Christian woman
he has gotten to know, but dismisses the notion: what he calls "the
chasm of race" (not, significantly, of religious belief) would make any
such union "a fatal blunder."

Yet these barriers do not prevent Levinsky or his fellow immigrants from feeling that they are at home in America. When "The
Star-Spangled Banner" is played at the Catskills hotel, Cahan writes,
the Jewish guests sing along wholeheartedly. "It was as if they were
saying: 'We are not persecuted under this flag. At last we have found a
home.'" For the first generation of American Jews, becoming American may have involved sacrificing Judaism, but it didn't require leaving the Jewish community. It was their children and grandchildren
who would face the challenge and temptation of breaking out into
America at large.

This process could begin even with children who were born in
Europe, provided that they came to America at an early enough age.
That was the case with Anzia Yezierska, who arrived in New York in

1890, when she was less than ten years old. Between 1920 and 1932, Yezierska published six works of fiction drawing on her experience of growing up on the Lower East Side, and achieved a temporary celebrity. One of her novels was turned into a silent film in Hollywood. But her work faded into obscurity over the next four decades, and it was not until after her death, in 1970, that a new generation of feminist scholars began to argue for her place in the canon. Today, Yezierska's novel *Bread Givers*, in particular, is recognized as one of the classics of American Jewish literature.

When *Bread Givers* was published in 1925, the world of the Jewish Lower East Side was already beginning to disappear. In 1924, the passage of restrictive immigration laws cut off the flow of new arrivals from Eastern Europe, while the Jews of New York had begun to move to other, more spacious neighborhoods. In telling the story of Sara Smolinsky, however, Yezierska resurrected the neighborhood as she had known it as a child in the 1890s. And she gave voice to a very different kind of Jewish experience than the one known to a successful public man like Abraham Cahan. For David Levinsky, the Jewish family is a wistful dream; for Sara Smolinsky, it is a living nightmare, one that she fights with all her considerable strength to escape.

Gender, of course, is one explanation for this difference. Arriving in America as a single man, David Levinsky is always the protagonist of his own story. Even before he gets rich, he has control of his destiny: he can decide what job to take, where to live, which marriage offers to accept or reject. It is taken for granted, by both the men and the women he encounters, that the wife's role in a marriage is to support the husband—initially by handing over whatever savings she might possess, and then by devoting herself to cooking, cleaning, and child-rearing. For both the men and the women of *The Rise of David Levinsky*, the freedom offered by America is the opportunity to form a traditional family, which is why David's own childlessness strikes him as such an important failure.

But to Sara Smolinsky American freedom is a much more subversive idea, which can be summarized in a phrase: "This is America, where children are people." She reaches this revolutionary conclusion after many years of being oppressed by her father, who manages through his tyranny and incompetence to ruin the lives of his wife and daughters. Yezierska mounts a strong indictment of what was not yet called the chauvinism of traditional Judaism, which is reflected in Reb Smolinsky's pronouncements: "The prayers of his daughters didn't count because God didn't listen to women. Heaven and the next world were only for men. Women could get into Heaven because they were the wives and daughters of men. Women had no brains for the study of God's Torah."

But Yezierska makes clear that Sara's revolt against patriarchy is not based primarily on feminist principle. Rather, it is an instinctive reaction to the way Reb Smolinsky has personally discredited the patriarchal ideal. He is guilty of the greatest sin an immigrant can commit: failure to "make it" in the New World. Of all the opportunities American life extends to the Jewish immigrant, he is unable to grasp a single one. When he tries to get rich husbands for his daughters, they turn out to be crooks and frauds; when he buys a grocery store, he is swindled with empty boxes and fake goods.

Ironically, the primary reason why Reb Smolinsky fails in America is that he refuses to make the sacrifice that came so easily to David Levinsky and most Jewish immigrants: he will not give up his Judaism. A Torah scholar, he clings to the traditional belief that such a scholar is the finest product, the ultimate justification, of Jewish society. It follows that he should not have to work for a living but should have his studies subsidized—if necessary, by the work of his wife and daughters, as was common among the learned elite of Eastern Europe. "Here I give up my whole life, working day and night, to spread the light of the Holy Torah. Don't my children owe me at least a living?" he complains.

Indeed, it would be possible to tell the story of *Bread Givers* as Reb Smolinsky's tragedy, rather than his daughter's. After all, he is trying to do the very thing that David Levinsky found too hard: to maintain Jewish traditions in a society that has no use for them. But in America, a Jewish scholar's life is no longer worth the sacrifices of his family. The title of the book tells the whole story: "bread giver" is

Yezierska's translation of the Yiddish expression meaning "provider" (what in English is usually called a breadwinner), and in America, for a man to fail as a provider is to fail absolutely. "If I were a widow, people would pity themselves on me," wails Sara's mother to her husband in her Yiddishized English. "But with you around, they think I got a bread giver when what I have is a stone giver."

Sara's sisters all submit meekly to Reb Smolinsky's rule, trapped by the belief that their obligation as good Jewish daughters is to support and obey their father. Their reward is to see their lovers banished and their lives ruined, growing old before their time. But things are different with Sara, the youngest, who is the most extensively shaped by her American environment. For her, authority must be justified on rational grounds, and when her father is unable to meet this test she makes her own declaration of independence, fleeing the family home and living on her own as a single woman.

Just how outrageous this step was, in the Lower East Side of the 1890s, is made clear by Sara's struggles to find a landlady willing to rent her a room. All respectable women, including her coworkers in a sweatshop, are convinced that only a woman who is sexually promiscuous would want to live on her own. They can hardly fathom Sara's feeling that a private room, after years of crowding in a tenement, is a moral necessity: "This door was life. It was air. The bottom starting-point of becoming a person."

"Becoming a person"—Yezierska's English version of the Yiddish word *mensch*, with all its overtones of decency and maturity—is Sara's goal, and it proves harder for her to attain than it was for David Levinsky to become a millionaire. Even poverty and struggle, for Cahan, feel like part of an adventure story, while for Yezierska they are bitter realities. Sara's modest dream is to go to college and become a schoolteacher, but to achieve it she must work a full day at a sweatshop, then attend night classes, and then stay up most of the night studying. She is always tired, hungry, and lonely; the only room she can afford is filthy and dark, and she doesn't have the energy to clean it. Few books are as successful as *Bread Givers* at conveying how difficult it is to rise out of poverty—the way it requires an almost inhuman self-discipline, as well as luck.

When she finally succeeds in gaining admission to an unnamed college outside of New York City, Sara is faced with the recognition that Christian America is another kind of hostile territory. For all that she has internalized American ideals of freedom and autonomy, Sara actually knows almost nothing about America itself. Older than the other students, poorer, and of course Jewish, she finds herself an outsider in paradise. Attending a college dance brings home the sense of her difference: "The whirling joy went on and on, and still I sat there watching, cold, lifeless, like a lost ghost. I was nothing and nobody. It was worse than being ignored . . . I had no existence in their young eyes." By the end of the novel, Sara has returned to New York as a schoolteacher, where she falls in love with her principal, a cultured Jewish man. Her dream of "being a person" remains an essentially parochial one, which requires a familiar Jewish environment to come true.

Ironically, Yezierska shows that what sustains Sara during her struggles is precisely her legacy from the father she hates. After all, she too cherishes the intellect, disdains money, and holds herself to a high ethical ideal; like her father, she is willing to withstand terrible pressures to keep to the path she believes is right. When she dismisses a rich suitor who offers to rescue her from poverty, simply because he is vulgar and materialistic, she is honoring her father's Jewish values. By the end of the novel, she is able to partly reconcile with her dying father, recognizing that she is truly his daughter: "Who gave me the fire, the passion, to push myself up from the dirt?" she asks herself. "If I grow, if I rise, if I ever amount to something, is it not his spirit burning in me?"

Like David Levinsky, however, Sara inherits the traditional Jewish admiration for intellect only in a secular form. Becoming a teacher is her version of becoming a Torah scholar (a path that was never open to women in Jewish tradition). Paradoxically, then, actual Judaism, in the obscurantist, patriarchal form represented by her father, represents an obstacle to achieving what Sara can still understand as

authentic Jewish values. That is why the book's ostensibly happy ending is belied by Sara's ominous image of her father, and all her ancestors, as a "shadow" and a "weight" that she must continue to bear.
The Jewish past has already become for Yezierska what it would
remain for future generations of American writers: a combination of
inspiration and burden, requiring a dialectical response. Jewishness
must be honored and escaped, preserved and transformed, all at the
same time. Literature itself would become one of the most important
ways of carrying out this spiritual balancing act.

Stories by Delmore Schwartz and *A Walker in the City* by Alfred Kazin

O NE OF THE MOST POIGNANT SUBPLOTS IN *THE RISE OF David Levinsky* concerns Lucy, the daughter of Dora, David's landlady and lover. Dora is an intelligent, thoughtful woman whose life provides no scope for the exercise of her gifts: what is expected of a Jewish immigrant wife is cooking and cleaning, not reading or writing. Cahan shows how Dora projects her own passion for self-improvement onto Lucy, whose schooling she absorbs at second hand. Dora makes Lucy repeat her lessons at home and engages her in English spelling contests as a way of improving her own speech. There is something almost vampiric about the intensity of the mother's desire to share her daughter's progress: "I want to know everything about her. Everything. I wish I could get right into her," Dora tells David.

Yet even as Dora clings to Lucy, she is doomed to fall behind her daughter in the race to become Americanized. Lucy's "manner of speaking, her giggle, her childish little affectations seemed to grow more American every day," Cahan writes. "She was like a little foreigner in the house. Dora was watching and studying her with a feeling akin to despair." The acme of Dora's ambition is to see Lucy achieve what she herself lacked: "My own life is lost, but she shall be educated," she insists. For Dora, true Americanization and independence involve two things: going to college and marrying for love, neither of which was possible for her. Lucy ends up fulfilling the first goal, but to Dora's distress, she rejects the second: as an adult,

Lucy chooses to marry a rich man for his money, rather than seek a soul mate. The lessons Lucy drew from her childhood of immigrant poverty were evidently the opposite of the ones her mother wanted her to learn.

From the very beginning of American Jewish literature, it was clear that the high expectations of immigrant parents would be fulfilled by their American children only in an ironic fashion. For the first American-born generation of Jewish writers, this irony would provide a central theme and tension. These writers were born in the first decades of the twentieth century and began to publish during the Depression years; they grew up speaking Yiddish at home and turned themselves into masters of English prose. In a sense, they were exactly the children to make a parent like Cahan's Dora proud, since they proved that Jews could participate in American culture at the highest level. Yet this journey into America inevitably meant a journey away from their immigrant Jewish forebears.

One of the first writers to express this generational predicament was Delmore Schwartz, whose precocious success, long decline, and early death made him a legendary figure in American Jewish letters. Born in Brooklyn in 1913, Schwartz came to prominence at the age of just twenty-three when his story "In Dreams Begin Responsibilities" was published in *Partisan Review*, the political and literary magazine that served as a major forum for advanced American Jewish writing. For readers of Schwartz's generation, this story provided what the critic Irving Howe remembered as "a shock of recognition." They were responding not just to the innovative form of the story but to the personal experience Schwartz had brought into literature for the first time: the experience of an American-born child who finds himself deeply alienated from the lives and values of his parents.

"In Dreams Begin Responsibilities"—the title is taken from a poem by W. B. Yeats—is a brief story in which an unnamed narrator sits in a dream version of a movie theater, watching as scenes from his parents' lives are projected on the screen. At first it is unclear how he could know the exact date of the scene he is witnessing: "It is Sunday afternoon, June 12th, 1909," he informs us. But as the story unfolds, it becomes clear that this is a key date in his family's mythology—the day his father proposed marriage to his mother.

The narrator's unease over what he is watching—he bursts into tears twice, causing a disturbance in the theater—quietly builds as the moment of the proposal approaches. Schwartz shows how his parents, even at what should be their moment of greatest intimacy, are fatally at odds with one another. His father is vain and boastful, lying about his salary: "My father has always felt that actualities somehow fall short," Schwartz writes. His mother is alternately submissive and stubborn, and small details foreshadow the way she will be dominated and disappointed by her husband. When the proposal takes place, the narrator imagines it happening almost by accident: the father is "puzzled, even in his excitement, at how he had arrived at the proposal, and she, to make the whole business worse, begins to cry."

It is at this juncture that the narrator rises out of his seat and lodges his protest: "Don't do it. It's not too late to change your minds, both of you," he shouts at the figures on the screen. "Nothing good will come of it, only remorse, hatred, scandal, and two children whose characters are monstrous." But the story does not endorse the narrator's demand. In its last lines, an usher scolds the young man making a disturbance in the movie theater: "Don't you know you can't do whatever you want to do?" the usher demands. The form of the story, split between screen and auditorium, allows Schwartz to communicate his divided consciousness. In his early twenties, he is simultaneously young enough to feel an adolescent's contempt and self-pity, and old enough to recognize that these feelings must be overcome. Symbolically, the narrator awakens from his dream to find it is the morning of his twenty-first birthday—the day he becomes a legal adult. It is time for him to grow up.

But for Jews of his generation, Schwartz suggests, growing up is complicated by the profound distance separating them from their parents. This predicament is dramatized in another of Schwartz's early stories, "America! America!," in which the author appears thinly veiled under the name Shenandoah Fish. It is a comic equivalent of his own incongruous name—the odd, unidiomatic Delmore, which his parents had thought sounded classy and British, coupled with the matter-of-factly Jewish Schwartz. Schwartz's very name bore witness to his predicament: he was shaped in the most intimate way by his parents' American ambitions, but they couldn't properly equip him to fulfill them.

As in "In Dreams," the main character of "America! America!" is an observer of the past—in this case, a listener, taking in his mother's stories as they sit together in the kitchen. These stories revolve around the history of another family, the Baumanns, whose trajectory in America is the opposite of what it is supposed to be: the immigrant generation is prosperous, while the American-born children are failures, frittering away their parents' achievements. Mr. Baumann, the father, is an insurance agent, an occupation which suits his talent for sociability and fine talk. He flatters himself that there is even something intellectual about his work, that he plays the role of "a sage although without rabbinical trappings." Respected and well-to-do, he is able to create a comfortable home for his sons, Dick and Sidney.

But the sons turn out to have inherited their father's easygoing temperament without his immigrant's drive to succeed. "The best preparation" for worldly success, Shenandoah's mother reflects, "was to be born into a family of thirteen children where there was never enough for everyone to eat." The Baumann children, however, were raised in American plenty, and so they are unprepared for struggle. Dick is a failure in business after business, while Sidney simply refuses to work, convinced that it is an injustice that he was not born rich. Schwartz suggests that their addiction to leisure is, ironically, the greatest compliment that could be paid to their parents, who succeeded in emancipating their children from the need for labor. "Sidney was to be admired," his mother reasons, "since in being unable to work he showed a sensitivity to *the finer things in life*."

What is most bitter, however, is that the young Baumanns have no appreciation of their parents' sacrifices, which made their own lives so easy. Sidney Baumann snobbishly insults his father's line of work, calling it "a gyp," and mocks him for wearing cheap shoes. This ingratitude, Schwartz suggests, is an egregious example of a feeling common to the children of Jewish immigrants, who "avoided and dreaded" bringing their friends home "because they were ashamed that their parents spoke broken English or a foreign tongue"—that is, Yiddish.

As he hears the Baumanns' story from his mother, Shenandoah grows guiltily aware that he is just as snobbish about his own family. As a budding writer—when the story opens, he has just returned from the requisite bohemian year abroad in Paris—Shenandoah naturally feels himself to be superior to his philistine parents. "The lower middle-class of the generation of Shenandoah's parents," Schwartz observes, "had engendered perversions of its own nature, children full of contempt for everything important to their parents." How could the generations think alike, when their experiences have been so different? "He reflected upon his separation from these people, and he felt that in every sense he was removed from them by thousands of miles, or by a generation, or by the Atlantic Ocean."

Over the course of the story, however, we see Shenandoah learning to adopt a humbler attitude toward the older generation. After all, he realizes, "nothing in his own experience was comparable to the great displacement of body and mind which their coming to America must have been." Even being a writer, he decides, is not properly a point of pride that should separate him from his family; rather, it is precisely as a writer that he should strive to understand them and speak to them. "He was sick of the mood in which he had listened, the irony and the contempt which had taken hold of each new event," Schwartz writes of his alter ego. "How different it might seem, if he had been able to see these lives from the inside, looking out." Schwartz's stories are parables about the difficulty of empathy, but they come down on the side of its possibility. In writing about his alienation from the past, he simultaneously affirms that it belongs to him, too.

In the same years when Delmore Schwartz was growing up in relative comfort, Alfred Kazin, born in 1915, experienced Jewish life at

the bottom of the socioeconomic ladder, in the Brownsville neighborhood of Brooklyn. Since the 1880s, Brownsville had been a center of Jewish settlement in New York. On the eastern fringes of the
city, still semirural in parts, it appealed to those looking to escape
the congestion of the Lower East Side. But the neighborhood was
synonymous with Jewish poverty; it was, Kazin writes in his classic
memoir *A Walker in the City*, New York's "rawest, remotest, cheap-
est ghetto."

By the time he published that book, in 1951, Kazin had come a
long way from Brownsville. A product of City College—the free public university that had been, since David Levinsky's time, the focus of
ambition for New York's Jewish youth—he published his first book,
a history of American fiction, at the age of twenty-seven. The appearance of *On Native Grounds* not only established Kazin as one of
the nation's leading literary critics, a position he would hold until
his death in 1998; it also announced, with its bold title, that Jewish
American writers were ready to claim their share in the nation's literary inheritance. Kazin was one of a cohort of Jewish critics who
spent their lives in service to the American classics.

But it was Yiddish-speaking Brownsville that was Kazin's real
native ground, and in *A Walker in the City* he returns to it with
ambivalent, intense emotions. "Every time I step off the train at Rock-
away Avenue," he writes, "an instant rage comes over me, mixed
with dread and some unexpected tenderness." It is the emotion of
an escaped prisoner returning to his cell, and Kazin suggests that
life in a Jewish immigrant neighborhood, for a boy with gifts and
ambitions, was a kind of captivity. He emphasizes the intense parochialism of such an upbringing, in which all of life was bounded by
a single city block: "Anything away from the block was good: even a
school you never went to, two blocks away."

It is never clear even to Kazin himself whether he needed to
escape Brownsville because he hated it, or because he loved it with
such frightening intensity. Certainly he never lets the reader forget
the poverty of Brownsville: he grew up sleeping on chairs near the
kitchen stove in winter, because the family couldn't afford to heat

the bedrooms. Some of his favorite adjectives for the neighborhood are "raw" and "gritty"; there were unpaved streets, dusty drugstores, and old farm buildings crumbling in the midst of the expanding ghetto. Yet *A Walker in the City* bears no trace of the resentment or desperation that is everywhere in Yezierska's *Bread Givers*. Rather, Kazin writes with celebratory tenderness about the tastes, smells, sights, and sounds of his childhood: pushcart cries, candy shops, handball games, the cables of the Brooklyn Bridge.

It was the quest for new experiences and sensations, Kazin suggests, that turned him into a "walker." The book is far from a conventional memoir; names and dates are scarce, and Kazin has no interest in continuous narrative. Rather, it is a kind of prose poem, a rhapsody of perceptions, memories, and discoveries; and the most important of these discoveries come during Kazin's escapes from Brownsville, on foot or by subway. "Beyond! Beyond!" he exclaims in one of the book's refrains. What lay just beyond the borders of the ghetto, he believed, was the real America: "I still thought of myself then as standing outside America." Psychologically, the great immigration that brought his parents and millions of others to the shores of America had not yet managed to penetrate the country's interior. To Kazin and the Jewish writers of his generation, the country they were born in remained excitingly, dismayingly foreign—a territory to be conquered through intellectual effort.

For Kazin, this effort led to a precocious interest in American literature and art. Like Schwartz, he was particularly fascinated by the period just before his own birth, when his parents had arrived in New York—as if understanding the recent past would help him to situate himself in history. He writes of suffering "an abysmal nostalgia for the city as it had once been," which is fed by visits to the American galleries of the Metropolitan Museum: "Dusk in America any time after the Civil War would be the corridor back and back into that old New York under my feet that always left me half-stunned with its audible cries for recognition." Significantly, Kazin's longing was directed toward the American past, not the Eastern European Jewish past that was his own family's history.

Exactly what it means to be a Jew, an American Jew, a Brownsville Jew, is one of the central questions of *A Walker in the City*. For
Kazin, Jewishness has to do much less with belief or practice than
with an overpowering sense of community. "Unthinkable to go one's
own way, to doubt or escape the fact that I was a Jew," he writes. "I
had heard of Jews who pretended they were not, but could not understand them. We had all of us lived together so long that we would not
have known how to separate, even if we had wanted to. The most
terrible word was *aleyn*, alone."

In these pages, we can already see Jewishness transforming from a
faith into an identity. Writing about the Judaism he knew in Brownsville, Kazin is largely dismissive: it was a shabby, boring affair, the
synagogue old and crumbling, the Hebrew lessons rote. Transgres-
sively, he reserved his spiritual enthusiasm for Jesus, whom he refers
to by the Hebrew version of his name, Yeshua. This is a signal example of how American conditions had changed the Jewish relationship
to the past: in the Old World, it would have been absolutely unthinkable for a young Jewish boy to rhapsodize about the Christian messiah in the way that Kazin does.

Yet for Kazin, Jesus is appealing not as a path out of Judaism, but
because he restores to Judaism the passion and spirituality lacking in
Brownsville. He was "our own Yeshua, the most natural of us all, the
most direct, the most enchanted." Elsewhere in *A Walker in the City*,
Kazin writes regretfully that there were no Hasidim in Brownsville to
offer a charismatic, ecstatic experience of Judaism. "There were my
people!" he exclaims, and it is easy to imagine Kazin, with his gift
for spiritual enthusiasm, making a good Hasid back in what he calls
der heym, "the home."

In the New World, however, there seemed to be no Jewish channel
for such emotions. For many Jews of Kazin's generation, left-wing
politics provided an alternative source of excitement and community,
and Kazin writes fondly about the socialist meetings and debates
that animated Brownsville life. But he is not truly passionate about
politics. He reserves his deepest self for aesthetic experiences, which
to him are the nearest equivalent to religious ones.

There is a close connection between the urgent intensity of Kazin's aesthetic sensations and his situation as a first-generation American. He is, after all, a kind of pioneer, born into a strange country that his family can do little to prepare him for. He must figure the world out as he goes along—like every child, only more so. That is why everything that surrounds Kazin in Brownsville strikes him as worthy of recording and reckoning with. As he writes, what he "felt in my bones about being a Jew" is that it entails "the fierce awareness of life to the depths, every day and in every hour: the commitment: the hunger."

The Adventures of Augie March and The Victim by Saul Bellow

AVIDITY FOR EXPERIENCE WOULD BE THE HALLMARK of the American Jewish writers of Kazin's generation, and none was more avid than Saul Bellow, the greatest of them all. In *The Adventures of Augie March*, the 1953 novel that made his reputation, Bellow's hero describes himself as "a sort of Columbus of those near-at-hand," and it was in this exploratory spirit that Bellow wrote about the American life that surrounded him. Lest there be any doubt about his commitment to the subject, *Augie March* begins with a declaration of nationality—"I am an American, Chicago-born"—and ends with the word "America," much as the Torah ends with the word "Israel." Bellow may not have had this scriptural precedent in mind, but it is symbolically apt: in his work, we witness America taking the place of the Land of Israel as the spiritual home of the American Jew.

The significance of Bellow's writing was not lost on its first Jewish readers. The critic Norman Podhoretz observed that Bellow "spoke for and embodied the impulse which had been growing among all the members of the second [American Jewish] generation . . . to lay a serious claim to their identity as Americans and to their right to play a more than marginal role in the literary culture of the country." It was Bellow's style as much as his subject matter that made this claim. The prose he invented in *Augie March* was an energetic hybrid of highbrow and slang—a self-conscious "accent of the future," to use Henry James's phrase. The famous first line of *Augie March* sets the tone for the syncopated eloquence that will unfurl over the book's nearly 600 pages: "I am an American, Chicago-born—Chicago, that somber city—and will go at things as I have taught myself, freestyle, and will make the record in my own way; first to knock, first admitted; sometimes an innocent knock, sometimes a not so innocent."

The sentence, with its self-conscious evocation of Huckleberry Finn and Walt Whitman, could not declare more clearly Bellow's intention to situate himself in the main line of American literature. That literature is Bellow's birthright, and he will not be dissuaded from claiming it, neither by gentile literary authorities nor by the alienation that, in Kazin and Schwartz, seemed to be the inescapable lot of the American Jewish writer. Over and over again in *Augie March*, Bellow insists that being born into a poor immigrant family does not disqualify him from participating in the most important and illustrious human experiences.

But as the story of Jacob and Esau teaches, the acquisition of a birthright is not always a straightforward process, and it certainly wasn't for Bellow. For one thing, Augie's opening declaration could not have been made by Bellow himself. He was not born in Chicago, the city whose great storyteller he became, nor even in the United States. Rather, he was born in 1915 in Lachine, Quebec, a suburb of Montreal, where his parents had temporarily settled before economic desperation sent them across the American border.

For Augie, becoming an American means becoming acquainted with the dark corners of America—the thieves, smugglers, abortionists, and con men who feature in many of his adventures, and from whom he receives a good part of his education. But his experience of these "somber" realities is by no means incompatible with embracing the highest traditions of Western civilization, which he discovers through his passionate, self-directed reading. Characteristically, Augie's introduction to the great books comes not in a lecture hall, but when he is recruited by a friend to steal textbooks from a store; he begins to read them before selling them to students.

Bellow knows that a Jewish boy growing up half wild in a Chicago slum might not seem like the natural audience for the Western

canon. Certainly the books Augie steals are not part of his Jewish inheritance, not the tomes that his ancestors spent their lives
studying. But for Bellow these are facts of no real importance. The
most American quality Augie possesses is his belief that things of
the mind are democratic, open to everyone who wants them. "First
to knock, first admitted," he says at the beginning of the book, and
Bellow was one of a generation of American Jews who were not
afraid to knock: "And what did I think of myself in relation to the
great occasions, the more sizable being of these books? Why, I *saw*
them, first of all. So suppose I wasn't created to read a great declaration, or to boss a palatinate, or send off a message to Avignon,
and so on. I could *see*, so there nevertheless was a share for me in all
that had happened."

It makes no difference to Bellow that these historic examples concern American founders, or German royalty, or French popes, who
could not have been more historically distant from his own forebears'
experience. For him, world culture is the possession of everyone who
can understand it, regardless of what we would now call their "identity." Nor does Bellow worry that Augie's own adventures could be
described, by an unfriendly observer, as shabby and inconsequential.
What matters is the quality of inner experience, not the outward
trappings of historical importance.

Augie himself starts out at the absolute bottom of the social scale,
the illegitimate child of an absent father and a mother who is mentally
impaired. His older brother Simon is a go-getter who will employ any
means to rise in the world, whether or not they are strictly legal or
ethical. His other brother, Georgie, is an "idiot" who will eventually
be consigned to a home. The only authority figure in the household is
a woman they call Grandma Lausch, although she is no relation but
only a boarder. Her tyrannical discipline keeps the family together,
for a time, but it is a hard school, in which Augie learns to value
freedom above all.

The picaresque episodes that make up the novel are united by
Augie's determination to preserve his freedom against all the people
and institutions that would take it away from him. Foremost among

these is work. Augie isn't shy of hard work; on the contrary, he goes through many jobs, from menswear salesman to coal-yard operator to smuggler of illegal immigrants. But the reason he has so many occupations is that he is unwilling to commit himself to any one of them. He is a seeker, and he regards settling down as a defeat. "I did have opposition in me, and great desire to offer resistance and to say '*No!*' which was as clear as could be, as definite a feeling as a pang of hunger," he admits, not without pride.

What Augie seeks is human greatness, and the surprising thing is that he so often finds it, even in the humble setting of Chicago's Jewish slums. Take William Einhorn, a neighborhood figure who is one of many substitute parents Augie encounters. Einhorn's arms and legs are paralyzed, so that he needs help to perform basic bodily functions. The actual substance of his activities is petty, if not laughable: he sends away for free samples to resell, enters newspaper and radio contests, and writes a newsletter for fellow sufferers called *The Shut-In*. Yet Augie insists that Einhorn "was the first superior man I knew," living proof of the possibility of human greatness even in reduced circumstances. With his plots and schemes, his ability to manipulate people and institutions, Einhorn demonstrates the same qualities that, in a king or general, would win historic fame. "I'd ask myself, 'What would Caesar suffer in this case? What would Machiavelli advise or Ulysses do? What would Einhorn think?' I'm not kidding when I enter Einhorn in this eminent list," Augie insists.

The refusal to accept diminishment, the insistence that life here and now is as full of possibility as any other time and place, is Bellow's American creed, which reflects the great contrast between the wide world open to him and the much narrower and more beleaguered environment his ancestors had left behind. Augie grows up hearing stories of the Old World from Mr. Anticol, the local freethinker, whose faith was destroyed when he witnessed a pogrom back in Europe: "From the cellar where he was hidden he saw a laborer pissing on the body of his younger brother, just killed. 'So don't talk to me about God,' he said. But it was he that talked about God, all the time."

Augie, on the other hand, almost never talks about God, not the God of the Torah at any rate. Judaism, for him, is local color, rather than a coherent intellectual or spiritual tradition that requires either allegiance or rejection. Religion is for the old: "the shaggy evening regulars" at the synagogue, "various old faces and voices, gruff, whispered, wheezy, heart-grumbled, noisily swarm-toned, singing off the Hebrew of the evening prayers." By contrast, the younger generation "had to be prompted when it came their turn to recite the orphans' kaddish." The ancient prayers are becoming unfamiliar to the American-born generation.

As for those who might deny his right, as a Jew, to claim an American identity, Augie dismisses them with lordly indifference. "Sometimes we were chased, stoned, bitten, and beat up for Christ-killers, all of us, even Georgie, articled, whether we liked it or not, to this mysterious trade. But I never had any special grief from it, or brooded, being by and large too larky and boisterous to take it to heart."

Being "stoned, bitten, and beat up" sounds like the kind of experience that might produce a complicated reaction to the fate of being born Jewish. If Augie refuses to admit this, it is not because Bellow didn't realize it, but because trauma and resentment play no part in the design of the novel. An Augie March who broods over his troubles or feels sorry for himself would not be the hero Bellow had in mind. After all, Augie rises above worse ordeals than neighborhood Jew-baiting, and once he goes out into the world, he never encounters any serious obstacle on account of his Jewishness. Indeed, he rejects the whole idea of his life being determined by the conditions of his origin. "If you're going to let it be determined for you too, you're a sucker. Just what's predicted," Einhorn lectures him.

That this was not the whole of what Bellow knew about American Jewishness can be seen by comparing *The Adventures of Augie March* with his previous novel, *The Victim*, which was published six years earlier, in 1947. Later in his career, Bellow liked to dismiss this novel as a kind of juvenilia, even though he was thirty-two years old when it appeared. But the book's powerful sense of constraint, which extends to both its language and its themes, is not just the sign of a writer who had not yet come into his full powers. It is also a deliberate artistic decision, suited to the very different understanding of Jewishness that Bellow wanted to express in this novel, written as it was in the years just after the Holocaust.

For Augie March, Jewishness is a fact but not an obstacle; for Asa Leventhal, the protagonist of *The Victim*, almost the reverse is true. Leventhal, a middle-aged New Yorker who works in a dull office job—he is a copy editor for a trade magazine—seems far less immersed in a Jewish milieu than Augie. Indeed, he has almost no milieu at all. Most of the book finds him in his office, alone in his apartment while his wife is away, or visiting the miserable Staten Island tenement where his brother's family lives. The novel takes place during a New York summer and gives an overwhelming impression of heat and discomfort; but the city also seems strangely underpopulated, as if the world was reflecting Leventhal's sense of alienation back to him.

A key difference between Augie and Leventhal is that the latter has an intense dread of poverty. Where Augie moves effortlessly from job to job, Asa will do anything to avoid losing the one he has, for he can never forget the time in his life when he was unemployed: "He had almost fallen in with that part of humanity of which he was frequently mindful . . . the part that did not get away with it—the lost, the outcast, the overcome, the effaced, the ruined."

It feels fateful, then, when a representative of that fallen world accosts him one day—a man who "looked like one of those men you saw sleeping off their whisky on Third Avenue, lying in the doorways or on the cellar hatches." Worse, it turns out that the man is certain Leventhal himself is responsible for his ruin. Kirby Allbee was a journalist who once helped Leventhal secure a job interview at the magazine where he worked. But Leventhal got into a fight with the man who interviewed him—Allbee's boss—and when Allbee was subsequently fired, he became convinced that Leventhal had done it on purpose to discredit him. He has spent years concocting an elaborate conspiracy theory, waiting for the moment when he will find Leventhal again and demand redress.

Like a Kafka hero—*The Victim* is plainly influenced by *The Trial*—Leventhal suffers from a persistent sense that he is trapped in a situation that is dangerous but not quite serious. Allbee is what we would now call a stalker, showing up at Leventhal's apartment late at night and running into him in public places as if by accident. But he is also a clownish drunk, full of self-pity and easy enough to fend off. Why, then, is he so unsettling? Why does Leventhal begin to doubt himself, wondering whether he actually was responsible for Allbee's ruin? "Illness, madness, and death were forcing him to confront his guilt. He had used every means, and principally indifference and neglect, to avoid acknowledging it and he still did not know what it was. But that was owing to the way he had arranged not to know," Bellow writes.

As it turns out, the true name of this secret guilt is Jewishness. Early in the novel, Leventhal clashes with his boss when he has to leave work early to help care for his sick nephew. "Takes unfair advantage. Like the rest of his brethren," Mr. Beard mutters. "I've never known one who wouldn't. Always please themselves first." The word "Jew" isn't mentioned, but there is no doubt which "brethren" Beard is talking about. Leventhal is well acquainted with the kind of low-grade anti-Semitic resentment from which Augie March's world appears quite free. Such hostility is calculated to induce paranoia in Jews, for they can never know which of their acquaintances harbors it, or when it will burst into the open.

So it is not exactly a surprise when Allbee's grievance turns out to be rooted in a similar kind of anti-Semitism. Allbee is convinced that the reason why Leventhal got him fired is that he once heard Allbee make an obliquely anti-Semitic remark at a party: he told a Jewish guest not to try to sing an old English ballad, because "it isn't right for you to sing them. You have to be born to them." This was, of course, the same attitude that many American literary authorities had toward Jewish writers, who they were certain could not write in the English language without distorting its spirit.

Leventhal naturally resents Allbee for making such a comment. But in Allbee's own mind, it is Leventhal's reaction to the offense that is truly culpable. In this way, a Jew's sensitivity to anti-Semitism becomes another sign of Jewish villainy: "You think that he burned me up and I wanted to get him in bad," Asa says to a friend who seems to take Allbee's side. "Why? Because I'm a Jew; Jews are touchy, and if you hurt them they won't forgive you. That's the pound of flesh." As their encounters multiply, Allbee lets drop further hints to Leventhal about the Jewish conspiracy that is not only out to ruin him, but to eject his entire WASP class from their place at the top of American society. "When I was born, when I was a boy, everything was different. We thought it would be daylight forever. Do you know, one of my ancestors was Governor Winthrop," Allbee rants. "It's really as if the children of Caliban were running everything."

As the novel develops—and *The Victim* is a short, taut book, less than half the length of *Augie March*—the teasing double reference of the title becomes clear. Is the victim in this story Leventhal, who is subjected to Allbee's persecution? Or is it Allbee, who is convinced that his anti-Semitism is only a response to Leventhal's persecution? Anti-Semite and Jew are locked in a mutual madness: "He had a particularly vivid recollection of the explicit recognition in Allbee's eyes which he could not doubt was the double of something in his own," Leventhal muses. At the end of the book, Allbee breaks into Leventhal's apartment, not to murder him, but to commit suicide there—as if to force Leventhal to accept that he is not the victim but the guilty party.

The fact that *The Victim* was written in the wake of the Holocaust is central to its conception and effect. But the annihilation of European Jewry is mentioned only once in the book, when Leventhal tries to shame Allbee: "I don't see how you can talk that way . . . Millions of us have been killed. What about that?" But Leventhal walks away without waiting for a response, and the magnitude of the Holocaust is never truly reckoned with in the book. The anti-Semitism Bellow conjures in *The Victim* is a metaphysical quandary rather than an immediate threat.

Indeed, there is something abstract and intellectual about *The Victim* that is related to its focus on Jewish identity, a subject that, at this phase of his life, did not deeply compel Bellow's imagination. Augie March, who takes being Jewish for granted, is a much more powerful character than Asa Leventhal, for whom it presents a problem. Perhaps the great liberating energy of *The Adventures of Augie March* came from Bellow's decision not to allow it to present a problem—to leap over its complexities in a "larky and boisterous" spirit. The energy and openness to experience of *Augie March* would be his finest rebuke to the idea that Jewishness should be considered a burden. On the contrary, in Bellow's work, Jewishness would be identified, for perhaps the first time in Western literature, with joy.

Stories by
Bernard Malamud

THE ADVENTURES OF AUGIE MARCH WAS PUBLISHED IN 1953 and won the National Book Award for fiction, inaugurating a golden age of American Jewish letters. Over the next twenty years, the National Book Award would be given to Jewish writers eight times (including twice more to Bellow himself). To a writer like John Updike, who belonged to the WASP majority that had historically dominated American literature, this sudden Jewish preeminence was almost as startling as it seemed to Kirby Allbee. Starting in 1970, Updike produced four books of stories about a fictional Jewish novelist named Henry Bech, who is clearly kin to figures like Bellow, Norman Mailer, and J. D. Salinger. "The book . . . had not so much been about a Jew as about a writer, who was a Jew with the same inevitability that a fictional rug salesman would be an Armenian," Updike explained, not quite politely. For a brief time, it could seem that to be an American novelist was to be a Jewish novelist.

Clearly, it was not just Jews reading these best-selling authors. In the mid-twentieth century, in the wake of the Holocaust and the founding of the State of Israel, Christian audiences conceived an unprecedentedly benign fascination with Jewishness. And American Jewish writers could communicate with these audiences because they themselves shared this fascination, which was born of estrangement. Jewishness for these writers no longer implied a religious belief or a linguistic inheritance. What, then, constituted their Jewishness? A question that could never have occurred to their European ancestors now became central for American Jews. How could they give meaning and content to an identity they could neither shed nor fully inhabit?

No American Jewish writer addressed such questions more intently than Bernard Malamud. The short stories collected in *The Magic Barrel*—published in 1958, another winner of the National Book Award—and *Idiots First*, published in 1963, appeared mainly in Jewish-flavored magazines like *Partisan Review* and *Commentary*. But they could also be found in *The Atlantic* and *Playboy*—a sign that Malamud's themes had crossover appeal. This was fitting, for running through his stories is the mysterious conviction that, as he put it in a 1973 interview, "all men are Jews, except they don't know it."

For this enigmatic statement to be meaningful, Jewishness cannot be what it was in the past, a determinate religious or national identity. Otherwise, it would be like saying that all men are Hindus or Japanese—a mere paradox. Rather, Malamud is implying that Jewishness is best understood as a metaphysical condition, a mode of the human spirit that is potentially open to all human beings to experience. This has the paradoxical effect of both elevating Jews— for they become people of special moral significance—and normalizing them—for there is nothing Jewish that non-Jews cannot find within themselves, "if they only knew it." Malamud's formula is thus perfectly expressive of American Jewishness, which has ceased to be an objective fact and become instead an elusive matter of inwardness.

What does being Jewish mean in Malamud's stories? On one level, it is a simple matter of having an Ashkenazi name and speaking an English shaped by the grammar and rhythm of Yiddish: "What's the matter you don't pull the shade up?" asks Davidov the census-taker in "Take Pity." More important, it almost always means being poor— often a poor storekeeper, like Malamud's own father. For Bellow in *Augie March*, as for Kazin growing up in Brownsville, poverty was a condition full of griefs, but one that did not preclude a life of vivid and significant experiences. But Malamud's poor Jews live in a gray and joyless world, where keeping going from day to day is the best they can hope for.

Often they don't achieve even that much: their stores go bankrupt, they get evicted from their tenements, they develop arthritis and can't keep working. Sam Tomashevsky, in "The Cost of Living," sees his little grocery driven to the wall when a new chain market opens up down the street: "After all the years, the years, the thousands of cans he had wiped off and packed away, the milk cases dragged in like rocks from the street before dawn in freeze or heat . . . the hours, the work, the years, my God, and where is my life now?" he laments.

But it is not simply being subject to misfortune that makes someone Jewish. Above all, it is the attitude they adopt in the face of suffering: a resigned expectation of victimhood, along with patient fidelity to an ethical code that the rest of the world has forgotten. In "The Death of Me," Marcus the tailor employs two workers who are always at each other's throats, a Pole and an Italian. He struggles to play peacemaker between them: "Why do you hate him and why does he hate you, and why do you use such bad words?" he pleads.

But in the end, neither of these men manages to kill the other; instead, it is Marcus who falls down dead, his Jewish heart unable to bear the strain of living surrounded by violence. He is literally too good for this world, and in the last lines of the story Malamud suggests that his fate was inevitable: "Although the old Jew's eyes were glazed as he crumpled, the assassins could plainly read in them, What did I tell you? *You see?*" For Malamud, it is the Jew who bears the burden of the world's guilt.

That the world does not appreciate this Jewish sacrifice only compounds its bitterness. Several of Malamud's stories feature Jews who try unsuccessfully to perform good deeds, sometimes while crossing ethnic boundaries. "Black Is My Favorite Color" is narrated by a Jewish man who falls in love with a black woman; after the couple is set upon by hostile black men in Harlem, the woman decides that an interracial relationship is simply impossible. The story, published in 1963 at the peak of the civil rights movement, has an unmistakable political resonance. Malamud implies that any Jewish attempt to make common cause with African Americans, as another oppressed minority, is doomed to failure.

Malamud suggests that the Jewish compulsion to benevolence can even become a kind of mania. "Take Pity" is the story of Rosen, an older man who develops a protective interest in a widow, Eva, and her young children. His attempts to help her, however, are all rejected, even as they grow more recklessly generous, from offers of advice to a loan to a proposal of marriage. Every time, Eva says no, leaving Rosen in a frenzy of stymied generosity: " 'Here,' I said to myself, 'is a very strange thing—a person that you can never give her anything. *But I will give.*' " Finally, he figures out a way to prevail in this strange struggle: he makes out a will leaving all his money to Eva and then kills himself.

Yet even this gambit, Malamud suggests, can be thwarted. The story takes the form of an interview between Rosen and Davidov, who is initially described only as a "census-taker." The setting is a "sparsely furnished" room that sounds like many another hovel in Malamud's fiction. But as the tale unfolds, and it becomes clear that Rosen is telling Davidov the story of his own death, the reader realizes that this is actually a kind of afterlife—a Jewish afterlife as dreary as the real life that preceded it. The story finishes with a startling, macabre touch, as Rosen looks out his window to see "Eva staring at him with haunted, beseeching eyes." "Go home to your children," Rosen cries, and the reader is left to wonder whether Eva, too, is dead—perhaps having committed suicide herself, as the ultimate checkmate of Rosen's stubborn generosity.

This quiet intrusion of the supernatural into ordinary life is a hallmark of Malamud's stories. Notably, the other world with which some of Malamud's Jewish characters make contact has nothing in common with traditional Jewish teachings or mystical doctrines. Yet it is always Jews who seem to experience it, and Malamud creates the impression that this spiritual susceptibility is another part of what it means to be Jewish. Indeed, in "The Magic Barrel," perhaps his best-known story, Malamud directly opposes conventional Jewish observance to the deeper and more genuine mysticism, infused by pity and suffering, that in his imagination is the true essence of being Jewish.

"The Magic Barrel" is rare in Malamud's work for focusing on a religious Jew, a rabbinical student at Yeshiva University in uptown Manhattan. Finkle is Orthodox, but sufficiently Americanized to feel reluctant and a little ashamed about consulting Salzman, an old-fashioned matchmaker. But his reasons for wanting to get married are unromantic and practical—he thinks it will be easier to get a pulpit if he has a wife—and he decides to see what Salzman has to offer.

Salzman is a mischievous and uncanny figure, hard to find when he's wanted but given to making abrupt, unexpected appearances. The women he tries to interest Finkle in marrying, however, are utterly prosaic, and they are not to his taste—either too old or too plain to suit his rather conceited sense of the wife he deserves. Finkle only begins to soften when he goes on a stroll with one of Salzman's clients—a woman much older than he had been led to believe—and realizes that the matchmaker has falsely built him up in her eyes as a "passionate prophet," a kind of religious genius. He is forced to admit, to her and to himself, that "I am not a talented religious person. I think . . . that I came to God not because I loved Him but because I did not." For the first time he begins to know the self-doubt that is the key to wisdom.

Finkle demonstrates how it is possible to be a Jew, even a rabbi, yet to lack the pity and otherworldliness that defines Jewishness for Malamud. This is the contradiction Finkle must resolve, with Salzman's magical help. He does so by falling in love—not for worldly reasons, this time, but helplessly and obsessively, with a woman whose photograph Salzman accidentally leaves behind. As it turns out, this woman is not a client but Salzman's own daughter, Stella, whom he has disowned for some nameless act of promiscuity: "She is a wild one—wild, without shame . . . Like an animal. Like a dog."

But learning this terrible truth only confirms Finkle's desire for Stella. What he needs to truly fall in love, and to become a real man of God, is to experience the pity and abjection that were missing from his Jewishness. Love of an unworthy woman will accomplish this for him: "He then concluded to convert her to goodness, himself to God." His transformation even takes physical form: "Leo had grown a pointed beard and his eyes were weighted with wisdom." Before, he had been clean-shaven, like a modern American; now he has a traditional Jewish beard. A Jew, Malamud suggests, must know suffering in order to become truly Jewish. The story ends with the rhapsodic meeting of the lovers, as the uncanny Salzman chants "prayers for the dead"; but Malamud doesn't tell us which will prevail, Finkle's faith or Salzman's curse.

The disjunction between actual Jews and essential Jewishness is taken even further in some of Malamud's most provocative tales. After all, if Jewishness is not a historical or biographical fact but a spiritual potentiality, there is no reason why only Ashkenazi immigrants from Eastern Europe should be able to possess it. In "Angel Levine," Manischevitz, a tailor suffering from a Job-like series of afflictions—his business burns to the ground, his son is killed, and his wife is deathly ill—is visited by an angel who offers to help. But while this angel bears the Jewish name of Alexander Levine, he takes the form of an African American man—an appearance that leaves Manischevitz confused and suspicious.

Manischevitz sends Levine away, but soon grows desperate enough to change his mind and go looking for him. His faith is further challenged when he sees the angel drinking and dancing in a Harlem nightclub. In this dream version of Harlem, he also finds a group of four black men studying Torah in a storefront synagogue and debating the nature of the soul. "But has dis spirit got some kind of a shade or color?" one asks, and another replies, "Man, of course not. A spirit is a spirit." And a spirit, for Malamud, is always somehow a Jewish spirit: Jewishness is the idiom of the divine, even when it is spoken by gentiles.

It is not until Manischevitz realizes this and declares his faith in Levine that the angel is able to heal his wife. The story concludes with a perfect statement of Malamud's Jewish universalism: "'A wonderful thing, Fanny,' Manischevitz said. 'Believe me, there are Jews everywhere.'" With this boldly naïve stroke, Malamud finds a way of reconciling the particularistic claims of Jewishness with the universalist ethics of America. A Jew is something everyone can become; anyone who knows suffering and humiliation—"How you have humiliated me," the angel reproaches Manischevitz— understands what it means to be Jewish. For Malamud, that is why the poor and the oppressed are, as it were, honorary Jews—even as some actual Jews don't qualify for the title.

This transformation of Jewishness into a moral and metaphysical quality was Malamud's solution to the problem of Jewish authenticity, which arose in the modern world wherever assimilation became a real possibility. In America, where the attraction of assimilation was overpowering from the first generation—where Jews shaved their beards as soon as they got off the boat, like David Levinsky—the quandary of authenticity was correspondingly acute. When a Jew looks inside, what does he find that can assure him that he is really Jewish? Can he lose this quality, and if so, can he regain it? The questions are at once earnest and absurd—just like the mysterious tales in which Malamud dramatized them.

Goodbye, Columbus and Portnoy's Complaint by Philip Roth

T O TURN FROM THE SYMBOLIC AND MELANCHOLY JEWS who inhabit Malamud's fiction to the outrageously vivid Jews of Philip Roth's is to cross a generational divide. While Bellow, Malamud, and Roth were often grouped together—Bellow wryly remarked that they were considered "the Hart, Schaffner and Marx of writing," alluding to a famous firm of Jewish clothiers—Roth was almost twenty years younger than the other two, and he came of age in a very different Jewish world. Where Malamud and Bellow were born to Yiddish-speaking immigrant parents and entered adulthood during the Great Depression, Roth was a second-generation American. Born in 1933, he came of age in a prosperous postwar America where Jews were beginning to move out of places like Brownsville and Humboldt Park.

This movement exposed Jews of Roth's generation to contradictory pressures. In the 1950s American Jews became more religiously observant, as part of a postwar trend that also affected Protestants and Catholics. By the late 1950s, writes the historian Jonathan Sarna, 60 percent of American Jews belonged to a synagogue, "a figure never exceeded and the only time in the twentieth century that more than half of America's Jews were synagogue members." This was a new way of formulating Jewish community, which emphasized membership in one of the three denominations that defined mid-century American Judaism—Reform, Conservative, or Orthodox.

At the same time, Jews developed a new sense that American

society—which, to Kazin in Brownsville, always seemed to be elsewhere—was more permeable than ever before. The decades after the Holocaust saw a historic decline in American anti-Semitism: "During those years," wrote one director of the Anti-Defamation League, American Jews "achieved a greater degree of economic and political security, and a broader social acceptance than had ever been known by any Jewish community since the Dispersion." Elite institutions that had barred or set quotas on Jews now began to open their doors. Most important, the younger generation of American Jews was rapidly discarding the historic taboo against marrying non-Jews. Rates of intermarriage, which had been less than 7 percent in the first half of the twentieth century, climbed to almost 50 percent in the 1980s.

For Roth, these changes translated into a new vision of Jewish life. His fiction not only portrays the new, assimilated Jewish middle class, usually in an aggressively satirical spirit; it also enacts the quandaries about Jewish identity that were becoming central to that class. Was being Jewish still in tension with being American? Why should Jews maintain the tribal loyalty that Roth decries? Perhaps Jewishness, which had lost its role as a religious identity for American Jewish writers almost from the beginning, was now destined to lose its social meaning, as well.

Yet the dawning of this possibility turns out to open new horizons of guilt, anxiety, and self-doubt. After all, to step outside the tight circle of Jewish life was to make a wager on assimilation that had signally failed to pay off in modern Europe. Roth is always haunted by the knowledge that even as he was growing up in safety in the Weequahic neighborhood of Newark, New Jersey, Jewish children in Europe were being killed in gas chambers. Which of these fates, Roth asked during his whole career, should shape the behavior and expectations of American Jews? Is the American welcome reliable, or should Jews continue to practice the strategies of caution that history had taught them? What would it mean for Jews to be truly at home in America?

Roth's commitment to airing these questions in fictional form already suggested his answer. Starting with his first book, *Goodbye, Columbus*, which appeared in 1959, Roth's instinct was to zero in on the most uncomfortable places in the American Jewish psyche and jab them with a diagnostic finger. To face down the intense criticism he received from many Jewish authority figures, Roth drew on his conviction that truth-telling is the writer's highest duty. And America, Roth believed, was a place where the Jewish writer could tell his truths without fear. Indeed, the recklessness with which Roth gave away his own secrets—about Jewishness, sexuality, and literary ambition—was a gauge of his trust in America.

That is the message of Roth's influential 1963 essay "Writing About Jews," in which he recounts some of the criticism that *Goodbye, Columbus* had received from rabbis and other community leaders, and indignantly rejects it. His only crime, he insists, is that he writes about Jews as honestly as any writer is expected to write about human beings. Yet some Jews believe that in doing so, "I had informed on the Jews. I had told the Gentiles what apparently it would otherwise have been possible to keep secret from them: that the perils of human nature afflict the members of our minority."

To such critics, Roth writes, "being conscious and being candid is too risky." But he rejects this as a misreading of American conditions. "If the barrier between prejudice and persecution collapsed in Germany, this is hardly reason to contend that no such barrier exists in our country," Roth insists. "The lives of Jews no longer take place in a world that is just *landsmen* and enemies. The cry 'Watch out for the *goyim*!' at times seems more the expression of an unconscious wish than of a warning: Oh that they were out there, so that we could be together in here!" The real challenge, Roth suggests, is for Jews to figure out what might unite them now that anti-Semitism no longer does the job.

What was it about *Goodbye, Columbus* that provoked such discomfort among some Jewish readers? Certainly there is an acerbic social comedy in the book's title story, a sharply observed account of class tensions among postwar American Jews. These are an undercurrent to the romance between Neil Klugman, a product of lower-middle-class Jewish Newark, and Brenda Patimkin, whose rich family lives in suburban Short Hills. Neil, who narrates the story, is attuned to all the little marks of status that place Brenda "above" him. She spends her summer lounging by the pool at a country club, while he is working in the dusty Newark Library. Visiting her house, Neil is struck by the refrigerator bursting with fresh fruit and the backyard full of expensive sporting goods, symbols of all-American bounty.

Implicit in all these distinctions is the question of whether Neil's family, which has remained in Newark, is more authentically Jewish than Brenda's. One of the early points of contention between them comes when Neil finds out that Brenda has had her nose "fixed." He teases her mercilessly about this attempt to remove the physical signs of Jewishness, to conform more closely to the American—that is, gentile—ideal.

Yet it is not the case that the Patimkins are fleeing Judaism. On the contrary, they are much more religious than Neil himself. Brenda's mother tries to pin him down about exactly which denomination he belongs to: "I'm just Jewish," he replies, as "I tried to think of something that would convince her I wasn't an infidel." The idea that one could be Jewish but not a synagogue-goer, which would have been commonplace to Kazin or Bellow, sounds anomalous in this corner of the postwar Jewish world.

But Roth suggests that it is the Patimkins whose social ascent has left them detached from the most authentic qualities of Jewishness. When Neil interacts with his aunt, whom he lives with in Newark, he finds her annoying with her Yiddishized English, her fussiness about food, and her dread of the unknown. But she is at least "just Jewish," in a way that the Patimkin children no longer seem to be. The difference comes to the fore in the comic scene that gives the story its title, when Neil is forced by Brenda's older brother Ron, a dull-witted athlete, to listen to a souvenir record album commemorating his glory days at Ohio State University. Roth expertly hits off the bathos of the album, but what's really significant is how deeply and genuinely Ron responds to its nostalgia: "And to you, Ohio State, to you Columbus, we say thank you, thank you and goodbye." In his unself-conscious acceptance of American kitsch, Ron is the most truly assimilated of all the characters in the story, and Roth leaves the reader wondering whether this adjustment to banality should be considered a success story or the opposite.

As Neil is drawn deeper into the orbit of the Patimkins, the possibility of marriage, and of joining the family's sink-manufacturing business, forces him into a decision about the kind of future he wants. Significantly, Neil, unlike many of Roth's later fictional protagonists, is not a writer, and so it is not in the name of literature or art that he can lodge a protest against conformity and philistinism. He must find a different ground for self-assertion, and the one he chooses is sex.

Neil and Brenda have no hesitation about entering into a sexual relationship, but she bridles at his suggestion that she go to a clinic to get a diaphragm. The issue, Roth makes clear, is less about propriety, or even sexual pleasure, than about dominance and control: "Just do it. Do it because I asked you to," Neil hectors Brenda. By demanding that she put his desires first, he challenges the advantages of wealth and status that give her the upper hand in the relationship. Brenda gives in, but has a trick of her own up her sleeve: with subconscious deliberation, she leaves the diaphragm at home when she goes back to college, and inevitably her mother discovers it. The scandal that ensues puts an end to their romance, as Brenda proves that, for all her seeming independence, she remains a Patimkin at heart, too conventional and status-minded to join Neil in his stand for sexual freedom.

A long road separates Neil Klugman from the satyr-like, sexually obsessed protagonists of Roth's mature work, from Alexander Portnoy in *Portnoy's Complaint* to Mickey Sabbath in *Sabbath's Theater*. But already in his first book, Roth makes clear that in the perpetual contest between sexual desire and social order, he is on the side of the former. Indeed, sexuality and artistic vocation are aligned, in Roth, as disruptive forces that are nevertheless legitimate. To be a good writer requires a stubborn faith in oneself, a willingness to trust one's own insights despite society's pressure to hide or moderate them. In just the same way, Roth sees fidelity to one's own sexual desires as a matter of principle.

What these forces have in common is that they are essentially individualistic. They require putting one's own true self before any consideration of what might be good for the community. Like Yezierska and Bellow, Roth enlists the individualistic force of the American creed as a counterweight to the obligations of Jewish community, which he sees as timid, conservative, and life-denying. Yet if Roth did not feel the strong claim of Jewish obligation, he would not have written so mischievously and passionately against it. For Bellow's Augie March, the right to an individual destiny was obvious and the claims of respectability negligible, partly because he was raised without a strong family to enforce them. For Roth, on the other hand, the right to be oneself is something that has to be constantly defended, using the weapons of comedy and aggression.

That is what he accomplished in the other stories in *Goodbye, Columbus*, where the book's real explosive power can be found. In "Writing About Jews," Roth dwells particularly on the story "Epstein," which deals with a middle-aged man's affair with a neighbor, and culminates in a slapstick scene where his whole family sees him naked and so are able to see that he has contracted a venereal disease. Against one particular rabbi who condemned Roth for writing about a Jewish adulterer, the novelist protests that "the character of Epstein happened to have been conceived with considerable affection and sympathy." Sexual self-assertion is always sympathetic to Roth, and he has no patience for the petty morality that can see Epstein only as a sinner. But the provocation of "Epstein" is mild compared to the other stories in the volume, particularly "Defender of the Faith" and "The Conversion of the Jews." Each of these tales offers a comic test of the limits of Jewish solidarity, asking whether an individual Jew is obligated to see himself first of all as a member of a collective.

In "Defender of the Faith," the question of whether Jews ought to be more loyal to one another than they are to America and its institutions is presented with provocative directness. The story is set during the last months of World War II and centers on Sergeant Nathan Marx, a veteran of the European theater who is now training recruits at an American army base. Marx is a Jew who has, through conspicuous heroism, disarmed anti-Semitism and proved himself to be a real American—although his commanding officer's insistence that he sees Marx as a soldier, not as a Jew, is implicitly self-refuting.

Preserving this hard-won Americanness becomes a challenge when Marx meets a new recruit called Sheldon Grossbart, who first forces Marx to acknowledge their shared Jewishness, and then starts to presume upon it to demand special treatment. Grossbart asks Marx to make sure that he and two other Jewish soldiers are excused from Friday night barracks-cleaning so they can attend prayer services. Reluctantly, Marx agrees, only to find that they spend the service horsing around. Similar requests for kosher food and then for a pass to attend a Passover Seder also turn out to be insincere ruses, in which Grossbart manipulates Marx's Jewish sentiments to gain personal advantage. Finally, Grossbart tries to meddle with the recruits' assignments to avoid having to fight in Japan. In disgust, Marx intervenes to make sure that Grossbart is sent into combat.

The exquisite discomfort of the story comes from the way Roth seems to substantiate, in the character of Grossbart, every anti-Semitic stereotype that American Jews like Marx try so hard to disprove. Grossbart is clannish, pushy, and cowardly; he thinks he deserves special treatment; he assumes Jews should help one another at the expense of gentiles. Of course, the story does not claim that all Jews are like Grossbart. On the contrary, Marx himself proves that Jews can be as patriotic and self-sacrificing as any American. Indeed, in the end it is Marx, not Grossbart, who deserves the title epithet: he is the defender of the faith in American values that Grossbart seeks to subvert. "You call this watching out for me—what you did?" Grossbart demands at the end of the story, to which Marx responds, "No. For all of us"—and that "us" both includes and transcends the Jews. The claims of Jewishness, Roth suggests in this story, cannot be allowed to interfere with the deeper claims of duty and fairness.

Of course, by suggesting that they sometimes do interfere, Roth is making a distinction that many Jewish critics of his story were eager to deny.

Notably, Judaism itself is not the faith that Grossbart seeks to defend. He is quite irreligious, using the obligations of Jewish holidays or dietary laws only as a transparent excuse to gain special privileges. Rather, Grossbart trades on mere Jewishness—an identity made up of family sentiment, insincere rituals, bits of Yiddish, and suspicion of outsiders. This kind of Jewishness, for Roth, is grounded in fear and hypocrisy, and deserves all the mockery it gets.

Ozzie Freedman, the rebellious Hebrew school student at the center of the story "The Conversion of the Jews," is a kind of Roth in miniature—someone who can't stop pointing out Jewish inconsistencies. He drives the rabbi crazy with his questions, precisely because they are good questions. If God can do anything, why couldn't he impregnate the Virgin Mary and be the father of Jesus? Less theologically, and more challengingly, "he had wanted to know how Rabbi Binder could call the Jews 'The Chosen People' if the Declaration of Independence claimed all men to be created equal." Here Ozzie spotlights the very same incongruity between Jewishness and Americanness that Roth dramatized in "Defender of the Faith." If Jews are supposed to be good Americans, how can they also see themselves as a community set apart?

Ozzie's rebellion comes to a head one afternoon in Hebrew school when he shouts at the rabbi, "You don't know anything about God!," and, in a blind rage, runs up to the roof of the synagogue. At first he has no intention of jumping off, but when he sees how upset the rabbi is, he starts to play with the idea—after all, annoying the rabbi is his favorite form of self-expression. Soon his mother arrives, the fire department brings a net, and Ozzie finds he is enjoying more attention than he has ever gotten. Finally, he takes advantage of this power by compelling the whole crowd, including the rabbi, to "say they believed in Jesus Christ—first one at a time, then all together." Only then does he consent to jump into the safety net.

Clearly, this story is a kind of parable of Roth's own position as a writer. Like Ozzie, Roth is impatient with Jewish pieties, evasions, and tribalism: he can't stop comparing the actual behavior of Jews with their professed beliefs and finding them wanting. Yet at the same time, Roth recognizes that there is something juvenile and solipsistic about this urge to provoke. "Is it me? Is it me ME ME ME ME!" Ozzie yells as he careens around the roof, naïvely expressing the self-assertion that Roth considers the highest literary and ethical value.

But the use Ozzie makes of his power, to humiliate and blaspheme, is proof of his immaturity. Indeed, in the end, what he manages to prove is that the Jewish community is more loyal to him than he is to it: they will do whatever is required to save his life, even betray their Judaism. What Roth intuits is that the highest American Jewish value is not belief in God—for Jewish communities in other times and places, it would have been preferable to become a martyr (or as Ozzie's classmates interpret the word, a "Martin") than to publicly confess Christianity. Rather, it is the community itself, its preservation and continuation, that is the most deeply felt obligation.

Just how strong the claims of that community were, even for a principled rebel like Roth, can be gauged by the extreme measures he employed to escape them. Ten years after *Goodbye, Columbus*, Roth published *Portnoy's Complaint*, an obscene satire on American Jewishness and its central bulwark, the family. The graphic sexual comedy of the novel—famously, the narrator Alexander Portnoy masturbates into a piece of liver, which goes on to become his family's dinner—helped to make it the biggest best seller of Roth's career: more than 400,000 copies were sold in 1969, the year of publication. Sixties audiences responded enthusiastically to the book's portrait of a man rebelling against family duty and conventional morality, in search of sexual pleasure and self-expression.

According to psychoanalysis, the battle of superego and id is a universal human phenomenon. But for Alexander Portnoy, it seems like a specifically Jewish fate. Looking back on his childhood in Newark, New Jersey, from the vantage point of his late thirties—an age and hometown he shared with his creator—Portnoy sees it as a conspiracy bent on inhibiting him. The many dietary prohibitions of Judaism, which may have had spiritual meaning for earlier generations, appear to him as arbitrary taboos, designed to instill self-distrust and suspicion of the world. This lesson in repression is reinforced by his mother, who loads the young Portnoy down with irrational guilt: in one comic scene, she stands outside the bathroom to monitor his bowel movements, concerned that he might have been sickened by eating junk food outside the house.

The idea that Jewish mothers were overbearing, and Jewish fathers correspondingly weak, was hardly Roth's invention. In *Portnoy's Complaint* he refers to "the Henny Youngmans and the Milton Berles breaking them up down there in the Fontainebleau," and the novel can be read as a cross between a psychoanalytic monologue and a stand-up comedy routine. The originality of the book lies, rather, in Roth's insistence that the comedy conceals a genuine psychic wound: "I am the son in the Jewish joke—*only it ain't no joke!*" Portnoy laments.

For Portnoy, as for Neil Klugman before him, sex is the battleground on which the struggle for independence must be fought. "LET'S PUT THE ID BACK IN YID!" he exclaims. "Liberate this nice Jewish boy's libido, will you please?" The frantic masturbation that consumes his adolescence is a kind of auto-emancipation, freeing him from the disabilities of Jewishness. "I grab that battered battering ram to freedom, my adolescent cock," Portnoy says. "My wang was all I really had that I could call my own."

But true freedom remains out of reach for Portnoy. His adult life remains a continual struggle between the dutiful, obedient, ethical side of his personality—which he associates with Jewishness—and the sexual, aggressive side, which yearns to break out into the wider world. That is why assimilation, the achievement of real Americanness, inevitably takes the form of sexual conquest: by having sex with non-Jewish women, Portnoy believes he can escape the psychological ghetto and achieve wholeness: "I don't seem to stick my dick up these girls, as much as I stick it up their backgrounds—as though through fucking I will discover America. *Conquer* America—maybe that's more like it."

Portnoy's adult life is a continuation of the same struggle that filled his adolescence: the fight between hedonism and duty. He appears to be a model citizen, someone his parents and his community can be proud of; yet he is also recklessly promiscuous. Portnoy is living a double life, rather than integrating superego and id in the way that psychoanalysis considers healthy, and the agonized comedy of the book makes clear that he is suffering for it. "Never mind some of the things I try so hard to get away with—because the fact remains, *I don't*," he assures us.

Yet even in *Portnoy's Complaint*, Roth does not display utter disaffection from the American Jewish family he so wildly satirizes. On the contrary, he is capable of writing about it with great tenderness, suggesting that perhaps the problem actually lies not in the Jews but in Portnoy himself. Toward the end of the novel, Portnoy waxes sentimental about the Sunday afternoon baseball games that the Jewish fathers of his Newark neighborhood used to play. Here, Roth suggests, was the sense of community and the healthy masculinity that Portnoy claims to have lacked. "Why leave, why go, when there is everything here that I will ever want?" he asks himself. But in order to become articulate, Roth the writer had to leave his community behind. That is one of the fundamental conditions of American Jewish literature, as of every literature: its love for the ordinary is condemned to the pathos of distance.

Stories by
Grace Paley

F OR THE INTELLECTUAL, SEX-OBSESSED MEN WHO POP-
ulate Philip Roth's fiction, becoming American is a matter of
energetic self-assertion—a determined break with Jewish community
in order to realize the promise of American freedom. Yet Roth's way
of making himself at home in America was not the only one available
to Jews, or Jewish writers, of his era. The stories of Grace Paley—
who was born in 1922, ten years before Roth—offer another vision of
what it might mean for Jews to become American, one that involves
not upward mobility and aggressive individualism but the forging of
new kinds of solidarity—with women, the working class, other white
ethnic groups, and African Americans.

Paley was an essayist and a poet, but her best-known work is the
three collections of stories she published at long intervals: *The Little
Disturbances of Man* in 1959, *Enormous Changes at the Last Min-
ute* in 1974, and *Later the Same Day* in 1985. In these stories, Paley,
like Bellow and Malamud, created an identifiably Jewish English by
blending what she called "the street language and the home language
with its Russian and Yiddish accents, a language my early characters knew well, the only language I spoke." One of her early stories,
"Goodbye and Good Luck," is an account of the life of Aunt Rose,
an elderly Jewish woman with a history in the Yiddish theater. Rose
speaks in the hybrid register that Paley described, eloquent but not
quite idiomatic: "In those noisy years I had friends among interesting

people who admired me for reasons of youth and that I was a first-class listener."

The need for Jews to create a voice that will be heard in America is the subject of one of Paley's best-known stories, "The Loudest Voice." To the young Shirley Abramowitz, who narrates the tale, Jewish family life feels like a conspiracy designed to keep her from expressing her natural exuberance. America, for her as for Yezierska's Sara Smolinsky, offers a way of outflanking domestic rigidity, with its patriarchal insistence that girls behave themselves. This is, after all, a country where free speech is a sacred value.

But it is also a Christian country, and the way Shirley ends up using her voice turns out to be ironic. She is cast as the Virgin Mary in a school Christmas pageant, on the strength of the loud, clear speech that her family urges her to tone down. Her parents are at odds over this piece of casting—her father tentatively accepts it, her mother is adamantly opposed, seeing the pageant as an attack on Jewishness, "a creeping pogrom." But Shirley and the other Jewish children cast in the pageant have no qualms; they simply enjoy the chance to show what good speakers of English they have become. Paley comically recounts the pageant using the names of the Jewish actors rather than their Christian roles: "Because of the terrible deceit of Abie Stock we came suddenly to a famous moment," she writes, counting on the reader to recognize that Abie is playing Judas. In the Old World, the figure of Judas was dreadful to Jews, since it inspired deep hatred on the part of Christians. In New York, however, the boundary between Christian and Jew is crossed playfully and innocently.

At the end of the story, it is left to Mrs. Abramowitz, Shirley's mother, to articulate the central irony of the pageant. The Jewish children turn out to be better at telling the Christmas story than the Christian children, because as immigrants and outsiders they need to raise their voices in order to be heard. The native-born children, Mrs. Abramowitz says, "got very small voices; after all, why should they holler? The English language they know from the beginning by heart . . . Christmas . . . the whole piece of goods . . . they own it."

To be accepted as Americans, Jewish immigrants have to use the American language better than the natives themselves—and, in fact, they do.

Channeling such voices is generally more important to Paley than telling a conventional story. In "A Conversation with My Father," she writes of her father pleading with her "to write a simple story . . . the kind Maupassant wrote, or Chekhov, the kind you used to write. Just recognizable people and then write down what happened to them next." But she is allergic to such writing—to "plot, the absolute line between two points which I've always despised. Not for literary reasons, but because it takes all hope away. Everyone, real or invented, deserves the open destiny of life." Her experimental or postmodern approach to narrative connects with her political commitment to liberation.

The connection is particularly close in a story like "Faith in a Tree," one of an intermittent series about Paley's alter ego, Faith Darwin. In these stories we see Faith dealing with the ordinary trials of family life, navigating between the demands of children, parents, and ex-husband. "Faith in a Tree" finds her in a Greenwich Village park, literally overseeing a group of children at play and conversing with the neighbors who walk by. Almost nothing actually happens—there is no dramatic coincidence or reversal of fortune, as in a Maupassant story—but as Faith interacts with her friends and children, Paley's prose conveys the trembling energy, hope, and fear of her historical moment, New York in the 1960s: "This *is* a great ballswinger of a city on the constant cement-mixing remake, battering and shattering," she writes.

For Faith, the idea of moving "up" in the world—"shot like a surface-to-air missile right into the middle class," as Paley writes in one story—and going to live among the Patimkins of Short Hills would be revolting. Her understanding of Jewishness involves a commitment to the difficult urban existence that most American Jews were happy to leave behind. But while the first generation of Jewish New Yorkers lived in Jewish slums, for Paley authentic city life involves what would later be called multiculturalism. "I dwell in soot and slime just so you can meet kids like Arnold Lee and live on this wonderful block with all the Irish and Puerto Ricans, although God knows why there aren't any Negro children for you to play with," Faith tells her sons.

Paley is poking fun, as she often does, at her own liberal idealism, yet she remains sincerely committed to it. In her stories, Jewish narrators alternate with Italian or Irish ones, all of them part of the same working-class sisterhood, all concerned with problems of marriage and family. Above all, Paley's solidarity belongs to the kind of women who populate her stories—unprosperous divorced mothers who make it through their difficult lives with stubbornness and good humor. The women in Paley's stories are unapologetically sexual and desirous—the Irishwoman who narrates "Distance" describes a neighbor as having a lover who "gave her great rattling shivers, top to bottom"—and they like men in general, even when they have trouble with individual spouses or lovers.

But they also don't take men quite seriously. In "The Used-Boy Raisers," we see Faith dealing tolerantly with her ex-husband and her current husband, whom she refers to, with slightly surreal humor, only as "Livid" and "Pallid." "I must admit that they were at last clean and neat, rather attractive, shiny men in their thirties," Faith reflects, and while the description is benevolent, it is also characteristically detached—as if it doesn't really matter, in the end, who she is married to or which husband is the actual father of her two sons. Paley's practical-minded feminism can be captured in a phrase from "A Woman Young and Old," when a mother scolds one of her daughters for stealing the other daughter's boyfriend: "Women should stick together. Didn't you learn anything yet?"

This native wisdom about the need for sticking together is the foundation of Paley's politics. "Faith in a Tree" ends with the arrival of anti–Vietnam War protesters in the park, which Paley describes as sparking a political awakening in Faith—a widening of horizons from the neighborhood to the nation and the globe. Faith's high-minded liberal politics are those of a whole generation of American Jews, and Paley shared them—she was a lifelong activist and frequent protester. In this vision, concern for humanity as a whole is morally superior to a narrow Jewish parochialism, which for Paley includes Zionism. While we often hear Faith Darwin's elderly parents worrying over the State of Israel, Paley's narrator in "The Used-Boy Raisers" declares: "You know my opinions perfectly well. I believe in the Diaspora, not only as a fact but as a tenet. I'm against Israel on technical grounds. I'm very disappointed that they decided to become a nation in my lifetime." Jews are meant to be "a splinter in the toe of civilization, a victim to aggravate the conscience."

Paley recognizes, however, that this idealistic Jewish universalism can have ironic effects when brought to bear in the real world. People of goodwill may end up blundering into social problems they don't understand, doing more harm than good. Paley offers a parable of such misguided intrusiveness in "Samuel," a brief story about a group of boys who are riding between subway cars. One of their concerned fellow passengers, worried that the boys might fall and get hurt, scolds them, but they respond by mocking her; whereupon another bystander, angry at their defiance, pulls the train's emergency brake—causing Samuel, one of the boys, to fall "head first to be crushed and killed between the cars." The desire to help people, Paley knows, can be hard to separate from the impulse to control and punish them—a temptation to which the high-minded liberal is especially prone.

That Samuel and his friends are black adds an important dimension to this dynamic. The woman who intervenes to scold the boys is hesitant at first because "three of the boys were Negroes and the fourth was something else she couldn't tell for sure. She was afraid they'd be fresh and laugh at her and embarrass her. She wasn't afraid they'd hit her, but she was afraid of embarrassment." This is the embarrassment of the Jewish liberal who finds that her benevolence isn't trusted or needed by those who are its objects—a theme that was highly salient to New Yorkers like Paley in the 1960s and 1970s, as relations between the Jewish and black communities broke down. The solidarity that Faith forges with her Irish and Italian neighbors remains paralyzed by suspicion when it comes to African Americans, who appear in her stories as figures of suspicion and resistance to her maternalism.

That is what happens in "The Long-Distance Runner," a surreal tale in which Faith goes on a jogging odyssey through New York City. She ends up back in "the old neighborhood"—Paley herself grew up in the Bronx—where she finds that the Jews have left and African Americans have moved in. Faith is now an interloper, and when she tells a local girl that she will take her in—benevolently, as Faith thinks; arrogantly, as the reader can see—she awakens the anger of a local crowd. To escape, she takes refuge in her old apartment, where a black woman, Mrs. Luddy, and her son Donald now live. At first they take her in and protect her, and Faith starts to cultivate Donald's writing ability: "Donald, I said, you are plain brilliant. I'm never going to forget you." But after living with them for days, they grow tired of her presence: "Time to go, lady . . . Time we was by ourself a little," Mrs. Luddy tells her plainly. Once again, Faith finds that there is a limit to what her benevolence can accomplish.

Paley's ability to ironize in fiction the very liberal convictions that she held in life is key to her stories' vitality. Her understanding of Jewish American destiny is similarly complex. At times she acknowledges that Jewishness may not divide easily into Americanness, that there is always a stubborn remainder: "Faith's grandmother pretended she was German in just the same way that Faith pretends she is an American," she writes darkly. Yet at the same time, she can grow earnestly sentimental about America, in all its difficulty and diversity. "I made an announcement to the sixth-grade assembly thirty years ago. I said: I thank God every day that I'm not in Europe. I thank God I'm American-born and live on East 172nd Street where there is a grocery store, a candy store, and a drugstore on one corner and on the same block a shul and two doctors' offices," she writes in "The Immigrant Story." After all, "to a Jew," Faith's father muses, "the word 'shut up' is a terrible expression, a dirty word, like a sin." And for Paley, America is above all the place where Jews are allowed to speak as freely and openly as they desire.

Stories by
Cynthia Ozick

I N 1970, A YEAR AFTER ALEXANDER PORTNOY BECAME a byword for Jewish neurosis, Cynthia Ozick appeared at a writers' conference in Jerusalem to launch her own, very different attack on the American Jewish condition. At the time, Ozick was little known; though she was in her early forties, she had published only one unsuccessful novel. But this did not discourage her, in her lecture "Toward a New Yiddish," from launching a frontal attack on her more famous peers—beginning with George Steiner, the polymathic literary critic. Steiner had appeared at the same conference in 1968 and given a talk in which he defended the diasporic condition as the essence of true Jewishness. For Steiner, exile had fostered the most noble element of Jewish modernity—the tradition of critical dissent that includes figures like Spinoza, Heine, and Trotsky.

Nor was Steiner alone in arguing that the Jews achieved a moral sublimity in exile that they could only forfeit by descending to ordinary citizenship in a nation-state. The equation of Jewish existence with an exigent alienation was a product of modern Europe, where Jews had never managed to integrate fully into any nation. But the promise of American Jewishness was that here, at last, Jews could live unexceptional lives.

For Ozick, however, it is a delusion to believe that the patterns of the Jewish past no longer apply in America. American Jews have not escaped Jewish history, and whether they realize it or not they are still living among strangers—a direct refutation of Grace Paley's

optimistic multiculturalism. "Write urgently—before the coming of
the American pogrom! How much time is there left? The rest of my
life? One generation? Two?" Ozick asks. Jews who do not feel this
pressure are "autolobotomized out of history."

This anxiety gives Ozick a unique perspective on American Jewish literature. "The problem of Diaspora in its most crucial essence
is the problem of aesthetics," she writes, and it is by thinking about
art that she thinks through the problem of Jewish destiny. For Ozick,
American Jewish writers are profoundly mistaken to believe that they
have entered into the mainstream of American literature, just as the
American Jew is deluded to think he has entered permanently into
American life. In the long run, she is sure, it is not America that will
remember or celebrate the Jewish writer. Only the Jews themselves
can preserve Jewish literature.

Ozick goes even further, arguing that no Jewish writer ever has
or ever will make a lasting mark in a non-Jewish literature or language. "There have been no Jewish literary giants in Diaspora," she
contends (though she acknowledges that this principle has trouble
accounting for a figure like Kafka). When Jewish writers write in a
Jewish context for a Jewish audience, they can become immortal.
But Jewish writers who attempt to assimilate into other cultures are
doomed to remain trivial, minor figures. "Nothing thought or written in Diaspora has ever been able to last unless it has been centrally
Jewish," Ozick concludes.

Naturally, then, Ozick wants her own work to be centrally Jewish,
in a way that she believes few of her peers, even the most celebrated,
have achieved. One obvious way that a text can be Jewish is to be
written in a language spoken primarily by Jews, like Yiddish. But this
does not seem to be an option for the American writer, since he or
she is condemned to write in English. To escape this dilemma, Ozick
calls for "a new Yiddish": not an abandonment of English, but a way
of writing English that will make it a language in which Jews can
address Jewish concerns. An authentically Jewish English literature
will be "liturgical," by which she means communally oriented and
religiously serious. Above all, Ozick is certain that Jewish art can-

not be art for art's sake, which she considers a form of paganism or idolatry: "The commandment against idols, it seems to me, is overwhelmingly pertinent to the position of the Jewish fiction-writer in America today."

Clearly, an American Jewish literature written according to Ozick's prescriptions would look very different from the actual canon. Writers like Malamud, Roth, and Paley were concerned with what it meant to be an American Jew, but for none of them did this involve immersion in Jewish texts or connection to Jewish history and theology. Can an American Jewish writer root herself in the Jewish past instead of the American present? This is the mission Ozick assigned herself in "Toward a New Yiddish," and over the following decade she wrestled with it in three collections of short stories: *The Pagan Rabbi* (1971), *Levitation* (1976), and *Bloodshed* (1982). Unlike Malamud, Ozick's Jews are not floating symbols of a moral condition. They are specific people who inherit a language and a religion: rabbis, Hasids, Yiddish poets. And the question her stories pose is whether there is any place for such people in the American imagination.

In "Envy; or, Yiddish in America," Ozick makes clear that Yiddish, at least, has no share in the American future. Edelshtein, the bitter, aging Yiddish poet at the center of the story, spends his days nurturing his resentment of a literary world that ignores him. Yiddish, which in the early twentieth century had millions of speakers in Europe and America, is now virtually a dead language. The American Jews now speak English, while the Eastern European Jews have been killed by Hitler. Edelshtein publishes his work in a magazine that keeps going through sheer inertia, but he has few readers, and no young ones.

The most tormenting irony of all is that he is totally obscure at a time when Jewish writers have never been more in demand in America. Yet Ozick, writing at the apogee of American Jewish literature, emphasizes that the popular Jewish writers actually have little knowledge of the Jewish past. They are foundlings, washed up on the shores of a new world with no interest in where they came from.

This condition, which felt so liberating to many American Jews, is for Edelshtein a shameful deracination. He finds writers "of Jewish extraction" to be "puerile, vicious, pitiable, ignorant, contemptible, above all stupid. In judging them he dug for his deepest vituperation— they were, he said, '*Amerikaner-geboren*,' " American-born.

What makes Edelshtein's resentment even worse, however, is that there is one Yiddish writer who actually has managed to reach a wide audience, if only in translation. This is Ostrover, whom Edelshtein derisively refers to as "Pig," and who is easily identifiable as a version of Isaac Bashevis Singer. The fact that Ostrover has managed to break out of the Yiddish ghetto proves that it is possible in principle to do so, which makes Edelshtein's own failure all the more bitter.

The plot of "Envy" is desultory—Edelshtein attends a reading by Ostrover, visits friends, and rants against his fate and the ignorance of American Jews. The only glimmer of hope emerges when he meets Hannah, the young niece of one of his friends, who miraculously recognizes Edelshtein's name and can even recite one of his poems. Immediately, he decides that Hannah must be his translator, the bridge over which his work can cross from the doom of Yiddish to the bright future of English.

But Ozick, who spends much of the story channeling Edelshtein's righteous wrath, proves equally adept at conveying Hannah's resentment of this vampiric figure who wants to take over her life. Despite her knowledge of Yiddish, Hannah shares the American Jewish hostility to the past: "All you people want to suffer," she says derisively of Edelshtein's fellow Yiddish writers. She expresses the secret wish that hides in the heart of the new American Jewish generation: "Die now, all you old men, what are you waiting for? Hanging on my neck . . . the whole bunch of you parasites, hurry up and die."

Hannah's ingratitude is terrible, and in the end it drives Edelshtein to strike her, thus destroying his chances of ever enlisting her as a translator. But Ozick allows us to see that ingratitude might be the only force that can free the young from the unbearable neediness of the old. American Jewry may be shallow, rootless, and ahistorical, but it is at least alive, which gives it unchallengeable rights over the dead.

The difficulty of separating literary ambition from mere lust for fame is at the heart of "Virility," a story that fuses Ozick's Jewish concerns with her equally searching feminist imagination. Can Jews ever occupy a central place in the Western literary canon? Elia Gatoff, a young Jewish immigrant newly arrived in New York, is determined to find out: he has conceived the ambition to become a poet, and he writes tirelessly even though he displays no particular gift. He was born in Poland, where the rest of his family was slaughtered in a pogrom, and learned to speak English when he went to stay with his aunt in England. But as the narrator, a skeptical newspaper editor, points out, "no one ever taught *her*"; the truth is that Elia has no roots in English and no sense of how to go about cultivating them. Instead, he fakes it, changing his name to "Edmund Gate" and collecting obscure words out of the dictionary. Though he submits his poems everywhere he can, they are unanimously considered terrible.

But soon something changes about both Edmund Gate and his poems. He becomes commanding and charismatic, his total self-belief winning over admirers; and the quality of his writing suddenly makes a dramatic improvement. In life and on the page, what impresses people above all is his masculine force—indeed, his books are titled *Virility*, *Virility II*, and so on. Reviewers praise his work with adjectives like "seminal and hard," "robust, lusty, male." He becomes a celebrated writer and goes on world tours, where he is besieged by female fans like a rock star.

It is only when he receives word of the death of his aunt Rivke back in England that Edmund's self-confidence disappears. As he finally reveals to the narrator, he has been keeping a secret: the poems he has passed off as his own were actually written by Rivke, who mailed them to him in batches. Now that she is dead, he won't be able to publish any new work. Urged to come clean by the narrator, Edmund decides he will publish the last remaining poems under his aunt Rivke's own name, under the title *Flowers from Liverpool*. But this time they receive very different reviews: "Limited, as all domestic verse must be. A spinster's one-dimensional imagination."

The moral of this mischievous parable is clear. A Jew can succeed in English literature if he disguises the fact that he is a Jew, just as a woman can succeed if no one knows she is a woman. This is a joke at the expense of the guardians of the male, WASP literary canon, who can be fooled so easily. But it also reveals Ozick herself as an anti-essentialist, who believes that gender and ethnicity have nothing to do with the imagination: a woman can sound just like a man, an immigrant like a native, a Jew like a Christian. And vice versa: after all, it is Ozick, a woman, who invented Edmund Gate, a man whose writing is a woman's masquerading as a man's. Words on the page transcend the blunt categories of identity. It is only feeble critics who need to know an author's gender or religion in order to place them appropriately.

"Virility" suggests that authenticity is not a meaningful term when it comes to literature, which means that Ozick's universalist aesthetics and her Jewish ethics are at odds. Some of her best stories explore this self-division, such as "The Pagan Rabbi," a fable in which she insists on the profound opposition of Jewishness to all the values we look for in art—beauty, pleasure, fantasy. To be authentically Jewish, she suggests in this story, means turning one's back on such values, while the Jew who tries to incorporate them into his life is doomed.

The mystery in this tale centers on Isaac Kornfeld, "a man of piety and brains," who we learn in the first sentence of the story has hanged himself in a park. Isaac conforms in every way to the traditional Jewish ideal: he is an Orthodox rabbi and a family man. It is the narrator of the story, Isaac's childhood friend, who has turned his back on his religious upbringing, to the point of marrying a non-Jewish woman. When the narrator visits Isaac's widow, Sheindel, she asks him about the gentile world with a combination of curiosity and disdain: "What are they like, those people?" To which he replies, in good American fashion, "They are exactly like us, if you can think what we would be if we were like them."

But Sheindel rejects this neat humanistic conclusion: "We are not like them," she insists. "Their bodies are more to them than ours are to us. Our books are holy, to them their bodies are holy." There is, she maintains, some essential difference in the Jewish character that makes it impossible for Jews to live in the same way as gentiles; and this difference has to do with the body, with sexuality and the senses. For a Jew to seek after these things too eagerly—the way that Roth's protagonists do, without apology—is, in Ozick's mind, a fatal error that can only bring punishment.

That is the fate of Isaac Kornfeld, who left behind scraps of writing that allow the narrator to piece together the reason for his death. In a fantastic twist that Ozick treats with perfect seriousness, it turns out that Isaac had become a pagan—and not in a metaphorical sense. "All our meditations and vain questionings . . . are expressed naturally and rightly in the beasts, the plants, the rivers, the stones," he rhapsodizes. Ultimately, he even has a sexual affair with a pagan goddess, a wood nymph named Iripomonoeia. But his joy is short-lived. One day, the nymph offers Isaac a vision of his own soul the way she sees it. It takes the form of "a quite ugly old man" who carries a bag full of books and reads an enormous volume as he walks along the road—a tractate of the Mishnah, the compendium of Jewish law. Text, Ozick's image suggests, is the only authentic way for a Jewish spirit to encounter the divine. "The sound of the Law is more beautiful than the crickets," Isaac's soul tells him.

By seeking the divine directly in nature, then, Isaac has not just betrayed Judaism. He has mistaken his own nature, which remains essentially Jewish even when he strives to escape it. That is why his punishment does not come from above, but from within: he kills himself because he realizes that a rabbi can never become a true pagan. To the narrator, Isaac's friend, his is a tragic fate. But Sheindel pitilessly turns her back on her dead husband, seeing him as a sinner who deserves his punishment. And by Jewish standards, Ozick implies, she is entirely correct. To cherish the world, the body, and the senses is to sin against Judaism.

It is not hard to see, however, that this binary opposition makes the notion of a Jewish artist impossible. If a Jew ceases to be Jewish when he or she cultivates beauty and the senses, then there is no place for Ozick's notion of a "liturgical" art, one that could reconcile Jewish demands with aesthetic longings. The Jewish artist is condemned to be like the pagan rabbi, a contradiction in terms.

In "Usurpation (Other People's Stories)," Ozick embraces and dramatizes this contradiction. Art is magic and magic is idolatry, she believes—and yet, as a writer, she longs for exactly that kind of sinful power. "I am drawn to what is forbidden," she acknowledges. "The Jews have no magic . . . oh, why can we not have a magic God like other peoples? Someday I will take courage and throw over being a Jew," she vows or threatens.

In this surreal, multiply symbolic story, the magic power of the artist is given physical form. It takes the shape of a heavy silver crown, "heavier than any earthly silver," which Ozick imagines being passed from one great writer to another. To be a writer, she suggests, is to want to usurp the crown, to take over the power and prestige of earlier writers. Indeed, in "Usurpation," the central image of the crown is itself borrowed, or stolen, from a story by Bernard Malamud, "The Silver Crown." Ozick's story even begins with her narrator listening to Malamud (who is not named) reading his tale at the 92nd Street Y in Manhattan. Ozick's narrator immediately feels that she has the right to take over and rewrite Malamud's story: "By the fifth paragraph I recognized my story—knew it to be mine, that is."

As the tale unfolds, in a series of dreamlike episodes and stories within stories, Ozick makes clear that there is something profoundly unseemly about a Jewish writer who desires the silver crown. This does not mean that no Jewish writers have possessed it: on the contrary, she imagines S. Y. Agnon (identifiable but unnamed, like Malamud) as one of its owners, as well as the early twentieth-century Hebrew poet Saul Tchernikovsky. For one writer to wrest the crown from another, Agnon advises a young aspirant, "it is necessary to be shy . . . All ambitiousness is hidden. If you want to usurp my place you must not show it, or I will only hang to it all the more tightly."

In the end, Ozick's narrator herself is forced to decide if she wants to claim the crown of art, with all its transgressive power. "Choose!"

demands the spirit of Tchernikovsky: "The Creator or the creature. God or god. The Name of Names or Apollo." Here is the very choice that faced Isaac Kornfeld, now transposed into explicitly artistic terms. To be an artist, Ozick insists, is to be an idol-worshipper, a traitor to Judaism. Yet her own love of art is so great that she replies, "on the instant," that she chooses Apollo. Immediately she gets her wish and begins to pour forth endless stories: "tellings, narratives and suspenses, turning points and palaces, foam of the sea."

But there is one last punishment in store for the Jew turned pagan. The story closes with a vision of the Heaven that awaits the Jewish writer, who feasts on Olympus, "nude at the table of the nude gods." Except that, in the story's last sentence, "the taciturn little Canaanite idols call him, in the language of the spheres, kike." Once again, Ozick insists that Jewish inauthenticity carries its own punishment. A Jew can never be a pagan or an aesthete, even if she tries; something will always come along to remind her that she has a different nature and a different fate. Assimilation, Ozick suggests, is not only ignoble but impossible.

Angels in America
by Tony Kushner

"**D**ESCENDANTS OF THIS IMMIGRANT, YOU DO NOT grow up in America, you and your children and their children with the goyische names. You do not live in America; no such place exists." If Cynthia Ozick had been in the Broadway audience on the opening night of Tony Kushner's play *Angels in America*, in 1993, it's easy to imagine her nodding in agreement at this sentence from the play's first speech. For most American Jewish writers, America is the great reality, and it is Jewishness that exists only in a doubtful fashion—as a memory, an obligation, a sentiment. Ozick, with her long historical perspective, sees America as merely an episode in a much longer Jewish story.

To the audience just embarking on the epic journey of *Angels in America*—which is composed of two plays, *Millennium Approaches* and *Perestroika*, and takes eight hours to perform—it might seem that Kushner is going to agree. This pessimistic verdict on the American Jewish experience is delivered by a rabbi at the funeral of a very old Jewish woman, Sarah Ironson—one of the last remaining members of the immigrant generation, "the last of the Mohicans" as he calls her. The passing of such a woman, and of her whole cohort— "pretty soon . . . all the old will be dead," the rabbi reflects—invites stock-taking. As the twentieth century nears its end, it is natural for a Jewish writer to ask whether the transplantation of Jewish life to America has been a success, and what price has been paid for it.

One way of tracing the evolution of American Jewish life is

through names. In his eulogy, the rabbi lists the names of Sarah's grandchildren—Lesley, Angela, Luke, Eric—and recoils at their foreignness: "Eric? This is a Jewish name?" For the rabbi, the adoption of such an Anglo-Saxon name is a sign of the way assimilation has erased Jewishness. But the irony is that the rabbi's own name—Isidor Chemelwitz—is equally foreign to Jewish tradition. If Isidor sounds like a Jewish name today, it is only because, like Irving, so many American Jewish men adopted it as a substitute for "Israel." From the beginning, as Abraham Cahan knew, Jewish life in America has consisted of adaptation. There is no such thing as purity or permanence, in names or anything else.

This impossibility of fixity is one of Kushner's central themes. The rabbi's opening speech proposes two contradictory ways of thinking about Jewish immigration to America. He lauds it as a heroic endeavor of a kind that the comfortable descendants of Sarah Ironson can never share: "Such Great Voyages in this world do not any more exist." At the same time, however, the rabbi derides this voyage as delusive, a change of place that failed to produce a change of character or destiny. Ashkenazi Jews, he claims, remain Eastern European on the inside: "Your clay is the clay of some Litvak shtetl." America claims to be a melting pot, where immigrants are remade into something distinctively new, but for the rabbi it is a "melting pot where nothing melted." American Jews are caught between two worlds, the lost authenticity of the shtetl and the impossible rebirth that America promises but withholds.

It is a surprising way for Kushner to begun a play whose subtitle announces that it is "a gay fantasia on national themes." The rabbi's speech has nothing to say about gay experience, and it denies the relevance of "national"—that is, American—themes, at least for Jews. Indeed, the first scene of *Angels in America* sounds like it belongs to a play that will be centrally concerned with Jewish experience. Yet as *Angels in America* unfolds, it becomes clear that Jews are just one of several peoples whose experiences and legends will play a part in the story. Prior Walter, dying of AIDS, is a WASP who can trace his ancestry back dozens of generations: as his name hints, he has had many prior incarnations, some of which appear to him in ghostly fashion. Joe Pitt, a Republican lawyer wrestling with his homosexuality, is a Mormon from Salt Lake City, a follower of an indigenous American religion.

At the center of this nexus of relationships is Louis Ironson—Prior's partner, Joe's lover, and the grandson of the dead Sarah. A gay New York Jewish intellectual, he is clearly the character closest to Kushner biographically, and the things he knows—about New York, politics, gay life, Jewishness—are the things Kushner expects the audience to know. A good example is his attitude toward Roy Cohn, the play's other main Jewish character. The historical Roy Cohn was a conservative Republican lawyer and power broker who served as an aide to Senator Joseph McCarthy. He was also a closeted gay man, which makes him, in Louis's eyes and the play's, a double traitor. Gays and Jews are both minorities exposed to hatred, which means that they have a special claim on the loyalty of their members: to deny belonging to the group is to ditch one's share of the common burden. In Louis's eyes, and Kushner's, that is exactly what Roy Cohn did when he helped secure the execution of Julius and Ethel Rosenberg, who stole atomic secrets and passed them on to the Soviet Union. For Kushner, Cohn's role in the Rosenberg case was a betrayal of Jewish solidarity, and by concealing the fact that he contracted AIDS he made a similar betrayal of gay solidarity.

Yet the power of *Angels in America* comes partly from the play's ability to transcend Louis's judgments. Roy is certainly a villain, but he is a charismatic villain like Richard III, who takes such delight in his own malice that he fascinates the audience. In one of the play's best-known speeches, he justifies staying in the closet, explaining that he cannot be a homosexual because he refuses to be one of the powerless: "Homosexuals are not men who sleep with other men . . . Homosexuals are men who know nobody and who nobody knows. Does this sound like me, Henry?" he angrily asks the doctor who has diagnosed him with AIDS.

Roy lacks any sense of idealism: to him, politics is a pure power struggle, "the game of being alive." This makes him the exact opposite of Louis, who has a rigid sense of the political virtue of his left-wing, anti-Reagan views. But precisely because he has high ideals, Louis can fail to live up to them. When his partner, Prior, becomes sick from AIDS, Louis abandons him. "There are thousands of gay men in New York City with AIDS and nearly every one of them is being taken care of . . . Everyone got that, except me. I got you," Prior says bitterly to Louis.

In his own way, then, Louis has committed an act of betrayal as grave as Roy Cohn's. And in a conversation with the aged rabbi we met in the first scene, Louis gropes toward the realization that his impeccably progressive politics and his personal cowardice may be connected. "Maybe a person who has this neo-Hegelian positivist sense of constant historical progress towards happiness or perfection or something, who feels very powerful because he feels connected to these forces, moving uphill all the time . . . Maybe that person can't, um, incorporate sickness into his sense of how things are supposed to go," Louis confesses.

The rabbi's curt response—"The Holy Scriptures have nothing to say about such a person"—emphasizes that Louis is living on the fault line between ancient and modern definitions of what it means to be Jewish. For Louis, being an American Jew means holding all the correct political views and hating all the right people, such as Roy Cohn and Ronald Reagan. But this view of history as a constant movement forward—"The world only spins forward," says Prior in the play's last speech—leaves Louis unequipped to deal with the kind of historical catastrophe that makes progress impossible to believe in. The AIDS epidemic is such a crisis, and Louis's abandonment of Prior suggests that secular liberal Jewishness is not resilient or deep enough to meet it. When this world fails to offer any cause for hope, the only recourse is what Jewish tradition calls the World to Come, the messianic era, when all earthly evils will disappear.

Ironically, the play's title is spoken by Louis as part of a statement of militant secularism: "There are no angels in America, no spiritual past, no racial past, there's only the political," he tells Belize. For Louis, this is an optimistic idea, because it means that America is capable of being perfected by politics; but Belize rebukes Louis for this shallow optimism, just as the rabbi rebuked him. As a black man, he cannot accept the Jewish narrative that sees America as a promised land, where things are constantly getting better. "I *live* in America, Louis, that's hard enough, I don't have to love it. You do that," Belize tells him later in the play.

In *Angels in America*, it is Prior who makes contact with the messianic realm and has a vision of a real angel. That is because Prior—dying, abandoned, humiliated by illness—is the character in most imminent danger, the one who needs an angel most desperately of all. And while Prior is a Christian, Kushner teasingly suggests that even for him, the divine realm is fundamentally Jewish. Hebrew is the sacred language in *Angels in America*, not just for Jews, but for all the characters. One sign that Prior is being approached by the divine—or else, as he thinks, that he is losing his mind—is that his nurse Emily starts speaking to him in Hebrew, a language that neither of them understands.

Those words are not identified in the play, but Kushner takes them from the Jewish prayer for the dead that is traditionally recited at the graveside. For audience members who recognize the prayer, this makes for an especially chilling moment, since it's as if the nurse is mourning Prior before he has died. Most audience members, of course, will not know what the nurse is saying. But the use of Hebrew suggests that, for Kushner, Jewish tradition continues to supply the language of the sacred. Jewishness, in Kushner's vision, is less a matter of fluency in Judaism than of proximity to the ultimate things. "Lou the Jew," as he ironically refers to himself, is Jewishly illiterate not simply because "I didn't even Bar Mitzvah," as he protests, but because he remains bound to a rational and secular worldview.

So it is doubly moving when, near the end of *Perestroika*, Louis is called upon to recite the mourner's Kaddish for Roy Cohn. At first he refuses: "I know probably less of the Kaddish than you do, Belize. I'm an intensely secular Jew," he explains guiltily. But as Kushner has already shown, Louis's discomfort with religion is fundamentally connected to his inability to face loss and defeat. He doesn't want to say Kaddish not just because he doesn't know the words, but because he has resolutely avoided any confrontation with death throughout the play.

When he does stumble through the words of the prayer—tutored by the ghost of Ethel Rosenberg—it is more than a return to parochial tradition. It is a recognition of the reality of death, especially of death from AIDS, which has claimed Roy's life and threatens Prior's. And it is an affirmation of the power of religion and ritual to make death tolerable, to incorporate it into a resilient and tragic view of life. Three Jews—Ethel, Roy, and Louis—are united in the face of terrible suffering and fierce political division, thanks to the enduring power of Jewish tradition. No wonder that when he finishes the prayer and Belize tells him he "did fine," Louis replies: "What are you talking about, fine? That was . . . fucking miraculous."

The play's most dramatic miracle, however, is the arrival of the Angel, who crashes through the ceiling over Prior's sickbed in an effect he describes as "very Steven Spielberg." As it turns out, however, this Angel is not exactly a representative of God. On the contrary, God is missing from Heaven just as he is missing from the earth, and the Angel says that what has driven him away is humanity itself. Angelic life is eternal, which means it never changes, but human life is historical, full of "voyages, no knowing where." The message that the Angel wants Prior to carry to the world, in her so-called "Anti-Migratory Epistle," is "YOU MUST STOP MOVING!":

Poor blind children, abandoned on the Earth,
Groping terrified, misguided, over
Fields of Slaughter, over bodies of the Slain:
HOBBLE YOURSELVES!
There is No Zion Save Where You Are!

The invocation of "Zion" is double-edged. Originally a Jewish term for the Promised Land of Israel, it was also adopted by the Mormons as a name for their promised land in Utah. But the definition of

Zion is that once it is reached, voyaging can stop and the chosen people can live in static felicity forever. This idea is central to both Zionism, which believes the only Jewish homeland is Israel, and American Jewishness, which sees America as a true and permanent home. In both places, the Jewish history of diasporic wandering is seen as a curse that has finally been lifted.

But Kushner's vision is anti-Zionist, in a metaphysical sense. He doesn't believe in fixity and purity but in movement and diversity, flux and change. That is why Prior rejects the holy book the Angel tries to give him—an echo both of Moses receiving the Torah and of Joseph Smith receiving the golden plates of the Book of Mormon. "We can't just stop," Prior tells the Angel. "We're not rocks. Progress, migration, motion is . . . modernity. It's *animate*, it's what living things do." This is true even if, as another character says, "what makes people migrate, build things," is "devastation": "Devastated people do it, people who have lost love." To be alive, Kushner suggests, is to accept both loss and progress, which together make up history.

That is why the only vision of paradise the play is willing to endorse is neither Jerusalem nor Salt Lake City, but San Francisco— a city that, at the time Kushner was writing, was famous as a gay mecca. "On every corner a wrecking crew and something new and crooked going up," Belize describes it to the dying Roy. Roy thinks that Belize is describing Hell, but he insists that it is Heaven: a place that is not pure and perfect, but hybrid and mutable. For Kushner, being able to see the beauty of this vision is the final test of political and spiritual virtue. The American Heaven is not a Jewish place, but it is a place where Jews belong—alongside Mormons, blacks, gays, and everyone else who is able to see the beauty of diversity. In this way, as the Angel puts it, "Heaven Is a City Much Like San Francisco"—or a country much like the America that, over the course of the twentieth century, the Jews both discovered and helped to create.

III

ISRAEL:
LIFE IN A DREAM

Only Yesterday by S. Y. Agnon ✧ The Diary of Hannah
Senesh ✧ *Khirbet Khizeh* by S. Yizhar ✧ *Where the
Jackals Howl* by Amos Oz ✧ *See Under: Love* by David
Grossman ✧ *Mr. Mani* by A. B. Yehoshua ✧ *Dolly City*
by Orly Castel-Bloom ✧ Poems by Yehuda Amichai

Only Yesterday
by S. Y. Agnon

I N 1908, THE NINETEEN-YEAR-OLD SHMUEL YOSEF Czaczkes left the small town of Buczacz, in Austrian Galicia, to make a new life in Palestine. He was one of about 35,000 Jews who settled in the Land of Israel, then part of the Ottoman Empire, during the decade before World War I, in what became known as the Second Aliyah. Many of these Jews were radicals driven out of the Russian Empire following the failed revolution of 1905. Militantly secular, they were contemptuous of the way of life of the pious Jews who had lived in the Land of Israel for generations, supported by charity from abroad. These young Zionists were inspired by the vision of A. D. Gordon, the Russian-born founder of the Labor Zionist movement, who wrote in 1911: "Every one of us is required to refashion himself so that the Galut Jew within him becomes a truly emancipated Jew; so that the unnatural, defective, splintered person within him may be changed into a natural wholesome human being who is true to himself." As a famous Zionist slogan put it, Jews must come to Palestine "to build and to be built."

But Czaczkes was a nascent writer, not an ideologue, and the path he took diverged significantly from the one that Labor Zionism prescribed. Rather than move to an agricultural settlement to work the land, he lived in the city of Jaffa, where he worked as an editor on a literary magazine. And while he was committed to the resurrection of Hebrew, the first Hebrew story he published was far from a Zionist fable. Its title, "Agunot," provided him with his pen name—S. Y.

Agnon—and hinted at the themes he would pursue for the rest of his long career, which culminated in the award of the Nobel Prize in Literature in 1966.

In Jewish law, an *agunah* is a wife whose husband has abandoned her without giving her a legal divorce. Because only a man can grant a divorce in Jewish law, women whose husbands failed or refused to do so were left in a legal limbo, unable to remarry. To this day, the *agunah* is a difficult problem for Orthodox Judaism. But in Agnon's story, the concept is used in a multivalent and ambiguous way. As the title, the plural form of *agunah*, suggests, there is more than one thwarted coupling in this tale.

The language of Agnon's story is rich and resonant, but its plot is simply told. A wealthy man in Jerusalem, Ahiezer, has one child, a daughter named Dinah. Like a princess in a fairy tale, she is "the pattern of virtue, and all the graces were joined together in her person." When the time comes for her to marry, Ahiezer searches far and wide for a worthy bridegroom, which for him means a great scholar. He finds what he is looking for in Poland, and Ezekiel, a young prodigy, is brought all the way to Jerusalem to marry Dinah. It looks like a perfect match: a rich, beautiful bride and a brilliant, learned groom.

Unfortunately, however, Agnon shows that both bride and groom have already given their hearts to others. Ezekiel is still in love with a girl from his hometown, while Dinah falls for Ben Uri, an itinerant artisan hired by her father to build a magnificent ark for his new synagogue. As soon as the wedding is over the marriage starts to fail, and by the end of the story Ezekiel has divorced Dinah and returned to Poland. Ahiezer, his hopes disappointed, leaves Jerusalem as well: "He had failed in his settlement there; his wishes had not prospered. He went forth in shame, his spirit heavy within him."

"Agunot" is a tale written, in the newly revived Hebrew language, by an idealistic new immigrant to Palestine. Yet it is not a story of pioneering young Zionists, or of the renewal of the Jewish spirit by contact with the land. Instead, it is a parable of failure, in which the Jewish life of Eastern Europe proves resistant to transplantation. The marriage fails in part because Ezekiel cannot truly leave Poland behind: "His feet are planted in the gates of Jerusalem, and stand on her soil, but his eyes and his heart are pledged to houses of study and worship abroad, and even now, as he walks in the hills of Jerusalem, he fancies himself among the scholars of his own town, strolling in the fields to take the evening air." In the end, Ahiezer must "go down" from the Land, reversing the process of *aliyah* or ascent.

If we ask who exactly the *agunah* in the story is, then, the answer cannot be Dinah, since she is granted a legal divorce. Rather, the abandoned spouse seems to be the Land of Israel itself, which cannot be mated with the Jewish culture and tradition of Eastern Europe. In the end, Jerusalem is left behind, while life continues in the old country. Yet Agnon was deeply committed to the Zionist project of renewing Jewish life in the Land of Israel. In the Nobel Prize address he delivered in 1966, he began by recapitulating the basic Zionist premise that life in Europe was a centuries-old mistake, a wrong that had to be corrected: "Because of that historical catastrophe when Titus the Roman Emperor destroyed Jerusalem and Israel was exiled from its land, I was born in one of the cities of Exile. But all the time I imagined myself as having been born in Jerusalem." Yet as the Israeli novelist Amos Oz observed, while these words of Agnon's were true, "their opposite is also true": it was the historical catastrophe of modern Eastern European Jewry that drove Agnon from the city of his birth into "exile" in Palestine.

What was the proper relationship between the new Jewish state and the long Jewish past? This question, which already haunted Agnon as a young writer, would become even more painful and urgent over the course of his lifetime. The first Zionists wanted to escape an Eastern European Jewish life they saw as decrepit and vulnerable. But even the most pessimistic of them could not have foreseen that by the time a Jewish state was achieved in 1948, that life would be totally destroyed by the Nazi genocide. Was this fate the ultimate ratification of the Zionist verdict on the Diaspora—that it was dangerous and enfeebled, a trap that had to be escaped? Or did it impose a new responsibility on Zionism, to preserve a Jewish legacy that would otherwise be lost?

This is one of the questions that haunts Agnon's masterpiece, *Only Yesterday*. As its title suggests, *Only Yesterday* is a backward-looking novel: published in 1945, it is set during the period of Agnon's first sojourn in Palestine between 1908 and 1912. By the time it was written, almost everything about Jewish life in Palestine had changed. The province had passed, at the end of World War I, from Turkish to British rule, and the British were committed, under the terms of the 1917 Balfour Declaration, to fostering Jewish settlement. While that settlement was violently resisted by the Arab population of Palestine, and while the British wavered in their commitment to Jewish immigration, the Jewish population grew sevenfold under British rule, to half a million. By the time the British quit the country, in 1948, the Jews were ready to create the State of Israel.

Agnon might well have written about the Second Aliyah in a spirit of nostalgia, since he was looking back at his youth in a vanished world. But any sentimentality about Zionism in *Only Yesterday* is undermined by Agnon's acutely realistic memory of what Jewish Palestine was like in those years, and by the unsettling moral implications of his story. The history of Zionism, as Agnon tells it, involves intoxicating freedom and heroic dedication, but also failure and alienation, material hardship and spiritual confusion. Like other modernist writers, he wanted his fiction to reflect the complexity of an age in which old certainties were eroding and new creeds rushing to take their place. Even in Palestine, a time and place where ideological fervor was almost a requirement for survival, Agnon somehow managed to remain skeptical, ambivalent—both a participant in the Zionist project and a detached observer of it. That constructive doubleness would be shared by many of Israel's great writers to come.

The pervasive irony of *Only Yesterday* is anchored in Agnon's treatment of his unheroic hero, Isaac Kumer. Isaac is a naïve, not very bright young man, a strange combination of innocence and passivity. The novel begins with a flourish of praise for him: "Like all our brethren of the Second Aliya, the bearers of our salvation, Isaac Kumer left his country and his homeland and his city and ascended to the Land of Israel to build it from its destruction and to be rebuilt by it." Yet when Agnon goes on to describe the way Isaac imagined life in Palestine, it becomes clear that his "ascent" is based on some serious misunderstandings. He thinks of it as a biblical land of plenty, full of fields of grain, orchards, and forests, rather than the harsh, poor, and remote province the reader knows it to be.

The question that hovers over the novel from the beginning is whether Isaac is a brave idealist or an unworldly fool. Zionism is an ideology, and any ideology—like any religion—can seem absurd to those who stand outside its charmed circle. To true believers, on the other hand, it is the skeptics and doubters who look absurd, unable to see an obvious truth. "If you will it, it is no dream," according to a famous Zionist slogan. But is it sane or reasonable to live in a dream? The novel is perpetually debating this question, showing us the beautiful certainties of the pioneers, then revealing the compromised actuality of Jewish life in Palestine.

It is posed again when Isaac, on board the ship to Jaffa, meets an elderly Jewish couple on the way to join their daughter in Jerusalem. They are classic religious pilgrims, whose motives are pious rather than Zionist. They are making *aliyah* not to build and be rebuilt, but merely, in Isaac's acerbic judgment, "to add dust to the dust of the Land of Israel." Yet their exchange leaves the reader wondering who is the true believer here and who is the realist. When the old man asks Isaac if he has any relatives in the Land, Isaac replies: "What do I need relatives for, all the Children of Israel are comrades, especially in the Land of Israel." To which the man replies, "In the Sabbath blessing, say that and we shall answer Amen, but on all other days it's hard to make it without a relative." Isaac turns out to have greater faith in his fellow Jews than the old man, who trusts in God but is skeptical of human beings. Zionism, in Isaac's ardent vision, is a renewed Judaism, whose adherents love and support each other in ways Jews have forgotten how to do. Agnon insists on the symmetry between the new ideology and the old religion, which the Zionists believed they were leaving behind.

It doesn't take long, however, for Isaac to realize that his dream of vines and fig trees was just that, a dream. The first thing that hits him when he gets off the ship is the unbelievable heat. His wool suit, which he wears in order to make the best possible impression, turns out to be totally unsuited to the climate of Palestine. It is a metaphor for all the adjustments he will need to make in his new life.

The first such adjustment comes right away, when Isaac goes to look for work on an agricultural settlement. Imbued with the religion of labor, he is certain that the only worthy activity for a pioneer is farming. But he learns that even Jewish landowners do not want to hire Jewish workers; they prefer Arab laborers, who, they believe, are more experienced, more obedient, and cheaper. As a result, Isaac is forced to linger in Jaffa, where he eventually picks up work as a housepainter. He makes a good living this way, but he fails to realize his initial hopes: He is living in a city, not cultivating the soil, and he is occupied with surfaces, not with roots.

This superficiality, Agnon suggests, is a fact of life in Jaffa. *Only Yesterday* shows that the cultural division in Israel between Tel Aviv, the secular, hedonistic coastal city, and Jerusalem, the ancient religious capital, goes back to the earliest days of Zionist settlement. (Indeed, it even predates Tel Aviv itself: the novel narrates the foundation of the Jewish metropolis, which began as a small housing development on the outskirts of Arab Jaffa.) The life Isaac falls into in Jaffa is in many ways recognizably modern and bohemian. His contemporaries in Greenwich Village would not be out of place among the cafés, the political and aesthetic arguments, the love affairs and all-night parties. It is a community of young men and women who have been liberated from parental authority and religious tradition. Isaac "behaved like most of our comrades," Agnon writes; "he didn't go to synagogue and he didn't lay *tefillin* and he didn't keep the Sabbath and he didn't honor the religious festivals."

For Isaac, the allure and the danger of this secular, modern life is embodied in Sonya Zweiering, a seductively androgynous woman whom he first gets to know as the lover of his friend, Rabinovitch. When Rabinovitch, thwarted in his attempt to earn a living in Palestine, goes back to Europe, Sonya decides to transfer her affections to Isaac. She, too, is a recognizable modern type: educated, fickle, and bored, she passes the time in love affairs because she can't commit to a career or relationship. It's no wonder Sonya prefers Jaffa, the city of slackers and bohemians, to Jerusalem, the city of rabbis.

Isaac, who has never even spoken to a woman he is not related to, finds himself entirely unable to cope with Sonya. After they become lovers, a development Agnon writes about elliptically, Isaac enjoys a period of unprecedented bliss: "Good were those days. But the days that came after were not good," Agnon writes ominously. "Blessed is he who had his first kiss with a maiden whom others had not yet kissed, and woe to him who kissed a maiden whom others had already kissed before him." While Isaac is naïvely consumed with guilt over having "stolen" his friend's girlfriend, as he sees it, Sonya has already gotten tired of him and is ready to cast him aside.

By suggesting that Sonya is an emblem of Jaffa, Agnon raises doubts, in the reader's mind and in Isaac's, about the true values of the Second Aliyah. Prompted by his breakup with Sonya, then, Isaac decides to leave Jaffa and try his luck in Jerusalem. This move gives Agnon a chance to describe a part of Jewish Palestine that most members of the Second Aliyah scorned, and in his portrait there is indeed much to dislike. The aridity of the climate in Jerusalem, where water is scarce and everything is coated in dust, is a clear symbol of its spiritual drought. The city is dominated by an ultra-Orthodox establishment that looks at Zionism, and at young secular men like Isaac, with suspicion and hatred.

Yet it is in this city of God that Agnon raises his sharpest challenge to the idea of God's providence. Isaac's life in Jerusalem is full of fateful coincidences, beginning with the moment he meets the elderly couple from the ship. They have come to Jerusalem to live with their daughter Rebecca and her husband, the fanatical Reb Fayesh, who spends his days issuing excommunications against his enemies. Rebecca and Fayesh have a daughter, Shifra, who is to Sonya as Jerusalem is to Jaffa: where Sonya was secular, seductive, and heartless, Shifra is pious, modest, and worthy of devotion. Isaac immediately falls in love with her, though he knows that her father would never accept a beardless Zionist as a son-in-law.

Inadvertently, however—or is it the hand of fate?—Isaac sets off a chain of events that will eliminate Reb Fayesh as an obstacle, while utterly transforming the course of the novel. One hot day, when he is working outside as a painter, Isaac sees a stray dog. Moved by an impulse he can't explain, he paints the words "Crazy Dog" on its back. He then abandons the dog—who comes to be known as Balak, which is both a biblical allusion and the Hebrew word for "dog" read backwards—to make his way in a world now turned inexplicably hostile. For of course, the Jews who can read Isaac's inscription believe that Balak is rabid, and every time he appears they flee or drive him away with stones.

Once Balak has entered the novel, Agnon seems reluctant to let him go; indeed, the dog runs away with *Only Yesterday* as if he had picked it up with his teeth. Isaac's story is repeatedly interrupted by chapters dealing with the dog, as he roams Jerusalem, hears a sermon, and wonders about his fate. Suffering hurts Balak into consciousness, forcing him to theorize about the reasons why everyone suddenly hates and fears him. He becomes a seeker:

> At that moment, all his suffering was naught compared to the search for truth. And once again he turned his head back to see what were those signs and what was the truth. But all his pains were in vain because he couldn't read. He was amazed and stunned. Everyone who sees me knows the truth about me, and I, who possess the truth itself, I don't know what it is. He shouted loud and long, Arf Arf Arf, this truth, what is it?

The power of Balak's story comes from the empathy with which Agnon enters the mind of this animal, capturing his bewilderment and need. Perhaps Agnon can do this because Balak is not unlike Isaac Kumer: both are passive, blown here and there by inner and outer forces, well intentioned but unable to master the world they live in. Was there something fated about the encounter of this particular man and this particular dog?

In any case, that fate turns out to be a grim one for both man and dog. Balak, who has been reduced to living in holes and eating scraps, finally grows into the label Isaac gave him, which now turns out to have been a prophecy: he contracts rabies and becomes truly "crazy." When he encounters Isaac again, just after Isaac and Shifra's wedding, he bites the man whom he remembers as the source of his curse, and Isaac falls fatally ill. On the brink of happiness, he dies miserably, and the words he had flung at the elderly couple on the boat turn out to fit him: he came to add dust to the dust of the Land of Israel.

Isaac's death is a shockingly bleak ending to the book, and it leaves the narrator himself with unanswerable questions. As much as it challenges traditional Jewish faith in divine providence, Isaac's death also challenges the Zionist belief in autonomy, in Jews seizing control of their own destiny. It is possible to do everything right, Agnon recognizes, and still fail to achieve autonomy; something as trivial as a dog bite can destroy the most committed pioneer. At the time Agnon was writing, in the early 1940s, Jewish Palestine had grown far beyond the meager settlements of 1908, and in many ways it was a triumphant success.

Yet the Jewish community was still in political limbo, caught between British suspicion and Arab hostility. Worse, they were forced to stand by helplessly as the Nazis annihilated the Jews of Eastern Europe, the world from which all the early Zionists came. The Jews of Buczacz, Agnon's hometown, were exterminated in Belzec in early 1943, the same year he finished writing *Only Yesterday*. Jewish self-emancipation succeeded only in partial and compromised terms, a far cry from the hopeful early visions of its pioneers. No wonder Agnon could not give his story a simple happy ending, as a propagandist or a socialist realist writer might have done. *Only Yesterday* is a Zionist novel that ends with a caution against hubris, and an acknowledgment that dreams never come true in quite the way they are supposed to.

The Diary of
Hannah Senesh

IN SEPTEMBER 1939, AS GERMAN AND SOVIET TROOPS
marched into Poland to divide the country between them, the
eighteen-year-old Hannah Senesh was making her way over land and
sea from Hungary to Palestine. It was the same journey Agnon's hero
had taken thirty years earlier, but those years had made a difference.
Where Isaac Kumer found a few Jewish pioneers clinging to survival
in the Land of Israel, Senesh was going to join a community almost
half a million strong, swelled over the previous decade by the arrival
of tens of thousands of refugees from Hitler's Germany. The growth
of Palestine's Jewish population had incited the antagonism of the
Arabs, who from 1936 to 1939 waged a violent campaign against the
Jews and the British, which came to be known as the Arab Revolt.
In response, in 1939 the British government issued a "White Paper,"
a policy directive that limited Jewish immigration to 15,000 a year
for the next five years. Just at the moment when the Jews of Europe
needed Palestine most, its gates were being closed to them.

Senesh was one of the lucky few who received a visa to come to
Palestine legally. She was selected by the Women's International
Zionist Organization because she was young, ideologically committed, and willing to undertake hard physical labor. Her destination
was Nahalal, an agricultural school where she would be trained in
the techniques of running a farm. Senesh spent two years there, followed by two years at Sdot Yam, a kibbutz on the Mediterranean
coast near Haifa. This was the rigorous process by which ordinary

European Jews became pioneers of a new country, and many of those who went through it went on to form Israel's social and political elite. In 1941, Senesh wondered in her diary whether that would be her fate: "I wonder whether I wasn't really meant to lend a helping hand in government? I've noticed at times that I have the ability to influence people, to comfort and reassure them, or to inspire them."

This prophecy would be fulfilled, but not in the way Senesh imagined. Her story has inspired and influenced Israel profoundly—she is a national heroine, with streets named after, her life taught in schools, and a few of her poems known to almost every Israeli. But she achieved this stature in death rather than in life. In 1943, Senesh volunteered to join a commando unit of Jewish soldiers that was being formed under the aegis of the British army to parachute into Nazi-occupied Yugoslavia. She was the only woman among the thirty-seven soldiers. To the British, the unit's mission was to rescue downed RAF pilots and help to organize partisan resistance; to Senesh herself, the primary goal was to make it to Hungary, home to a million Jews—including her mother—whose lives were imperiled after the Germans occupied the country in March 1944. Soon after crossing the Hungarian border, however, Senesh was captured, imprisoned, and tortured. She was executed by firing squad on November 7, 1944, when she was twenty-three years old.

Senesh only spent about four years in Palestine, from late 1939 to early 1944, and she was on the periphery of public events there. But her diary—which she began to keep in Hungarian in 1935, and continued in Hebrew until the end of 1943—offers an important record of this critical period in Israel's prehistory. The personal and ideological transformations that she underwent in that time make her representative of a whole generation of Zionists—thousands of young men and women who were seized with an irresistible impulse to leave their homes and families and try to build a new society. Senesh's diary shows that such historic efforts didn't come without a significant personal cost. Indeed, like many great Israeli books from Agnon's onward, the diary focuses on the challenging individual realities that belied the nation's grand collective hopes.

Senesh began keeping her diary when she was thirteen years old, living with her mother, grandmother, and older brother in an assimilated, middle-class household. Her father, a playwright of some renown, had died suddenly when she was only eight. In the diary's first years, Senesh focuses on ordinary subjects like school, travel, and her admirers among the boys she knew (to her disappointment, she never found someone to admire back). But even at this age she had a feeling that she was not cut out for an ordinary life. "I would rather be an unusual person than just average," she wrote in August 1936, not long after her fifteenth birthday. "When I think of an above-average man I don't necessarily think of a famous man, but of a great soul . . . a great human being. And I would like to be a great soul. If God will permit."

Initially, however, this longing had nothing to do with politics, for which the young Senesh had only a fearful loathing. Rather, she suspected that if her destiny was greatness, it might take the form of becoming a writer, following in her father's footsteps. But while her diary and poems would indeed become famous, Senesh was not a natural writer of narrative, and her diary doesn't display the curiosity or love of detail that bespeaks a future novelist. In this it offers a striking contrast with the much more celebrated diary of Anne Frank, which was being written in Amsterdam while Senesh was keeping hers in Palestine. With Anne, the reader has the sense that if she had lived she would certainly have become a writer of importance, even if the diary itself never saw the light of day. With Hannah Senesh, it is primarily the history she lived through and helped to make that ensures her claim on posterity. This difference mirrors the one between Anne's universalism, which appeals to readers of every background, and Senesh's committed Zionism, which makes her a specifically Israeli and Jewish heroine.

Exactly what made Hannah Senesh become a Zionist is a question the diary doesn't really answer. She appears to have converted virtually overnight. In the earlier part of the diary, she seldom writes about Jewishness and has no real interest in Jewish observance, something that remained true until the end of her life. But she was made aware early on that Jewishness set her apart in Hungarian society. In one small but telling episode, Senesh was elected to an office in her school's literary club, only to see the election annulled because positions weren't open to Jews. "Only now am I beginning to see what it really means to be a Jew in a Christian society," she writes in June 1937, shortly before her sixteenth birthday.

It was in March 1938, when Nazi Germany annexed Hungary's neighbor Austria, that Senesh was struck for the first time by the real danger facing Europe's Jews. But it was hard, the diary shows, to know what if anything Jews could do to help themselves. Her brother Gyuri asked some of his classmates who were "Arrow-Crossers"— members of Hungary's fascist, anti-Semitic party—"to look after Mother and me if there should be any trouble," a request that struck her as hopelessly naïve. But it is also deeply poignant: Gyuri did not yet believe that a murderous ideology could overcome personal relationships with individual Jews.

It is against this background of tension, fear, and hopelessness that Senesh writes, almost offhandedly, about her conversion to Zionism. "I don't know whether I've already mentioned that I've become a Zionist," begins the diary entry for October 27, 1938. "The word stands for a tremendous number of things. To me it means, in short, that I now consciously and strongly feel that I am a Jew, and am proud of it." But Senesh was unusual even among Zionists in her immediate conviction that she must emigrate to Palestine—a goal that many Zionists were happy to pursue from afar. For a young woman facing an uncertain future both personally and politically, this concrete goal served as a source of purpose and direction. "I am immeasurably happy that I've found this ideal, that I now feel firm ground under my feet and can see a definite goal toward which it is really worth striving," she writes.

Remarkably, even as Europe moved toward war, Senesh managed to make her plans a reality: less than a year after this diary entry, she was in Palestine. Over the next four years, the diary becomes a chronicle of her life there, which was outwardly undramatic—she did nothing but go to school, learn Hebrew and farming, and engage in hard, tedious labor. The interest of the diary lies, rather, in Senesh's continual struggle with doubts over whether immigrating to Palestine had been the right decision. From the outside, her story looked like a Zionist fable with a happy ending: a Jew flees a continent on the brink of Holocaust and finds a new life in the Jewish homeland.

But two questions haunted her, both of which carried wider implications for the Zionist project. First, Senesh wondered whether she had done right to save herself while leaving her mother to face the war alone. Zionism was meant to be the redemption of the whole Jewish people, but it had turned out to be the work of a vanguard, which now found itself cut off by war from the Jews left behind in Europe. The young pioneers who went to Palestine could do nothing to save their people from Hitler, just as Senesh could do nothing to protect her mother in Budapest. "I can think of nothing now but my mother and brother," she writes in January 1943. "I am sometimes overwhelmed by dreadful fears. Will we ever meet again? And one question keeps torturing and tormenting me: Was what I did intolerable? Was it unmitigated selfishness?"

The other doubt in Senesh's diary, which keeps coming back despite her earnest efforts to suppress it, has to do with her own hopes for the future. She had grown up in a bourgeois intellectual family, a good student with dreams of becoming a writer. Moving to Palestine meant exchanging her comforts and ambitions for the life of a manual laborer. "Today I washed a hundred and fifty pairs of socks," she writes in February 1942. "I thought I'd go mad. No, that's not really true. I didn't think of anything." Tending to chickens and washing clothes were essential tasks on a kibbutz, but they left Senesh with little time or energy for intellectual development—though in one entry she records how, after a tiring day, she tried to grapple with Kant's *On Perpetual Peace*, in a poignant symbol of the high-minded ambitions that drove the kibbutz movement.

Did serving the Zionist cause and the Jewish people require the complete sacrifice of any hope for individual achievement and personal satisfaction? Senesh often feared that it did. At the Nahalal agricultural school, she writes in April 1940, she learned about "root cells, which are the first to penetrate into the earth and prepare the way for the entire root. Meanwhile, they die." She immediately saw the parallel with herself: "Shall our generation become such root cells, too?"

Seen against this psychological background, it becomes easier to understand Senesh's decision, in 1943, to volunteer for the mission that would end in her death. As a novice Zionist back in Hungary in 1938, she had enjoyed a sense of certainty and purpose that she lost amid the compromised reality of life in Palestine. Becoming a soldier would give her back that meaning. It would liberate her from tedious work and assign her a crucial role in the Zionist struggle, and it would allow her to feel that she was doing something to help the Jews left behind, including her mother. No wonder that as soon as she heard about the planned mission, in February 1943, she felt called to enlist: "I see the hand of destiny in this just as I did at the time of my *aliyah*," she wrote in her diary. That September, in the middle of army training, Senesh confirmed that despite all her doubts and fears, she believed her life had unfolded exactly as it was supposed to: "In my life's chain of events nothing was accidental. Everything happened according to an inner need."

One of Senesh's fellow soldiers recalled that on the day she set off for Hungary, she pressed into his hand a Hebrew poem she had written, "Blessed Is the Match." Just four lines long, it offers a metaphor for the sacrifice she was about to undertake: "Blessed is the match consumed in kindling flame," it begins and ends. In fact, Senesh's death did not ignite any flame in Nazi-occupied Hungary. In concrete terms she gave her life for nothing, and it's possible to view the entire mission as a mere gesture. But in a longer perspective, Senesh's death achieved the same thing as the similarly hopeless rebellion mounted by the Jews of the Warsaw Ghetto in 1943, whose leader Mordecai Anielewicz wrote in his last letter: "The dream of my life has risen to become fact . . . Jewish armed resistance and revenge are facts." Senesh, too, gave her life to prove that Jews did not have to await their fate, that they could take up arms against their enemies—a cardinal principle of Zionism, and one that Israelis would have to rely on again and again.

Khirbet Khizeh
by S. Yizhar

BEFORE SHE LEFT ON HER MISSION, HANNAH SENESH composed a letter of farewell to her brother, who arrived in Palestine just before she departed. In it she tried to explain her attitude toward the Land of Israel: "I love it because it is ours. No, not ours, but because we can make ourselves believe it is ours." The hesitation is telling: after all, how could the Jews believe the land was theirs when it was already home to another people?

In the early days of Zionism, it was possible for Jews to imagine that their arrival in Palestine would be welcomed by the Arab population. In his 1902 novel *Old New Land*, Theodor Herzl included an Arab character, Rashid Bey, whose function is to testify that the Arabs will embrace and benefit from the Jewish "new society." "Would you call a man a robber who takes nothing from you, but brings you something instead? The Jews have enriched us," he reassuringly insists. But while individual Arab landowners did profit from selling their land to Jewish settlers, it did not take long for the Jews to recognize that their presence was rejected by virtually the whole Arab population of Palestine. As early as 1891, a delegation of Palestinian Arabs petitioned the Ottoman sultan to prohibit Jewish immigration.

When the British conquered Palestine in 1917, then, they were inserting themselves into a situation already fraught with hostility. In November of that year, the British government issued the Balfour Declaration, stating that it would "view with favor" the cre-

ation of a "national home" for the Jews in Palestine. This was the
biggest political victory earned by Zionism so far, even though the
Declaration went on to state that "nothing shall be done which may
prejudice the civil and religious rights of existing non-Jewish communities in Palestine." For the next thirty years, the British would
try to thread this needle with meager success. In effect, their method
in governing Palestine was to alternately appease and intimidate the
rival populations.

Finally, in 1947, Britain resigned its mandate and turned the problem over to the United Nations, which endorsed the division of the
territory of Palestine between two states, one Jewish and one Arab.
The partition plan embodied in UN Resolution 181 called for the
creation of a small Jewish state, whose population would in fact be
almost evenly split between Jews and Arabs—500,000 of the former
to 450,000 of the latter. Even so, the Jews, who had by now evolved
their own governmental organization and semiofficial army, agreed
to the plan, seeing it as their best chance at realizing the Zionist
goal of self-determination. Meanwhile, the Arabs, consistent with
their position from the beginning of the conflict, rejected partition.
No sooner had the resolution been adopted, at the end of November 1947, than armed conflict began—an all-out battle between two
communities that had been covertly at war for years. At the same
time, the surrounding Arab states declared their intention of invading
Palestine to ensure an Arab victory. When the State of Israel was offi-
cially declared on May 14, 1948, the armies of Jordan, Syria, Egypt,
Saudi Arabia, and Lebanon mobilized against it. Just a few years
after the Holocaust, the possibility of Jewish defeat and annihilation
was very real.

But the war known in Israel as the War of Independence resulted
in a Jewish victory. The victory came at a high price—of the 600,000
Jews in the new state, some 6,000 were killed in the war—but the existence of Israel was secured, and its borders were expanded from the
original UN map. Far from settling the Arab-Jewish conflict, however,
the war of 1948 only introduced a new and even more bitter chapter.
For during the war, some 700,000 Palestinian Arabs were made ref-

ugees, fleeing their homes in what was now Israel to the surrounding Arab countries—including Jordan, which had annexed the West Bank territory originally designated for an independent Palestine.

In late 1948, the thirty-two-year-old writer Yizhar Smilansky was a soldier in the Israeli army, fighting on the southern front against the invading Egyptians. In the course of the campaign, Israeli forces conquered a number of Arab villages, and the order was given to destroy them so that their inhabitants could not return. Soon after the war's end, in the summer of 1949, Smilansky—writing under his pen name, S. Yizhar—used his experience in one such village as the basis for a novella, *Khirbet Khizeh*, which would become one of the most important and controversial literary records of the war. In this short book, Yizhar records a day in the life of a soldier who, against his own moral scruples, takes part in the expulsion of a civilian Arab population from the title village.

Khirbet Khizeh is a fictional place and the book is a highly stylized literary work, yet Yizhar insisted that it was based closely on fact: "Everything . . . is reported accurately, meticulously documented," he said years later. And *Khirbet Khizeh* was widely read: a best seller upon publication, the book was made part of Israel's national high school curriculum in 1964 and was filmed for television in 1978. Yet as the Israeli historian Anita Shapira has written in an essay on the book and its legacy, "many Israelis still react as if the subject didn't exist, was unknown, or is under wraps—best not mentioned."

The book's first line seems to acknowledge that its subject matter is too painfully fresh in the memory to be handled directly. "True, it all happened a long time ago, but it has haunted me ever since," says the unnamed narrator, as if he were about to relate a tale from the distant past. In fact, Yizhar was writing barely six months after the events in question, as his first readers would have known perfectly well. It is as if he had to project his story forward to some indefinite future, to increase the distance between himself and his memories, in order to convince himself that it was permissible to write about these things at all. Even then, he emphasizes that he is writing about Khirbet Khizeh only because he has no choice.

It is this insistence on simply telling the story—saying what happened and how it felt, rather than explaining, justifying, or contextualizing—that gives the book its disturbing power. The language of testimony can be heard right from the start, when Yizhar's narrator offers what is ostensibly a direct quotation from the order his outfit received on the day in question. Their mission is to "assemble the inhabitants of the area . . . load them onto transports, and convey them across our lines," after which they are to destroy the village's stone buildings and huts. At the same time, the men are ordered not to engage in any "violent outbursts or disorderly conduct." This is not to be an outbreak of vengeance, but a military operation carried out by professionals. Yet this distinction between legitimate force and illegitimate violence provokes a bitter irony in the narrator. He and his fellow soldiers are expected to "burn-blow-up-imprison-load-convey" with "a restraint born of true culture," as if that could ennoble or justify their actions.

Worst of all, this restraint was meant to be a sign of "the Jewish soul, the great Jewish soul." Yizhar was an admirer of A. D. Gordon, the idealistic exponent of Labor Zionism, and throughout the book he writes with almost hallucinatory intensity about the land of Israel itself—the physical terrain that was to be the setting for remaking the Jewish soul. Yet now, in wartime, the protection of the Zionist achievement required acting in a wholly different spirit. Instead of generous enthusiasm, there must be a hardening of the heart. The mood of *Khirbet Khizeh* is that of the soldier in wartime, a combination of boredom, contempt, hostility, and occasional fear. The episode related in the story comes late in the war, after a year of fighting, and by the time we meet these Jewish soldiers they have succeeded in dehumanizing the enemy in their own minds. "Forget these Ayrabs—they're not even human," one soldier scoffs.

What sounds at first like loose talk, the boasting of bored soldiers, is soon shown to have real consequences. As they approach the village, the platoon sees that the inhabitants have started to run away. Their orders are to let civilians leave, but the soldiers egg each other on to start shooting at the fleeing Arabs. Yizhar records the almost childish eagerness of the soldiers as they take turns at the machine gun—"Get 'em, a little to the right"—as though, we would say now, they were playing a video game rather than trying to kill human beings. Yizhar's honesty compels him to record the excitement of killing—"The thrill of the hunt that lurks inside every man had taken firm hold of us." The narrator even takes part in the hunt, shouting out instructions to the machine gunner to help him take aim. At the same time, paradoxically, he rebels inwardly against something he knows is deeply wrong: "Let him miss, oh, let him miss them!" he prays. Yet this remains a silent prayer. Yizhar is not telling a story of heroic resistance, only of inward scruple, which ends up having no effect. If no one gets killed during this shooting spree, it's only because of good luck and bad aim.

The company soon moves on to the work of emptying the village, rounding up any remaining inhabitants. Unsurprisingly, this means women and children, the old and the sick, since all the men of fighting age have already left. As Yizhar cunningly shows, this heightens the soldiers' sense of guilt, since there is no way to construe the expulsion as any kind of combat against a worthy enemy. But their guilt is camouflaged as disgust, which makes it easier to bear. When they come across two old women who have been left behind, the soldiers react with nausea: "What could you do with them but spit in disgust, and not look, and run from here—the horror! The horror!" But as this line suggests, with its echo of Kurtz's famous exclamation in Joseph Conrad's *Heart of Darkness*, the real horror here is not the victim, but the victimizer.

Yizhar offers a profound insight into the psychology of atrocity. It is not because the target of violence is repulsive that she becomes a target; rather, she must be made repulsive in order to be targeted. The soldiers must also change the way they think about themselves in order to carry out acts that their own consciences reject. After rounding up prisoners, one soldier asks, "How many pieces do you have?" Rather than seeing this as a sign of his toughness, Yizhar describes it as an attempt to convince himself that he is tough. Another form of self-justification is the soldiers' repeated insistence that, whatever they are doing to the Arabs, the Arabs would do worse to them if given the chance.

The incidents that follow in the story are all minor, small scale. There is no battle, no culminating act of violence, certainly no massacre. Rather, we see the soldiers pick up a man here, a woman there, and then load them onto trucks to be sent away. The process is interrupted only by a few incidents—the soldiers encounter a horse with snared legs and help to free it; a truck struggles to cross a flooded road; a soldier snatches off an Arab woman's head scarf. The escalating tension of the novel is entirely internal, having to do with the narrator's attempts to repress his own horror at what is happening.

While the narrator's comrades seem untroubled by what is happening in Khirbet Khizeh—if anything, they are only impatient for more violence, more decisive action—Yizhar allows the narrator himself to channel the reader's growing dismay and doubt. And as this feeling grows, it takes more provocative forms. As he observes the group of refugees, the narrator reflects, "their appearance and their gait recalled nothing so much as a confused, obedient, groaning flock of sheep." The image inevitably reads as a reference to the Jews killed in the Holocaust, who were said to have gone "like sheep to the slaughter." Have the Jews, Yizhar implicitly asks, exchanged roles with their former persecutors? Are they now the war criminals—and if so, are the Palestinians the new Jews?

The question becomes still more explicit near the end of the story, when Yizhar invokes the heavily loaded term "exile": "I had never been in the Diaspora—I said to myself—I had never known what it was like . . . but people had spoken to me, told me, taught me, and repeatedly recited to me, from every direction, in books and newspapers, everywhere: exile . . . Our nation's protest to the world: exile! . . . What, in fact, had we perpetrated here today?" Zionism was supposed to be the negation of exile and everything it had meant to the Jews for two thousand years: powerlessness, victimhood, the longing for home. Now the Jews were back in their own land, rulers of their own destiny—and their first act was to exile another people, condemning them to the same fate. Was this the only way the Jews could be redeemed? If so, was it truly a redemption at all?

Khirbet Khizeh offers no simple answer to these tragic questions. Yizhar insists that the narrator's moral revulsion at what happens in the village remains a personal, instinctive reaction. He does not say that the Arabs should not be expelled, merely that he himself doesn't want to take part in the process: "If it had to be done let others do it. If someone had to get filthy, let others soil their hands. I couldn't. Absolutely not." But this cannot be the last word, since the narrator knows that he will benefit from the expulsion—perhaps he even requires it, if he wants to live in a secure Jewish state. If to will the ends is to will the means, and if Yizhar is a Zionist, how can he disassociate himself from the War of Independence and everything it involves?

Near the end of the novel, the narrator pronounces a kind of curse on his own comrades and people: "Khirbet Khizeh is not ours. The Spandau gun never gave us any rights." Yizhar concludes with a prophecy that the injustice he has documented will be avenged. This vengeance will take the form of undying Palestinian hatred, as the narrator reflects when he sees the look in the eyes of a boy being deported from the village: "Something was happening in the heart of the boy, something that, when he grew up, could only become a viper inside him."

Still more darkly, Yizhar suggests that the Jews have earned divine punishment. The last sentence of the book imagines a day in the future when "God would come forth and descend to roam the valley, and see whether all was according to the cry that had reached him." It is an allusion to the book of Genesis: "And the Lord said, Because the cry of Sodom and Gomorrah is great, and because their sin is very grievous, I will go down now, and see whether they have done altogether according to the cry of it, which is come unto me." The judgment on the cities of the plain was, of course, total destruction. Just months after fighting to establish the State of Israel, Yizhar fears that it will deserve the same fate.

Where the Jackals Howl
by Amos Oz

O N NOVEMBER 29, 1947, THE UNITED NATIONS VOTED to partition Palestine into two states, one for Jews and one for Arabs. By the time the vote took place, it was after midnight in Jerusalem, where the eight-year-old Amos Klausner listened to the roll call of nations along with a crowd of his neighbors. More than half a century later, long after he had changed his last name to the Hebrew "Oz"—"strength"—and become Israel's most famous novelist, he wrote about that night in his memoir, *A Tale of Love and Darkness*. He remembered how his father whispered to him in the darkness about an episode from his childhood in Vilna, when his own father had been attacked by a gang of schoolboys and stripped of his trousers. "But from now on," Oz's father tells him, "from the moment we have our own state, you will never be bullied just because you are a Jew, and because Jews are so-and-so. Not that. Never again." It was, Oz writes, the only time he ever saw his father cry.

This was the promise that it was up to Oz's generation to redeem. Centuries of Jewish weakness and humiliation must be erased by the toughness of the first native-born Israelis. This generation became known as "sabras," after the desert fruit that is tough and prickly on the outside but sweet within. And Oz, whose chosen name demonstrated his allegiance to the ideal of Jewish strength, would become the great novelist of this generation and its experience. Yet his work would not build up the Zionist myth, but question and explore it. What does it mean, Oz asks, to be born into someone else's dream?

As he explains in his memoir, Oz was equipped by birth and upbringing to ask that question, since he was not at all a sabra by nature. On the contrary, he was born in 1939 into a lower-middle-class intellectual family in Jewish Jerusalem, surrounded by people who uneasily straddled the European past and the Israeli future. In his mother's bedtime stories, Oz was introduced to a distant, vanished Eastern European world, with all its loveliness and menace: "I was in the east, but my heart was in the farthermost west." Oz ironically inverts the famous lines from the medieval Hebrew poet Yehuda Halevi, who yearned for the east, the Land of Israel, while living in the farthest west, Spain. Now that the Land of Israel had been attained, it was Diaspora that became the object of dream and fantasy.

For the young Oz, becoming Israeli required an intense internal struggle to break free of his family, with its habits and values. "They were so alien, so burdensome," he wrote of his parents and their whole generation. "They belonged to the Diaspora. They were the generation of the wilderness. They were always full of demands and commands, they never let you breathe. Only when they are dead will we be able to show them at last how we can do everything ourselves."

Oz saw life in Jerusalem as a cul-de-sac, cut off from the main road to the Zionist future. That future was being built not in cities, but in the country, and above all on the kibbutz. At the conclusion of *Only Yesterday*, Agnon salutes the first kibbutz pioneers as "our brothers, the elite of our salvation," expressing an admiration that would become a major Zionist theme. The kibbutz was a collective farm settlement governed on socialist principles, where all property was owned in common. An invention of the fervent, self-sacrificing idealism of the Second Aliyah pioneers, the kibbutz proved to be the perfect solution to the economic problems that bedeviled the earliest Jewish settlements. It was also part of a geopolitical strategy: kibbutzim were founded along the borders of Jewish Palestine, and during the 1948 war they were the first line of defense against the invading Arab armies. The young Oz naturally saw the kibbutz as the place where real Israeliness was being forged.

But he was far from being pioneer material. In a comic episode in his memoir, he writes about how he and his father attempted to conquer the wilderness, on the smallest possible scale, by planting a vegetable garden in their yard. After great effort, they managed to scratch out a few rows in the packed soil, only to see their seedlings die immediately. The father tried to console his son by purchasing grown plants and planting them in the garden, pretending they had grown up overnight; but then these plants died as well. Like Isaac Kumer, the Klausners were hopelessly unfitted to live out the Labor Zionist dream.

Unlike Isaac, the young Amos Klausner would not stop trying, even if it meant breaking with his family. The catalyst for this break was the suicide of his mother when he was thirteen years old. The following year, he changed his name and moved to Kibbutz Hulda, a settlement in central Israel. He would live there for more than thirty years, marrying and raising a family, living modestly as part of a communal regime even as he became one of the most famous figures in the country.

Toward the end of *A Tale of Love and Darkness*, Oz remembers how on the kibbutz "I took up writing again, when no one was looking, feeling ashamed of myself . . . surely I hadn't left Jerusalem for the kibbutz to write poems and stories but to be reborn, to turn my back on the piles of words, to be suntanned to the bone and become an agricultural worker, a tiller of the soil." But it turned out that literature, inwardness, and complication, all the familial and Jewish inheritances he wanted to discard, could not be gotten rid of so easily. The new Jew was still connected to the old Jew, child to parent, Israel to Eastern Europe.

Indeed, the utopia of the kibbutz turned out to breed new kinds of complexity and difficulty, which Oz made it his mission to turn into literature. At first, he worried that the kibbutz was a barren terrain for fiction. How could such a small world—a few hundred farmers, living in the middle of nowhere—sustain the kind of drama that a writer needed? Surely he would have to get out, to go to Paris or London or at least Tel Aviv, in order to gain the worldliness that a novelist needed.

What released Oz from this dilemma, he writes, was the discovery of a Hebrew translation of *Winesburg, Ohio*, the classic book of short stories by the American writer Sherwood Anderson. Anderson's character studies, which revealed the loneliness, eccentricity, and passion brooding underneath the surface of respectable small-town life, became the models for the stories Oz wrote in the early 1960s, when he was in his early twenties. Writing just one day a week—all the time he was initially allowed by the kibbutz, which determined the work schedules of its members—Oz produced the material for his first book, *Where the Jackals Howl*, published in 1965.

Like many of the classics of Israeli literature, *Where the Jackals Howl* offers a subversive view of Israeli life. Oz was writing from the heart of what was, in a sense, Israel's aristocracy: the socialist pioneers who founded the kibbutz and their children who were brought up there. The narrator of these stories uses the first-person plural, as if to express both the solidarity and the parochialism of the kibbutz elite; this is the voice of an insider. But even though he had arrived at Kibbutz Hulda as a teenager, Oz never really succeeded at gaining access to its inner circle. This double perspective, combining intimacy and estrangement, made him the perfect person to write about the kibbutz, since it allowed him to see what was genuinely new and strange about its way of life. And what he discovered was something very different from the propaganda-poster image of simple pioneers that had enchanted him as a young man in Jerusalem.

For Oz in *Where the Jackals Howl*, the most important fact about the inner life of the kibbutz is its sense of vulnerability. The jackals whose voices can be heard in the night, prowling just outside the borders of the settlement, return again and again throughout the book, becoming more than just dangers to the livestock. They embody a primal chaos that is always threatening to overturn the precarious order of the kibbutz: "Beyond the fence lived another world, which silently yearned by day and night to raze the house to the ground, gnawing slyly and with infinite patience, like a stream slowly eating away at its banks."

In a concrete sense, of course, the "other world" that longs to destroy the kibbutz can be understood as Oz's way of writing about the Arabs. He is acutely aware that the land on which the kibbutz stands was Arab land in the recent past, and that its old owners are still determined to reclaim it. The kibbutz thus serves as a microcosm of the State of Israel itself, a country surrounded by enemies longing to "raze the house to the ground." The sense of existential threat was fundamental to the Israeli experience, especially before the 1967 war, when the state was just ten miles wide at its narrowest point.

But it is not the external threat to the kibbutz's survival that concerns Oz in *Where the Jackals Howl*. In these stories, rather, the jackals seem to voice a danger that arises from within: the threat of psychological chaos and moral transgression. The kibbutz is not just an attempt to assert control over the land; even more, it is a form of control over its members' lives and feelings. Its rigorous socialist doctrine is an expression of pure superego, forbidding people from expressing the selfishness, competitiveness, desire, and envy that drive so much human interaction. Obedience to the doctrine is ensured by the constant mutual surveillance of a small community. As Oz would write in his second book, the kibbutz novel *Elsewhere, Perhaps*, "Everyone here judges, everyone is judged, and no weakness can succeed for long in escaping judgment . . . That is why each and every one of us is forced to wage war against his nature. To purify himself. We polish each other as a river polishes its pebbles."

Labor Zionism saw itself as a break with religious Judaism, but it is not hard to see that this model of communal life—a small, homogeneous community charged with observing a strict law—is in fact quite similar to the way most Jews had lived in the villages of Eastern Europe. Indeed, in an essay on kibbutz literature, Oz described the founders of the kibbutzim as men who "had lost their religious faith and abandoned the religious commandments, but they had not given up their devotion and drive and their thirst for the absolute: to be attached to a single, great, final and decisive truth, that found detailed expression in innumerable rules and regulations, both great and small, in everyday life." In other words, socialism served the same function for these rationalist, atheist Jews that the Torah did for their pious ancestors. It is an ethical ideal that represses what Judaism calls *yetzer hara*, "the evil inclination."

But where repression flourishes, there will inevitably be rebellion and transgression as well—a religious truth that Freudian psychoanalysis reformulated for a secular age. This is why, in Oz's stories, the kibbutz has the atmosphere of a moral hothouse where luxuriant vices grow in secret. There is a young writer's truth-telling impulse at work here, a desire to show what really goes on beneath the official surface. But Oz's tone is never merely satirical or debunking. Rather, he portrays the kibbutz as a place where human nature, placed under unusual stress, assumes strange and significant new forms.

Inevitably, sexuality is one of the primary zones of conflict in *Where the Jackals Howl*. The kibbutz encourages marriage and monogamy—this is one of the few areas of life that have not been radically communalized. Yet this sexual economy does not succeed in satisfying all desires, and it is haunted by frustrated and illicit sexual impulses. The title story shows what happens when such impulses suddenly erupt. Here we are introduced to an ugly middle-aged bachelor, Matityahu Damkov, who lures a teenage girl, Galila, to his room by promising to give her a set of paints—a rare luxury sent from abroad.

His motives are made plain enough when he starts to tell her about his previous life, back in Eastern Europe, where he was in charge of a stud farm. In graphic detail, he describes the procedure for getting a stallion ready to mate: he is sexually starved until he is ready to go mad, then released to vent his passion on the first mare he sees. In the blunt symbolism typical of this early book, Oz makes it clear that Damkov is describing himself in this portrait. An unmarried man and a perpetual outsider, he is ready to erupt with sexual violence.

It is not until after Matityahu and Galila have sex—it is hard to say whether it's against her will—that he makes an even more explosive revelation, telling her that he is her real father. At first Galila rejects this claim, and Oz leaves it unclear whether or not Mattityahu is speaking the truth; but by the end of the story she seems to have accepted it, calling her lover "Father." Desire, Oz suggests, is capable of overturning all taboos, even the most primal. The incest theme returns in another story, "Strange Fire," where a woman seduces her daughter's fiancé, after revealing to him that she used to be married to his father. This secret makes her the young man's quasi-stepmother, and turns his intended marriage into a kind of brother-sister incest.

In the context of the kibbutz, the crime of incest takes on a special meaning. This is a society where the fathers, the founders, retain an inordinate degree of prestige and power. They were the ones who brought the kibbutz into being out of nothing, in godlike fashion. What's more, they are the ones who enforce its strict communal regime. There is no way to escape them either morally or physically, since children grow up to live in the same community, under their parents' watchful eyes.

For the fathers and mothers to commit incest, then, is the ultimate symbol of their domination, their unwholesome power. Oz sees the kibbutz in terms not unlike those Freud used to describe primitive human society in *Totem and Taboo*—a primal horde, where all the women were the property of the patriarch and his sons were left isolated and humiliated. Freud speculated that the rebellion of the sons against their overweening father was responsible for the establishment of civilization, and for its taboo on incest. Religion, Freud believed, had its origins in the sons' sense of collective guilt for the murder of their father.

Just so, many of the young characters in *Where the Jackals Howl* are governed by an intense guilt toward their parents, whom they can neither escape nor overcome. It seems almost inevitable that the book concludes with a retelling of the story of Jephthah, the biblical judge who sacrificed his own daughter in order to fulfill a vow to God. The sabras, Oz implies, had grounds to feel that they were sacrificed to their parents' ideological ambitions. In the story "On This Evil Earth," Jephthah is portrayed as a savage warrior who combines the biblical precedents of Cain and Ishmael: "I say to you cursed be your love, O God, and cursed be my love of you," he prays.

When the sons do attempt to live up to their fathers' expectations in *Where the Jackals Howl*, the consequences can be disastrous. That is the case in "The Way of the Wind," which features the familiar constellation of an overbearing pioneer father, Shimshon Sheinbaum, and his overshadowed son, Gideon Shenhav. The names in the story are already significant: like many sabras, including Oz himself, Gideon has Hebraized his last name, which suggests both an attempt to escape his paternal inheritance and a desire to live up to the image of the new Jew. Gideon is a sabra, born on the kibbutz, bearing all the expectations of his father—and failing to meet them: "He did not shine at work; he did not shine in communal life. He was slow of speech and no doubt also of thought."

It is to compensate, or overcompensate, for his weakness that Gideon insists on volunteering for the paratroopers, the most elite outfit in the Israeli military. The story takes place on a day when Gideon's unit is to parachute near the kibbutz where he grew up. It is supposed to be his moment of triumph and vindication, when he shows the world, and his father, that he has become a heroic soldier. So intent is he on being conspicuous that during the jump, Gideon deliberately pulls his backup chute so that he will stand out from the other parachutists. In doing so, however, he sends himself off course and ends up stuck on an active power line, in full view of the whole kibbutz.

To his father's humiliation, Gideon is unable to bring himself to cut the cords of his chute and fall to the ground. Instead, a young and mischievous boy named Zaki tries to climb the utility pole and cut the cord for him; but before he can do so, Gideon deliberately electrocutes himself on the power line. It is a simple tale, told with the inevitability of a Greek tragedy: Gideon's weakness leads to hubris, and hubris brings punishment. Born into any other environment, Gideon might have led a normal life; on the kibbutz, with its particular historical and familial power structures, he is doomed.

Gideon Shenhav fails to become a soldierly superman, but other characters in *Where the Jackals Howl* succeed, and Oz suggests that they are hardly better off. One of the common Israeli complaints about the sabra generation was that they had failed to inherit their parents' ethical idealism. Born into war and conflict, they were often perceived by their elders as nihilistic and inarticulate. The historian Amos Elon describes "a stark, intensely introverted, icy matter-of-factness in the young that contrasts sharply with the . . . rather verbose emotionalism of their elders."

Oz represents such a figure, with all the ambivalent feelings he inspires, in "The Trappist Monastery." Itcheh, brave and brutish, is the hero of his army unit, famous for exploits in battle, such as single-handedly clearing out a cave full of enemy soldiers. Arrogantly certain of his superiority, he condescends to the "general-duty men," the orderlies whose job is to serve the frontline troops; and he is domineering with women, including his girlfriend Bruria, whom he alternately paws and ignores. In the martial culture of the young State of Israel, he represents virtues that no one can challenge; the community needs him in order to survive, and he knows it.

The first part of the story takes place as Itcheh is leading a group of soldiers on a reprisal raid against an Arab village. Rather than describing the action, however, Oz shows us the scene back at the army base, where Nahum, an orderly, is wooing Bruria with a bizarre, masochistic fantasy. He imagines Itcheh coming back from combat severely wounded, so that Nahum has the chance to save his life with an emergency operation. Only in this way will the huge imbalance in their status be rectified; only then will Nahum be able to stand up in Itcheh's presence as a man. It will even offer him a kind of sexual fulfillment, by allowing him to play a role in Itcheh and Bruria's lives: "You'll get married, live happily ever after . . . And I shall continue to love you both from a distance."

The system of values that exalts Itcheh leaves no room for someone like Nahum, who is meek and introverted. Once again, Oz concentrates on the losers in Israeli society, the ones who cannot live up to the ideal of the new Jew. And once again the loser ends up taking a self-destructive revenge on those who humiliate him. When Itcheh returns from battle, triumphant and unharmed, Nahum tells him a lie, saying that Bruria has run off with another soldier. Inflamed, Itcheh insists that Nahum accompany him in pursuit of the couple. But they drive so fast and recklessly that their jeep breaks down, and they find themselves alone, at night, with enemy soldiers nearby. In taking revenge on Itcheh, Nahum has endangered himself. Worse, he has put himself totally in the power of a man he despises, thus confirming the power imbalance between them. Martial heroism like Itcheh's, Oz suggests in this story as throughout *Where the Jackals Howl*, is a double-edged sword: the qualities of toughness and over-bearing confidence that built the State of Israel might also end up dooming it.

See Under: Love
by David Grossman

F ROM THE BEGINNING, ZIONISM'S PROMISE WENT HAND
in hand with a dark prophecy. Jews who came to Palestine would
be reborn as fearless and capable pioneers, but those who did not
would pay a terrible price. And the Holocaust vindicated this diag-
nosis of the European Jewish future in the most brutal terms. The
future Israeli prime minister Moshe Shertok observed that "events
have totally proven the Zionist position on the solution to the Jewish
problem. Zionism predicted the Holocaust decades ago." Yet at the
same time, the Holocaust represented a catastrophic failure for Zionism, which had not been able to rescue the Jewish people in time.

Politically, too, the Holocaust had a double legacy. It made the
creation of a Jewish state possible, as the world grew convinced that
the Jews needed and deserved a homeland, in part to absorb the
hundreds of thousands of refugees languishing in displaced persons
camps after World War II. But it also meant that that state would
take a far different shape than Zionism had originally envisaged. By
1949, one-third of the Jewish population of Israel were Holocaust
survivors; and since virtually every Ashkenazi Jew in Israel was just
one or two generations removed from Eastern Europe, almost all of
them lost family members in the Holocaust. The first native-born
Israeli generation was cut off from its past in the most concrete sense.
"This is a generation with no grandfathers and grandmothers," said
Gideon Hausner, the prosecutor in the trial of Adolf Eichmann.

The novelist David Grossman was born in Jerusalem in 1954.

Seven years old when the Eichmann trial was broadcast on the radio, he recalled it as a formative experience for Israeli children of his generation. It served as their introduction to the terrible loss at the heart of twentieth-century Jewish identity. This was a loss, Grossman wrote in an essay, "which we did not understand at the time and which is still being deciphered throughout the course of our lives. Perhaps what we lost was the illusion of our parents' power to protect us from the terrors of life. Or perhaps we lost our faith in the possibility that we, the Jews, would ever live a complete, secure life. And perhaps, above all, we felt the loss of the natural, childlike faith—faith in man, in his kindness, in his compassion."

Grossman was not a child of Holocaust survivors—his father had immigrated to Palestine before World War II and his mother was born there. But this did not mean that the Holocaust failed to cast a shadow over his family. Indeed, he writes about his childhood in terms similar to those used by the children of Holocaust survivors, emphasizing the mysteries and silences that surrounded him. "My generation, the children of the early 1950s in Israel, lived in a thick and densely populated silence," he recalled. "In my neighborhood, people screamed every night from their nightmares. More than once, when we walked into a room where adults were telling stories of the war, the conversation would stop at once."

In his 1986 novel *See Under: Love*, Grossman asked whether that silence can ever really be filled. Can anyone—in particular, for Grossman, can any writer—truly understand what happened to the Jews of Europe during World War II? And if one does achieve such understanding, what price must be paid for it? The questions clearly have their roots in those childhood silences that Grossman remembers, and which are experienced in the novel by the main character, Shlomo "Momik" Neuman. Over the course of the book, we see Momik grow from an acutely imaginative and vulnerable boy into a man very much like the author—a writer whose life seems irreparably scarred by his early fixation on the Holocaust.

In parallel to Momik's story, we also read Momik's stories—fantastic inventions inspired by his Holocaust obsession, full of magical realist techniques, in which a man turns into a fish or a child lives a complete human life span in twenty-four hours. The very extravagance of these conceits is itself a kind of polemical statement. From the beginning, writing about the Holocaust tended to adopt a quiet and unadorned style, suited to a subject that resisted any kind of literary embellishment. Theodor Adorno famously said that writing poetry after Auschwitz was barbaric, and a similar ethic informs the literary style of writers such as Primo Levi and Elie Wiesel, who want only to tell their stories as clearly and unaffectedly as possible. For Grossman to write about the Holocaust in the way he does, then— in floridly experimental language reminiscent of James Joyce, or in wildly inventive fables like Gabriel García Márquez—is a challenge to this literary decorum. The book's style recapitulates its central question: Is it possible for the literary imagination to be equal to the Holocaust?

As a grown man, Momik spends a lot of time at Yad Vashem, Israel's Holocaust memorial and research center. On one visit there, he meets Ayala, who reveals to him the existence of a secret room called the White Room. In this magical space, there are no books; the only thing the visitor can learn there is what he himself brings to the imagination of the Holocaust: "And in this room you find the essence of those days . . . but the wonderful thing is that there are no ready-made answers there. Nothing is explicit. It's all merely possible."

The White Room is plainly a metaphor for the writerly imagination, which must finally confront the Holocaust alone and unaided. This is a perilous undertaking, since the more one attempts to understand evil, the more one risks being deformed by it. In the second section of *See Under: Love*, we catch glimpses of the adult Momik as husband and father, and see how his closest relationships are paralyzed by his obsession with the Holocaust—both the knowledge of what has already happened and the possibility that it could happen again. "I want to be ready next time it happens," Momik tells his wife. "Not just so I'll be able to break away with a minimum of pain from others, but so I'll be able to break away from myself. I'd like to be able to erase everything inside that could bring me excruciating pain if it were obliterated or degraded."

But the only way to be utterly detached from life and love is to be dead; and isn't cultivating this kind of death-in-life simply a surrender to the Holocaust, a way of becoming its belated victim? The question has societal implications, for it suggests that Israel, founded on the memory of the Holocaust and living in anticipation of a possible future annihilation, cannot possibly develop in a natural and human way. Grossman has been a sharp critic of Israeli politics and society in his journalistic writing, but in *See Under: Love* current political questions do not arise. It is as a Jew and a human being, much more than as an Israeli, that Momik must confront the Holocaust, and this is another expression of Grossman's quiet radicalism. In the White Room, there are no crowds, flags, or armies to mediate between the individual and the memory of the Holocaust. Everyone must confront its evil alone.

Which is not to say that *See Under: Love* could have been written in any other country. The first of the book's four sections, which deals with Momik's childhood in 1950s Jerusalem, evokes a society in which the Holocaust is pervasive, as it could be nowhere but in the Jewish state. The problem facing Momik is that this memory, which makes everyone so fearful and sad, is never openly named or explained. Even the words "Europe" and "Poland" are never mentioned. To Momik, the place grown-ups come from is simply known as "Over There, a place you weren't supposed to talk about too much, only think about in your heart and sigh."

Like the young Amos Oz, who grew up fascinated by the fairy-tale landscape of a Europe he never saw, Momik knows that he will never understand his parents or his world unless he figures out the secret of Over There. So he must become a detective, trying to piece together clues and references. The problem is that he takes everything much too literally: when he hears someone mention "the Nazi Beast," he believes that this is an actual animal, "a huge dinosaur that once lived in the world which everyone was afraid of now. But he didn't dare ask anyone who or what."

When Momik is told by a well-meaning adult that "the Nazi Beast could come out of any kind of animal if it got the right care and nourishment," he takes this metaphor at face value. He decides to build a menagerie in his basement, filling it with all the animals he can trap—pigeons, cats, a jackal—and starving them until the Nazi Beast finally emerges from hiding. Every time he descends into the dark cellar to examine the animals, he is forced to confront his deepest fear, the Nazism he will spend a lifetime trying to understand. This fear takes an obvious toll on the boy, breeding obsessive-compulsive habits (he develops a system of using his fingers to count the letters in every word he says) and a nameless, all-encompassing anxiety.

Finally, Momik brings an old man who survived the Holocaust down to see his menagerie, hoping that the smell and appearance of "a real Jew" will succeed in bringing out the Nazi Beast. Real Jews, Momik reflects angrily, "seem to like it even when you hurt them and when you laugh at them and they're miserable, they've never done anything in their whole lives to fight back, they just sit there . . ." In this crude fashion, Momik both expresses and exposes a cherished myth of Israeli society—the idea that the new Israeli Jew was qualitatively different from passive Diaspora Jews.

In the second section of *See Under: Love*, glimpses of Momik's adult life are mingled with an extended narrative about Bruno Schulz, the great Polish writer, whose reputation rests on two books of short stories. The circumstances of Schulz's death are particularly hideous to Grossman. He had been adopted as a "personal Jew" by an SS officer, whose house he was decorating with murals; when his protector killed a Jew "belonging" to another SS man, that officer killed Schulz in retaliation, supposedly with the words, "You killed my Jew, now I've killed yours." For Grossman, this episode reveals the way Nazism could reduce human personality to a mere unit in an obscene system of barter. "The horrible thing for me about the Holocaust is the way every trace of individuality was obliterated," Momik reflects.

It is to right this injustice, to restore and demonstrate the power of the individual imagination, that Grossman weaves a fantastic tale about Schulz's fate. In this version, Schulz was not murdered but managed to escape to the seaside, where he dove into the water and joined a school of salmon on their journey through the ocean. Schulz learns how to tune in to the signal—Grossman gives it an invented name, "ning"—that tells the school of salmon where to go; he even grows gills and starts to transform into a fish himself. Grossman weaves into this tale details about the adult Momik, who is half inventing it, half recalling it. In this way, we are able to see that the fearful, obsessive boy of the first section has grown into an anxiously self-protective and emotionally repressed adult, unable to give himself fully to his wife and child.

Schulz names the central issue at stake in the novel when he tells Momik: "Whosoever kills another human being destroys a uniquely idiosyncratic work of art which can never be reconstructed." This is the challenge that Momik sets himself as a writer: Is it possible to reconstruct, even partially, a life and mind destroyed by the Nazis? It is closely related to the challenge facing him as a man: Can he fully entrust his own mind and heart to the people around him, knowing that they are vulnerable to destruction? *See Under: Love* itself becomes Grossman's answer: if the book is good enough, imaginative enough, humane enough, then it will prove that life is worth living, even in a world where the Holocaust is possible.

In the last two sections of *See Under: Love*, Grossman makes that challenge his explicit subject, through the story of Anshel Wasserman, who is—like Momik and Schulz—a kind of writer. When the young Momik meets him, Wasserman is a muttering, inarticulate old man whose only comprehensible utterance is a name, "Herr Neigel." All Momik really knows about him is that he had once been a popular writer of stories for children. His tales dealt with a band of adventurers known as "the Children of the Heart," who traveled the world fighting villains and escaping from dangers.

On this slender basis, the adult Momik constructs a scenario involving Wasserman, who is a prisoner in a concentration camp run by an SS officer named Neigel. Wasserman, in this fantasy, is for some reason unable to die, no matter how many times he is killed by the

Nazis. Yet after working as a *Sonderkommando*, a prisoner in charge of disposing of the bodies of murdered Jews, Wasserman can't stand living any longer. So, like a reverse Scheherazade, he makes a deal with Neigel, who turns out to have been a devoted fan of the Children of the Heart. He will invent a new story involving those characters, which he will tell Neigel every night. His reward, however, will be not life but death: each night after finishing his story, Neigel will shoot him in the head, in the hope that finally he will be able to die.

This is an extremely dark premise, in which life seems to have only a negative value: it is the occasion for indescribable suffering, something to escape at any cost. But as the game goes on and Wasserman weaves his tale, it becomes clear that he has an ulterior motive. "People are like flies . . . the stories they are told must be like flypaper," he reflects, and the story he tells Neigel is meant to entrap him in a particular way: it is meant to awaken his humanity. Here is the ultimate test of the storytelling imagination—not to save the life of a Jew, but to turn a Nazi into a human being.

Neigel is aware of Wasserman's plan, and he scorns it: "If you had a knife in your hand, even a little jackknife, it would be a lot more convincing and effective than the millions of words you're going to chatter here." This is entirely consonant with the Zionist view that the safety of the Jews cannot be secured by mere words; when dealing with a hostile world, only the ability to physically defend oneself matters. But Wasserman has the daring to disagree. He wagers that it is possible to provoke empathy even in the most hardened foe. In the laboratory-like conditions of *See Under: Love*, the power of narrative can be at least hypothetically vindicated.

It is to this end that Wasserman tells the most devastating story of all, the tale of Kazik. Grossman casts this story in yet another innovative form: the final section of *See Under: Love* takes the form of an alphabetical encyclopedia, in which Kazik's life is related, not in a consecutive narrative, but in an ingeniously constructed collage. As Wasserman tells it, the Children of the Heart are now old men and women trapped in the Warsaw Ghetto. Mysteriously, they find themselves entrusted with a newborn child, Kazik, who soon demonstrates a strange power: he is living at a hugely accelerated rate, so that he will pass through a complete human life span in one day.

As he relates the stages of Kazik's life, and the associated trials and adventures of the Children of the Heart, Grossman also relates the effect that Wasserman's story is having on Neigel. Slowly but surely, the heartbreaking tale of Kazik does penetrate the SS man's brutal exterior, and he starts to confide in Wasserman about his private life and his family. Finally, the entwined stories of Kazik and Neigel reach a double catastrophe, when both end up committing suicide: Kazik, in despair over the possibilities of a brief life passed entirely in the Warsaw Ghetto; Neigel, when he realizes that he has regained too much of his humanity to function any longer as a reliable Nazi. In this way, Wasserman has his revenge at last. He has told a story so moving and terrible that it can even pierce the heart of a concentration camp commandant.

It is an ironic conclusion to a novel that places so much faith in the power of literature. Storytelling about the Holocaust, Grossman suggests, cannot counter its evil, or eliminate its memory from the world. All stories can do is bring that evil home to us, in so vivid and terrible a way that life in this world becomes impossible. Literature might be equal to the Holocaust only in the sense that it can make its reality too painfully immediate to bear.

This ambiguity continues to the very last page of *See Under: Love*, where we read about the wishes that the Children of the Heart expressed when they first discovered the newborn Kazik. They wish for him to "grow up manly and brave and willing to believe," and not to be "poisoned" by the hatred surrounding him. Above all, Wasserman says, "All of us prayed for one thing: that he might end his life knowing nothing of war . . . We asked so little: for a man to live in this world from birth to death and know nothing of war."

For Kazik, of course, this hope is impossible, since he spends his brief life span surrounded by World War II. But for Grossman's Israeli readers, it carries another kind of irony. After all, the Jewish state, born out of the memory of the Holocaust and dedicated to ensuring that the Jewish people will never again be destroyed, has spent its entire existence in the midst of war. Zionism, Grossman suggests, has been unable to fulfill the minimal requirement for a good human life: peace. In this sense, Zionism represents not a break with Jewish history, the way its founders intended, but the translation of Jewish history into a new setting, carrying all the old traumas and challenges with it. The memory of the Holocaust ensures that "here" can never be truly detached from "Over There," the Israeli future from the European past. All the immense imaginative resources Grossman employs in *See Under: Love* turn out not to liberate the reader or the writer, but to trap them in the White Room, where the horror of history must be continually reenacted.

Mr. Mani
by A. B. Yehoshua

IN THE 1940S, THE YOUNG AMOS KLAUSNER WAS GROW-
ing up in Jerusalem's Kerem Avraham neighborhood and attending Gymnasia Rehavia, one of the first modern high schools in Jewish
Palestine. Among his fellow students was Avraham Yehoshua, who
was born three years earlier, in 1936. But Yehoshua—who, as A. B.
Yehoshua, would rival Oz as one of his generation's leading Israeli
novelists—had a very different relationship to the city they shared.
Oz's family had arrived in Jerusalem not long before he was born,
and he felt that they still had one foot in Europe. The same was true
of most of the Zionist settlers who arrived in Palestine during the
early twentieth century.

Yehoshua's family, on the other hand, had been living in Jerusalem
for five generations. They were Sephardic Jews, whose ancestors had
settled around the eastern Mediterranean following the expulsion
of the Jews from Spain in 1492. The continual presence of Jews in
Jerusalem since ancient times was one of the Zionist movement's key
claims to the Land of Israel—proof that the Jews had never forfeited
their presence or their rights there. But the long-standing Jewish
communities of Jerusalem also presented an ideological problem for
Zionism. For one thing, their connection with the Land was rooted
in Judaism, rather than the secular nationalism promoted by Zionism. For another, they had long coexisted with Palestine's Arab population, which the new Zionist immigrants could not do, thanks to
their large numbers and political ambitions. From the point of view

of a family like the Yehoshuas, the State of Israel was just the latest development in their relationship with the holy city of Jerusalem, one that had existed long before the state and might, in theory, continue after it.

In his 1989 novel *Mr. Mani*, Yehoshua shows that this perspective could powerfully unsettle the usual Zionist ways of thinking about Jewish history. The novel surveys six generations of the Mani family, who, like the Yehoshuas, are Sephardic Jews resident in Jerusalem since the 1840s. In each generation, there is a Mr. Mani who manages, usually by the skin of his teeth, to carry forward the family line and name. Yet the book is ingeniously structured so that the Manis are seldom allowed to speak for themselves. Rather, each chapter takes the form of a transcript of a conversation between people whose destinies intersect with a member of the Mani family. (Actually, the transcript includes only one side of the conversation, rendering it effectively a monologue, with occasional indications of the reaction of the listener.) Not until the last chapter, set in 1848, do we encounter the earliest Mr. Mani, whose story turns out to explain some of the recurrent patterns we have seen shaping his descendants' lives throughout the book.

The first of these narrations takes place in Israel in 1982, where a twenty-year-old woman named Hagar is heard talking to her mother, a widow whose husband was killed in combat years before. Hagar lives in Tel Aviv, leading the kind of pleasantly aimless existence common to young people in prosperous cities throughout the modern world—taking a few college classes while conducting a romance. Her lover, Efrayim, who is currently serving in the army in Lebanon, is the father of the child Hagar has just discovered she is carrying; and here, too, she is casual in a modern way, neither ashamed of being pregnant outside marriage nor unduly concerned with how to raise the child when it is born. After all, she grew up in the progressive-minded, ultra-secular environment of the kibbutz, where her mother still lives. In short, Yehoshua presents Hagar as a typical secular Israeli, a Jew who has been successfully emancipated from the moral and religious burdens of Jewish tradition. At one point in her narrative, she reveals that she doesn't know that a minyan, a group of ten men, is needed in order to recite the mourner's prayer, the kaddish— an elementary fact about Jewish observance that would have been known to all her ancestors.

Hagar ends up leaving the free, modern life she lives in Tel Aviv in order to experience the very different atmosphere of Jerusalem— a city that, for Yehoshua as for Agnon, is inescapably religious and bound to history. In Jerusalem, she begins to have an odd sensation: "this new feeling . . . that I've never had before, which is that I'm not so alone anymore but part of a much bigger story that I don't know anything about yet because it's only beginning." This is a kind of metafictional joke, of course, since Hagar is literally a character in the first chapter of a novel. But it is also, Yehoshua implies, an awakening to the fact that, though she tries to forget it, the modern Israeli ineluctably belongs to a very long story. For Hagar this is not just the story of the Jewish people, but specifically the story of the Mani family. Her lover's full name is Efrayim Mani, and what brings her to Jerusalem is a request from him: he is concerned that he can't reach his father on the phone and asks Hagar to check on him.

This father, Gavriel, is the first Mr. Mani to appear in the novel, and from the start he is a mysterious figure. He is in mourning for his mother, who has just died—it is for her funeral that the minyan needs to be assembled. But this doesn't seem to explain the state of suicidal despair in which Hagar finds him when she travels to Jerusalem and confronts him in his apartment. She finds that Mr. Mani has taken down the rope from the window shade and fashioned it into a noose; if she hadn't arrived when she did, he might have hanged himself. "He couldn't control this impulse he had to do away with himself every evening . . . [T]hat thought wasn't his own but came from someone or somewhere else," Hagar muses, planting a clue that will be followed up as Yehoshua takes the reader back into the Mani family's history.

Over the several days of her visit, Hagar and Mr. Mani act out a weird psychodrama, in which she follows him around Jerusalem and sleeps in his apartment in order to keep him under surveillance.

There is something uncanny about the way the two strangers from different generations are drawn together, apparently in spite of both their wills, as if they are acting out a fated pattern. After all, the biblical Hagar was the young handmaiden who was given to the older Abraham so that he could father a child, just as this Hagar is pregnant with Mr. Mani's grandchild. Equally uncanny, Yehoshua suggests, is Hagar's developing relationship with the city of Jerusalem itself. Even when she attempts to leave Jerusalem, she finds herself turning back, as if her destiny demanded that she stay there.

Hagar's narration is inconclusive—the reader never does discover what's wrong with Mr. Mani, and she ends up losing the pregnancy that united her fate with the Mani family's in the first place. But later on, Yehoshua writes, Hagar gets pregnant by Efrayim once again, and this time she bears a son, Roni. While Efrayim wants nothing to do with her or the child, Mr. Mani becomes a regular visitor, thus fulfilling the role fate seems to have cast them in. Hagar has carried on the Mani family line, and Mr. Mani becomes a surrogate father to his own grandchild. It seems like a very modern story of an improvised, blended family.

But as *Mr. Mani* unfolds, it becomes clear that the constellation of events and relationships that draws Hagar and Mr. Mani together is neither modern nor accidental. Rather, the themes of their story return in each generation of the Mani saga, going back to the 1840s: difficult pregnancies, absent fathers, intergenerational attraction, obsessions and suicidal tendencies. All of these stories unfold against the background of Jerusalem, a city that, in its gloomy fatefulness, seems to influence the Manis' fate like a dark star. "Jerusalem? A small, poor, harsh city," says the narrator of a later chapter, who visits the city in 1899. "And yet, oddly enough, it does not seem remote. There is nothing provincial about it. Nor will there ever be."

The idea that what seems provincial can actually be the center of the world influences Yehoshua's treatment of Jewish history. The years spanned by the novel, 1848 to 1982, were full of events that are now in the history books, yet the Manis play no role in any of them; they are always at a tangent to history. Gavriel Mani's father,

Efrayim, dies in World War II, but not in the Holocaust: he is on a boat full of refugees that is accidentally sunk by a British bomber. Efrayim's father, Yosef, is present in Jerusalem during the capture of the city by the British in 1917, the event that ultimately made possible the creation of Israel. But he ends up being deported by the British for being a political nuisance, and so he plays no role in building the Jewish state. Yosef's father, Moshe, attends one of the Zionist Congresses in Basel where Theodor Herzl set out his plans for the Jewish state. But he ends up committing suicide in Beirut, where he has been driven by his romantic obsession with a younger woman.

In each generation, the Manis stubbornly refuse to embody the collective fate of the Jewish people. Instead, they are chased by their own private, familial Furies. Not until the novel's last chapter, however, does Yehoshua actually entrust the narration to a member of the Mani family—Avraham, who is the first of the dynasty to settle in Jerusalem, and the first to have his life consumed by an obsession. In his case, this is both an erotic fixation on a particular woman and a determination to continue his family line—desires that merge when his son dies childless and Mr. Mani takes it upon himself to make sure his daughter-in-law becomes pregnant. "The world would have its Manis after all," Avraham declares grimly, even if it requires incest to make that happen. It is a kind of mirror image of the fate of the first Mr. Mani we meet, back in 1982 in the first chapter, who also ends up being, in a different sense, the father to his own grandchild.

Indeed, *Mr. Mani* is a novel full of hidden correspondences, which help to create its dreamlike atmosphere. In the 1980s, Hagar ends up in a maternity ward in the old city of Jerusalem—which is where Moshe Mani had his maternity clinic a hundred years before. Yosef Mani is arrested by the British during World War I because he insists on crossing enemy lines to make speeches to the Arabs, haranguing them about the need to come to terms with the impending Jewish state. He doesn't know that he is following in the footsteps of his ancestor and namesake, who is fixated on the idea that the Arabs of Palestine are descended from ancient Jews, and spends his life lecturing them about the need to come back to Judaism. Biblical echoes, too, permeate the book. Yosef Mani ends up being killed by a mob on the Temple Mount as his father Avraham watches; the Temple Mount, in Jewish tradition, is the same Mount Moriah where the biblical Abraham went to sacrifice his son Isaac.

These deep continuities in the Manis' story also help Yehoshua emphasize how much has changed in Jerusalem and the world between 1848 and 1982. Avraham Mani inhabits a world saturated in Judaism—speaking a language full of biblical references, serving as disciple to a wise rabbi, numbering the years according to the Jewish calendar. His descendant Roni, Hagar's son, will grow up knowing almost nothing about Judaism. It is an acute irony, then, that it is Roni who will experience what Avraham could only have prayed for: he will live in a Jewish country. Yet it is impossible to read *Mr. Mani* and come away thinking that this Zionist achievement is the teleological goal toward which Jewish history has been tending. The Manis' home—the home, Yehoshua suggests, of Jewish destiny—is not the State of Israel, which appeared overnight and could vanish just as quickly, but the city of Jerusalem, which endures forever.

Dolly City
by Orly Castel-Bloom

O NE OF THE MOST HOPEFUL PASSAGES IN AGNON'S *ONLY Yesterday* depicts the founding of Tel Aviv in 1909. It began as a neighborhood of sixty houses built on the sand dunes outside Jaffa, but by the time Agnon came to write about it in his novel, it had grown into Israel's biggest city. Today, it is the center of a metropolis that is home to 3.5 million people, almost half of the country's population. "The tourists think Tel Aviv was like that from the beginning and each one of her forefathers, the builders of Tel Aviv, attributes the splendor of Tel Aviv to himself," Agnon writes. But he sees the city as something more like a miracle, a fulfillment of the divine plan: "Tel Aviv became Tel Aviv by the life force of the living God."

In the provocative and surreal novel *Dolly City*, by Orly Castel-Bloom, however, it comes to seem more like the work of a devil. Published in 1992 at the beginning of Castel-Bloom's career, the book offers a vision of Tel Aviv as Dolly City, a place where all the achievements of modernity—skyscrapers, railways, hospitals—are exaggerated to the point of nightmare. "Dolly City, a city without a base, without a past, without an infrastructure. The most demented city in the world," Castel-Bloom writes, turning the city's point of pride—its newness, its self-createdness—into a token of artificiality and insanity.

If Grossman uses magical realism and absurdism to convey a tragic depth of feeling, Castel-Bloom renders those same techniques sinister by vacating them of all sentiment. What is left is a fearful portrait of a modern society that both is and is not Israel. Indeed, Dolly City can be taken as Castel-Bloom's dystopian portrait of any modern metropolis, bristling with four-hundred-story skyscrapers yet full of violence and decay. "All the streets in Dolly City are one-way streets, but everybody drives in all directions anyway," comments Dolly, the novel's mad narrator, after whom the place is named. This suggests that it is in part a projection of her disordered mind rather than a real location. Yet Dolly's vision is deeply rooted in Israeli myth and reality, making the identification of Dolly City with Tel Aviv inevitable.

In a sense, the novel can be read as Castel-Bloom's satiric rewriting of Theodor Herzl's 1902 novel *Old New Land*, the book that gave the city of Tel Aviv its name. Where Herzl imagines the utopian Jewish society of the future, Castel-Bloom offers a dystopian reflection of the one that has actually come into being. Similarly, where Agnon introduced the early, idealistic pioneer A. D. Gordon as a character in *Only Yesterday*, so Castel-Bloom features a character named Gordon who mouths the tenets of Labor Zionism—its love of the soil and everything natural. Accordingly, he mistrusts Dolly City, which in the light of the Labor Zionist ideal can only look like a perversion—a prison where Israelis are kept away from the land that should be their source of spiritual renewal. "Dolly City is not a place to put down roots or start a farm. It's not a place," Gordon complains.

But by the late twentieth century, Castel-Bloom suggests, this kind of romantic ideology can only appear obsolete and absurd. Where Agnon's Gordon was a saintly figure, Castel-Bloom's Gordon is an antiquated hippie who injects chlorophyll as if it were an organic substitute for heroin. When Castel-Bloom writes that Gordon "felt connected to the history of the world, especially the history of the Jews," this only marks him as an alien in the world of Dolly City, where history has vanished and even the notion of family has been profaned. "All the babies in Dolly City are adopted, the little bastards. All the mothers in Dolly City are fucked up, screwed up," rants Dolly.

This is the voice of the novel—Dolly's obscene, uncontrollable monologue, which stops at nothing in communicating her sense of dislocation and rage. She records a series of transgressive episodes in which she commits cartoonish acts of violence that carry no gravity or consequence. Child abuse, mutilation, torture, crucifixions, multiple murders: *Dolly City* makes room for them all, like a story by the Marquis de Sade. But it is the weightlessness of this violence that makes it truly disturbing. In the postmodern anti-world of *Dolly City*, there is neither morality nor law, not even the law of cause and effect.

In particular, the moral strictures of Judaism are absent. This is obvious from the first page, where Dolly performs a version of a biblical sacrifice. "In very ancient times, in the land of Canaan, righteous men would sacrifice bigger animals than this to God. When they cut up a lamb, they would be left with big, bloody, significant pieces in their hands, and their covenant would be a real covenant," Dolly reflects. Her own sacrifice, by contrast, involves a goldfish, which she cuts to pieces, burns with a match, and swallows. This is at the same time an act of blasphemy and a sign of disappointed religious yearning. The only form Judaism can take in Dolly City is parodic and absurd, like everything else.

The plot of *Dolly City*, such as it is, involves Dolly's discovery of a baby boy abandoned by the side of the road in a plastic bag. This boy, whom she calls "Son," immediately falls prey to Dolly's perverted maternal instinct, which makes her abnormally concerned for his well-being. Because she is a kind of doctor—she claims to have trained at the University of Kathmandu, and conducts animal experiments in her apartment—Dolly is able to demonstrate her concern for Son by performing countless unnecessary surgeries on him. "Even though the child was a hundred percent healthy, I decided to cut him open. I succumbed to the chronic doubt from which I suffer," she confesses.

Here is maternal instinct exaggerated to the point of horror. What's more, in the name of protecting Son, Dolly convinces herself that violence against her perceived enemies is fully justified. At one point she plans to kidnap an Arab baby and steal its kidney, in order to transplant it into Son. "An Arab baby. They hate us, we hate them," she muses, in a twisted reflection of what Castel-Bloom sees as an endemic Israeli sentiment. In the end, however, she decides to take revenge on an even greater enemy, the Germans. She visits an orphanage in Düsseldorf and tries "all the kidneys of all the forty babies of the proper age . . . Some of them died on me. I left them lying there with their guts spilling out, and took a coffee break," Castel-Bloom writes in camp-horror style.

But perhaps, Castel-Bloom suggests, this kind of madness is the price of being Israeli. One of the surgeries Dolly inflicts on the young Son involves carving a detailed map of Israel on his back: "The sight of the map of the Land of Israel . . . gave me a shiver of delight. At long last I felt that I was cutting into living flesh. My baby screamed in pain—but I stood firm," Dolly gloats. The power of the image comes from its literalization of the Zionist ideal. Dolly has found a way of making the connection between the Jew and the Jewish state ineffaceable.

And is the metaphor really so outrageous? After all, when Son grows up, he is inevitably drafted into the armed services—in his case, a through-the-looking-glass version of the Israeli navy, where he fights in a bizarre and unexplained war against France. If the state can demand the sacrifice of a child's life, why shouldn't a mother have the right to prepare him for it? During Dolly's visit to an asylum, one inmate says, "The state should pay for the psychiatric treatment of its citizens, since the state was responsible for unbalancing their minds."

"Crazy people like saying that the craziness is stronger than they are. Not me. I may be crazy, but it's not stronger than I am," Dolly insists. *Dolly City* insists on a perverse kind of admiration for its heroine, who is able to survive a mad world by responding to it with an equally ferocious madness. At the end of the book, she believes that this will to survive is her true legacy to Son: "I knew that after everything I'd done to him—a bullet or a knife in the back were nothing he couldn't handle." Here is the same desperate insistence on toughness that plays such an ambivalent role in the work of Oz and Grossman—a toughness that deforms even as it makes survival possible. The pathos of *Dolly City* lies in its defiance of ordinary human feeling, as if desensitization were the only possible response to a world, a country, and a city that are simply too hard to live in.

Poems by
Yehuda Amichai

F ROM AGNON TO CASTEL-BLOOM, MODERN HEBREW
literature is obsessed with the gap between the Zionist ideal and
the experience of the individual Israeli. How can the individual preserve a private sense of reality in a time and place defined by abstract
political ideas and grand historical movements? This question lies at
the center of the work of Yehuda Amichai, who is widely considered
Israel's greatest poet. "The twentieth century was the blood in my
veins," Amichai writes in an early poem, and he is constantly aware
of being situated in history—the history of the modern world, of the
Jews, and of the State of Israel, with their sometimes conflicting,
sometimes overlapping coordinates.

Amichai's biography prepared him for this role, since he shared
many of the central experiences of his Israeli generation. Born Lud-
wig Pfeuffer in Germany in 1924, he immigrated to Palestine with
his family in 1936 as part of the wave of German Jews fleeing Nazi
persecution. Ten years later, he made the classic Zionist gesture of
taking a new Hebrew name to suit his new identity: Amichai means
"my people lives," a powerful statement to make just after the Holocaust. As a young man he served in the British army during World
War II, and then in the Palmach, the elite commando unit of the
defense forces of pre-state Israel. He would also see active service in
the Sinai campaign in 1956 and the Yom Kippur War of 1973. Upon
his debut as a poet in the early 1950s, he was recognized in Israel as
one of the major literary voices of his generation.

Ironically, however, the element in Amichai's work that enabled him to play this role was precisely his resistance to the collective. There is nothing remotely official about Amichai's writing, and his poems are the opposite of anthems or slogans; they always speak in a skeptical, individual voice. His language is colloquial yet rich in imaginative metaphor, allowing him to set his own experience against a very wide historical and religious background. Biblical figures and dialogues with God mingle in Amichai's work with intimate scenes of lovemaking and everyday epiphanies.

Living in an intensely political society, it was particularly important to Amichai to preserve a zone of independence from the strong claims of Zionist solidarity. In "King Saul and I," for instance, he expresses the same discomfort with the Israeli military ideal that Amos Oz dramatized in the stories of *Where the Jackals Howl*. He turns the biblical king into a symbol of authority and valor, only to mark his own profound distance from such a heroic type: "He is a dead king. / I am a tired man."

This "tiredness" is a reaction to the superhuman demands placed on Amichai's generation in the tasks of immigration, state-building, and war. War is a frequent subject of Amichai's early work, but he always writes about it in a civilian spirit, emphasizing the loss and waste of combat and the human need for peace. One such poem is titled after its refrain, "I Want to Die in My Bed." Coming from a man who was a soldier in four wars, this sentiment has a real force: it is not just a plea for survival, but a rejection of the cult of sacrifice. The best way to honor the dead, Amichai suggests, is to honor ordinary, unglorious life.

For Amichai, the area of life that symbolizes individual freedom and privacy is the erotic. From youth until old age, he writes vividly about sex and desire, about women he has loved and the places where they came together. Love, he often suggests, is both an escape from the pressures of history and a response to them: "In the middle of this century we turned to each other / With half faces and full eyes / like an ancient Egyptian picture," he writes, as if the posture of lovers facing one another is timeless and renders them immune to time.

In another poem Amichai writes, "Every day of our life together / Ecclesiastes cancels a line of his book." Ecclesiastes is one of the most pessimistic books of the Bible, the one that declares, "All is vanity." The lovers' passion serves to rebut this dark view, offering proof that human life can be full of goodness.

Yet even here, the mention of Ecclesiastes situates Amichai's love poems in a Jewish context. The history he would escape is always present. How could it be otherwise for a poet writing poems about sex in the Jews' holy tongue? In the ongoing debate about whether Zionism was a break with the Jewish past or a continuation of it, Amichai comes down firmly in the latter camp. Raised in an Orthodox family—he explained that it was easy for him to speak Hebrew in Palestine, because he had studied it so intensively at Jewish schools in Germany—Amichai abandoned religious observance, yet remained a profoundly religious writer. But his Jewishness is full of paradoxes. He is able to write with intimacy, even love, about a God who does not exist.

"I declare with perfect faith / That prayer preceded God. / Prayer created God," Amichai writes, borrowing the refrain of a Jewish prayer that lays out the fundamental articles of belief, as articulated by Maimonides in the twelfth century. In the twentieth century, Amichai suggests, a revision is needed. God must now be understood not as humanity's creator but as its creation, a myth we have invented for our own purposes. Yet the poet continues to insist that this God plays an important role in our lives. Even as we create him, he creates us, since our ideas of God help to determine our ideas about who we are and how we should live. God and human beings and prayer are bound together in a cycle without end, which continues to revolve even in an age of unbelief.

For Amichai, the key obstacle to traditional Jewish belief is the fact of the Holocaust. In one poem, he describes the tattooed numbers on the arms of concentration camp survivors as "the telephone numbers of God, / numbers that do not answer." This is a characteristic Amichai metaphor, fusing a serious subject with an everyday image, so that religion and history cease to be solemn abstractions and enter into the texture of ordinary life. But Amichai does something even more audacious than denying God: he asks the reader to pity God, describing him as a father who has lost his children. In this way, Amichai simultaneously affirms an ancient Jewish idea and revolutionizes it: God is still "our father, our king," in the words of a Jewish prayer, but now he is a sovereign without power, who has to look on helplessly as his people suffer. In this way, Amichai reveals himself as a profound post-Holocaust theologian, even as he writes, "After Auschwitz, no theology."

Amichai thinks of Israel as a God-haunted place, especially in Jerusalem, where he spent most of his life. To live in Jerusalem is to live in a dreamscape, a hallucination: "Jerusalem's a place where everyone remembers / he's forgotten something / but doesn't remember what it is." A real place that is also a living symbol, the city represents the extreme tension inherent in Zionism itself. There is something exhilarating about living so directly at the center of history, in a country defined by the grandest ambitions and the most dire tragedies. This condition is responsible for much of the energy and scope of Amichai's work: he is plugged into a powerful current, and he is strong enough to let it flow through him. Yet just as he prefers peace and love to war and heroism, Amichai dreams of a time in which the oldest Zionist ambition—to become a normal people in a normal country—will be fulfilled. After a century of historic achievement, this ordinariness remains, in the title of one of his poems, "The Greatest Desire."

IV

MAKING
JUDAISM MODERN

Three Addresses on Judaism by Martin
Buber ✧ *Religion of Reason out of the Sources
of Judaism* by Hermann Cohen ✧ *Judaism as a
Civilization* by Mordecai Kaplan ✧ *Halakhic Man*
by Joseph Soloveitchik ✧ *God in Search of Man* by
Abraham Joshua Heschel ✧ *To Mend the World*
by Emil Fackenheim ✧ *Standing Again at Sinai*
by Judith Plaskow

Three Addresses on
Judaism by Martin Buber

"WHY DO WE CALL OURSELVES JEWS? BECAUSE WE are Jews? What does that mean: we are Jews?" With these words, delivered to an audience of students in 1909, Martin Buber laid down a challenge that would echo through the twentieth century. For Jewish tradition and those who still lived within it, Buber's questions were unnecessary. Such Jews knew why they were Jews: they were part of God's chosen people, descendants of the Israelites who had received God's Torah and were bound to live by it. While this fate could be burdensome, it was also the highest spiritual privilege.

But for the majority of twentieth-century Jews, faced with the pressures and opportunities of secular modernity, Buber's questions were unavoidable. If one is born Jewish but doesn't practice Judaism, speak a Jewish language, or live in a Jewish community, what does it actually mean to call oneself a Jew? For imaginative writers in Europe, America, and Israel, it was possible to answer these questions without directly confronting religious belief. But for theologians and philosophers like Buber, it was not a vague Jewishness but Judaism itself whose beliefs and doctrines, texts and practices, had sustained the Jewish people for thousands of years. Could these things be given new life for the twentieth century?

In 1909, the thirty-one-year-old Buber was already one of German Jewry's leading thinkers about this question. The descendant of rabbis, Buber had a secular university education and fell early under the spell of Friedrich Nietzsche, whose books convinced him of the need to discover new sources of value and meaning. But unlike many Jewish intellectuals of his generation, Buber believed that renewal could take place within Judaism, by cultivating the resources of a tradition modern Jews had become estranged from. That was his goal in three lectures he delivered to the Bar Kochba Society of Prague, a Jewish student organization, between 1909 and 1910. These lectures, collected in the book *Three Addresses on Judaism* in 1911, caused a sensation among the younger generation of German-speaking Jews. Among Buber's listeners in Prague were several who went on to become leaders of the Zionist movement, as well as the then-unknown Franz Kafka.

The power of Buber's addresses came from his willingness to acknowledge what much of this audience felt, that the Judaism they knew was spiritually bankrupt. In the first lecture, "Judaism and the Jews," Buber insists on this point. Judaism may have had real meaning for their ancestors, but for modern Jews it had become "the most miserable slavery," compulsory and burdensome. Neither the Orthodox Judaism of practice and observance nor the Reform Judaism of decorous worship and ethical idealism could speak to the true spiritual needs of the young.

In subsequent lectures Buber would imagine ways to change this situation, to restore urgency and authenticity to Judaism. But in "Judaism and the Jews," he is less interested in Judaism as a religion than in Jewishness as a nationality. Here, too, he argues, there is something missing in the modern Jew's identity. He belongs to the Jewish people as a historical fact, but this fact has no definite meaning for him. At a time when nationalism was on the rise among all the peoples of Europe, Buber notes that the Jew alone was deprived of "all the elements that might constitute a nation for him . . . land, language, way of life." For the Jew in Diaspora, there is no match between these things and what Buber calls "the community of his blood."

Today, blood (like its related term, race) is a discredited concept, both scientifically and politically. But for Buber, blood is something very real—an essence that unites the Jewish people despite all differences of time and place, determining their national character and the way they respond to the world. It is at the same time physical—what we might now call genetic—and historical, shaped by collective experience over time.

This Jewish character includes nobility, "the element of the prophets, the psalmists, and the kings of Judah," but also disgrace, the "pain, misery, and humiliation" that have been the lot of the Jews in Diaspora. Buber has a low opinion of the Jewish character that has been formed by persecution. Though he is an intellectual himself, he particularly objects to Jewish intellectuality, which he sees as a defense mechanism that allowed Jews to feel superior to the gentiles who mistreated them. "For centuries," he laments, "we did not hit back when our face was slapped." The result was that Jews became too mental and not physical enough—"out of touch with life, out of balance, inorganic."

Such ideas were common among the Zionists of Buber's time, whose goal was not just a Jewish national home but the creation of a new Jew, free from the psychological deformities of exile. Yet Buber's analysis of the Jewish predicament does not issue, as one might expect, in a simple exhortation to emigrate to Palestine. (He himself didn't move there until 1938, when he was driven out of Germany by Nazi persecution.) Rather, what he has in mind is an inner spiritual transformation that can take place anywhere Jews happen to live. When Buber urges the Jew to "purify himself from the dross of foreign rule," this doesn't mean rebelling against the political rule of foreign governments, but rejecting foreignness as an inner temptation by defining oneself as a Jew first and foremost: "Whoever, faced with the choice between environment and substance, decides for substance will henceforth have to be a Jew truly from within." To be an authentic Jew, for Buber, means choosing to be what one is, rather than passively accepting it.

Already in "Judaism and the Jews," it is clear that Buber's thinking tends to fall into dualistic patterns: environment versus blood, foreign versus native, mind versus body. In the second lecture, "Judaism and Mankind," he heightens this dualism still further, suggesting that the condition of being split between opposing influences and desires is an essential Jewish trait. "The yea as well as the nay dwell in the Jew," Buber writes. Once again, he acknowledges the shame and negativity that some modern Jews feel about their heritage. But he emphasizes that Jewish defects go along with great virtues. Jewish history presents "contrasts most extreme . . . a most courageous truthfulness alongside a deep-seated mendacity, ultimate readiness for sacrifice next to greediest egotism."

Yet such Jewish division is always accompanied, Buber insists, by a striving for unity through the "expulsion of the negative." Indeed, Buber sees the origin of Judaism's religious genius in its powerful urge to overcome duality and achieve oneness. "Just as the idea of inner duality is Jewish, so is the idea of redemption from it," he writes. It follows that individual Jews, as well as whole periods of Jewish history and thought, can be judged by whether they promote unity or succumb to duality.

For Buber, Jewish creativity is always associated with the striving for unity and synthesis. This criterion yields the paradoxical result that some of the most creative, and therefore most authentic, Jewish thinkers are those who rebelled against Judaism itself. For Buber, the heretical seventeenth-century thinker Benedict Spinoza was a great Jewish spirit, while the whole of rabbinic Judaism, which sustained the Jewish people for two thousand years, was in some sense anti-Jewish. Rabbinic Judaism, with its focus on law and textual study, is to Buber merely "poverty-stricken, distorted, and sickly," its authority "directed against creativity itself, against all that was free, new, change-producing."

The argument of "Judaism and Mankind" builds to a climax in Buber's direct challenge to his audience. Which kind of Jew, he demands, are they going to be? Will they belong to the *Urjuden*, the "elemental Jews," who long for spiritual unity and strive to achieve it, or to the *galut* Jews, the Jews of exile, who are inauthentic, alienated, slaves of a rote tradition? The disparagement of the *galut* Jew was a staple of Zionist thought, but once again Buber employs Zionist concepts in unusual ways. Exile, for him, is not a political or geographic condition but a spiritual one. It is perfectly possible to be a *galut* Jew in Palestine, just as one can achieve elemental Jewishness in Germany. What matters is that the individual Jew make a decision to embrace unity in his own spirit, and in so doing fulfill Judaism's mission to "proclaim a world in which dualism will be abolished."

In the third lecture, "Renewal of Judaism," Buber makes explicit how different his definition of renewal is from those current among European Jews in his time. Many believed that the renewal of Judaism required modernizing it, which in effect meant making it more like liberal Protestantism. Reform Judaism, which was born in Germany in the early nineteenth century and became the dominant form of worship among assimilated German Jews, involved jettisoning much of traditional Jewish practice and redefining Judaism as an ethical creed. Buber can sympathize with the desire to free the modern Jew from tradition, but he dismisses Reform as "not a renewal of Judaism, but its perpetuation in an easier, more elegant, Westernized, more socially acceptable form." Better to be a rote follower of a tradition that is at least really Jewish, he writes, than to enlist in the "feeble" assimilationist program of Reform Judaism.

One alternative to assimilation was Zionism. But while Buber had a long connection with the Zionist movement, he makes clearer than ever in this third lecture that Zionism alone is far from adequate to his dream of renewal. The creation of a Jewish home in Palestine, Buber writes, would have many beneficial effects on Jewish life, psychologically, politically, and culturally. But spiritually, it is not enough: "It could not guarantee a renewal of Judaism in the absolute meaning of the word." It's even possible that the "pathetic inner chaos" of Jewish life in Diaspora is the most fertile ground for such a renewal, on the principle that the worse things get, the closer the Messiah must be.

But Buber's most daring move of all is his reclamation of Jesus as a Jewish figure, in defiance of the age-old beliefs of Jews and Christians alike. Original Christianity, he writes, "could with greater justification be called original Judaism." Jesus is the heir of the Jewish prophets in his dedication to the messianic ideal, which Buber calls the "unity-idea." Indeed, Jews' "superstitious horror of the Nazarene movement," he argues counterintuitively, is itself a manifestation of "*galut* psychology." By allowing Christians to claim Jesus as their own, Jews submit to a historical injustice and a misrepresentation of Judaism.

What twentieth-century Judaism needs, Buber concludes, is a comprehensive spiritual renewal, "to regain living Judaism." But if one were to ask exactly what this renewal will look like or what concrete actions it involves, Buber admits he has no answer: "What the nature of this future synthesis will be . . . of this no word can be said." In the *Three Addresses*, then, he finds himself in the odd position of a revivalist preacher who has nothing to revive. Since traditional Judaism is in his view sterile and obsolete, he can't demand that Jews return to keeping kosher and observing the sabbath (which Buber himself did not do). On the other hand, he can hardly expect all of his readers to make themselves into religious geniuses like Jesus and Spinoza. Buber is left in a position that would be shared by many Jewish thinkers in the twentieth century: unable to go back to the Judaism of the past, uncertain how to create the Judaism of the future, yet passionately committed to the task of giving Jewishness a new meaning.

Religion of Reason out of the Sources of Judaism
by Hermann Cohen

MARTIN BUBER SPOKE TO AND FOR A RISING GENER-
ation excited by the promise of Zionism. But for Hermann
Cohen, the leading Jewish philosopher of the older generation, Zionism looked more like a threat to the goal to which he had devoted his
life: an authentic Jewish existence among the nations of Europe. Born
in Germany in 1842, the son of a cantor, Cohen trained to become a
rabbi before changing paths to become a student of secular philosophy. He managed to secure an appointment as a university professor
at a time when that career was all but closed to Jews, and he emerged
as one of the leading philosophers of his time, known for his influential interpretation of the work of Immanuel Kant.

At the same time, Cohen was a vocal defender of Judaism against
the rising chorus of intellectual anti-Semitism, arguing that Jewish
and German identities were compatible. In an essay on "Germanness and Jewishness," written in 1915 as the world war raged, Cohen
declared that German Jews believed in and demonstrated "German
predominance in the deepest domains of all intellectual and spiritual
life." Yet Cohen was no assimilationist, if that implies a desire to
discard Jewishness in favor of some other identity. On the contrary,
he believed that it was essential for Jews to preserve Judaism. But
this required understanding what Judaism really is: not a nationality
based on blood, as Buber would have it, but a sublime ethical creed
whose role is to assist in the progress of all mankind. And for this

purpose, it was necessary for the Jews to live among other peoples, not to withdraw into an atavistic nationalism of their own.

Cohen died in the spring of 1918, just months before World War I ended with the defeat of Germany. His last book was published the following year, serving as his final word on the subject of Judaism's true nature. How he understood that nature is suggested by the book's title, *Religion of Reason out of the Sources of Judaism.* Religion, for Cohen, is not a matter of irrational belief or mystical experience. On the contrary, there is such a thing as a "religion of reason," which teaches universally valid moral principles. And it was Judaism, Cohen argues, that first introduced this religion of reason to the world. Studying "the sources of Judaism"—which for Cohen primarily means the Bible, but also the Talmud and later Jewish philosophy—enables us to see how Judaism evolved from a primitive religion based on myth and animal sacrifice into the sublime moral ideal that is its true essence and destiny. Like Maimonides eight hundred years earlier, Cohen wants to show that Judaism properly understood is not only compatible with reason, but its necessary complement.

For the most part, *Religion of Reason* does not deal with contemporary Jewish issues, at least not directly. Rather, it is an abstract analysis of the basic concepts of Judaism as Cohen understands them, using biblical sources to explore ideas like revelation, sin, and law. Yet it is unmistakable that Cohen's concept of Judaism reflects the highest aspirations of many European Jews of his time, especially those in sympathy with the Reform movement. To be Jewish, in Cohen's understanding, is not to owe loyalty to a Jewish people or nation, in ways that might complicate the obligations of citizenship in a modern European state. "The meaning of Jewish nationality," he writes in the book's introduction, "is determined by religious Judaism. The latter is the only Judaism."

But religious Judaism, for Cohen, is not necessarily defined by the laws and rituals that constituted Jewish observance for centuries. Rather, its essence is ethical monotheism, which for Cohen is Judaism's unique contribution to world history. "I do not assert that

Judaism alone is the religion of reason," Cohen writes. On the contrary, one of his chief arguments is that Judaism is a source of principles that are common to all mankind. But Cohen does insist that the moral core of Western civilization comes from its Jewish roots.

Judaism's strict adherence to ethical monotheism sets it apart from the Greek and Christian traditions that are usually thought of as the wellsprings of European culture. The Greeks were polytheists, of course, and for Cohen even the Christian idea of the Trinity is a deviation from the purity of the monotheistic idea. Because of this, both traditions are prone to the temptation of pantheism—the belief that there is no clear distinction between God and the world, because everything that exists is part of God. The Christian belief that God became a man violates the first principle of monotheism, which is that God is a "unique" being, essentially different from everything he created. "The position of monotheism leads to the consequence: 'Nothing is beside me.' Cosmos and nature are negated," he writes.

But if God is radically unique, how is it that humanity ever comes into relationship with him? This question had spurred much Jewish thought over the ages, from the rationalism of Maimonides to the mysticism of Kabbalah. The key, for Cohen, is that human beings can never have knowledge of God; they can only "acknowledge" him, and this acknowledgment takes the form of love. That is why "love for the unique God" is the primary Jewish duty: "You shall love the Lord your God with all your heart and all your soul and all your might," says Deuteronomy. This is the opposite of the Greek philosophical view of God, which holds that he can be known intellectually, but is not the kind of being that receives or deserves love. The Jewish God, on the other hand, is a "person," which is why human beings can be in relationship—or, as Cohen says, "correlation"—with God. The giving of the Torah on Mount Sinai showed that God wants to create such a relationship with humanity.

For modern minds, Cohen knows, the story of Sinai is problematic because it describes a miraculous intervention by God in the course of history, and we are no longer as ready as our ancestors to

believe in miracles. The Bible itself appears to modern critical scholars as a human document, not a divine one. But while Cohen is no
fundamentalist, he believes that modern biblical criticism tends not
just to explain the Bible, but to explain it away. It is true that the
Bible was the work of human beings using the language and concepts
available to them in their time; but Cohen insists that this is not the
whole story. What really matters in the Bible is not its supernatural
elements, but "the inner, relentless chain of the motivation of ideas"
that led Judaism from its origins in myth to the "religion of reason"
that it became. Monotheism is an evolving idea, one that leads the
Jewish people toward an ever purer and more rational understanding
of God and morality.

Such a transformation, Cohen argues, took place with regard to the
Jewish understanding of creation and revelation. Creation appears in
Genesis as a process that occurred once, at a definite time in the past,
because God decided for inscrutable reasons that the earth should
exist. But this "marvel of the temporal beginning," Cohen writes, is
the product of "myth," similar to the creation legends found in all
cultures. Later Judaism, with a more properly monotheistic understanding of God, no longer sees creation as a onetime event. Rather,
it is a constantly renewed process, as God continues at each moment
to sustain the universe. "One marvels not so much at the beginning,
but rather at the constancy in becoming, the permanency in change,"
Cohen explains. In this way, the Jewish believer's mind is directed
away from miracle and mystery and toward law-governed, everyday
nature, which is the true expression of God's creativity.

Similarly, Cohen downplays the importance of the revelation at
Sinai, which was traditionally seen as the foundation of Judaism
itself, the miracle that guaranteed the truth of the Torah. But "the
tendency of revelation," Cohen writes, "is to detach its meaning from
the *fact* on Sinai and base it rather on the *content*." We don't have to
believe that God appeared to Moses in cloud and thunder, an event
that can only be known to us through hearsay. Rather, the Torah's
sublime moral vision is what authenticates its divinity: "Revelation
proves itself in its wisdom and reason." In this way, Cohen shifts the

essence of religion from faith, which requires us to believe things we can't know, to reason, which enables us to know God through his works and his commandments.

What is the knowledge that Judaism teaches? For Cohen, it is nothing but morality: "Pure monotheism," he writes, is "identical" with "pure morality." God's goodness is what the Bible calls holiness, which for Cohen is preeminently a moral status, not a ritual or mystical one. When God says in Leviticus, "Thou shalt be holy, for I am holy," this is nothing more or less than an injunction to be moral: "The holy spirit is the spirit of moral action."

Cohen goes on to offer a hypothetical account of how Judaism's moral message helped to create modern ethical consciousness. Notably, he argues that religion was more effective in this task than Greek philosophy, which remained too abstract and rationalistic to ignite a passion for doing good. The Greek moral ideal was Stoicism, a method of living with suffering and misfortune without allowing them to overwhelm you. But Stoicism could never have discovered compassion as a moral emotion that confers an obligation to improve the lives of others. For the Greeks, pity is merely a feeling that has to be transcended in order to achieve emotional peace; at best, Cohen writes, it is a reflex.

For Judaism, on the other hand, pity lies at the center of morality. Without pity, we see one another simply as what Cohen calls "the next man"—isolated individuals with no mutual connection or obligation. Pity, however, transforms the next man into what Cohen calls "the fellowman," and in becoming my fellow he becomes my responsibility. Without mutual pity, or what today might be called empathy, there can be no true human community: "Religion achieves what morality fails to achieve. Love for man is brought forth."

Still, the notion of the fellowman contains an ambiguity that is troubling for Cohen. The Torah's laws bind Jews with obligations to one another; they are fellowmen because they are part of the same people. But the charge that Jews are particularistic, that they place loyalty to their own above loyalty to the state or the human race, would seem to undermine Cohen's belief that Judaism is a universalistic faith. That is why Cohen strenuously argues that, in fact, Judaism does not inculcate a special obligation toward fellow Jews: "The acknowledgment of the other as the fellow countryman only arose from a biased misinterpretation." To make this counterintuitive claim, he draws attention to several passages in Deuteronomy that discuss the legal status of the "stranger," the non-Israelite living in the Land of Israel. Justice must be done to the stranger just as much as to the Israelite.

As Judaism developed, Cohen argues, the concept of the stranger was broadened into that of the "Noahide"—the non-Jewish peoples descended from Noah, the only survivor of the Flood. Jewish tradition holds that God made a covenant with Noah, binding his descendants to obey seven laws, including those against murder, adultery, and idolatry. For Cohen, "the concept of the Noahide is the foundation for natural law." Every rational creature can discover and obey the Noahide precepts without the benefit of divine revelation. In this sense, the historical evolution of Judaism was toward an ever more inclusive vision, until finally God's covenant with Israel becomes simply a symbol of his love for humanity as a whole: "In Israel God loves nothing other than the human race."

But pity is only the first stage of the development of conscience, according to Cohen. Pity recognizes injustice in society, but not in the self; it calls for social action, but not individual repentance. That is why Judaism had to cultivate a second stage of morality, in which the attention of the individual is turned inward upon his own motives and actions. To accomplish this, Cohen argues, it had to overcome the ancient Israelite understanding of animal sacrifice, the ritual through which man could atone for his sins and achieve reconciliation with God. The task of the biblical prophets was to redefine atonement, not as a cultic or ritual idea but as a psychological and ethical one. The prophets told the Jewish people that what God wanted from them was not rituals but repentance: "Your appointed seasons My soul hateth; they are a burden unto Me; I am weary to bear them," God says through Isaiah. For Cohen, Yom Kippur, the Day of Atonement when Jews afflict their bodies by fasting, is meant to express the great truth that "repentance is in earnest only in the recognition and taking upon oneself of suffering."

Along with the value of suffering, Judaism embraced the idea of a future in which suffering would be abolished. This was the origin of messianism, another central Jewish concept which, Cohen believes, has been misinterpreted by Christianity. Initially, Jews imagined the Messiah as the anointed successor of King David, a monarch who would come to restore the fallen Jewish kingdom and triumph over its enemies. But this figure gave way in time to the "suffering servant" of Isaiah, who conquers not through might but through meekness. Finally, the Messiah achieves a "total liberation from . . . national patriotism," becoming instead a universal redeemer who comes to end suffering and death, while bringing all the nations of the world to worship the one true God. Cohen cherishes the verse in Isaiah which proclaims, "For mine house [that is, the Jerusalem Temple] shall be called a house of prayer for all peoples."

Whether the topic is creation, revelation, sin, or redemption, Cohen's thought in *Religion of Reason* always moves in the same direction: away from whatever appears parochial or supernatural in Judaism, and toward whatever can be understood as universal and rational. For Cohen, this is the very same movement that can be seen in the unfolding of Judaism throughout its history, from primitive Canaanite myth through the Torah, the prophets, the Talmud, Maimonides, and down to the twentieth century. Stage by stage, Judaism disencumbers itself of particularism and superstition, until it becomes—not unlike the philosophy of Kant—a rigorous moral message aimed at all rational creatures. As Cohen puts it, "monotheism claims that not every people may have its own peculiar God, but that there is one God for all peoples, as there is one mathematics for all peoples."

But this sublime vision raises an important question about the role of Judaism in the twentieth century—or, more precisely, about the obligation of the individual Jew. If Judaism is understood as a religion of reason addressed to all mankind, then why does it have any particular claim on people who happen to be born as Jews? Why should Jews follow commandments, observe holidays, and preserve their communal identity, if Israel is simply a metaphor for humanity?

This very same question had been raised by earlier Jewish rationalists like Philo and Maimonides, who insisted that the commandments remained binding on Jews, even if they were best understood as metaphors or symbols rather than actual expressions of the divine will. But Cohen, living in a secular, modern society, isn't so sure. In his chapter on "The Laws," which bears most directly on the contemporary Jewish issues of his time, he hedges on whether Jewish law is still binding on Jews. After all, the purpose of the Torah is "the continuation of religion," and under modern conditions, it's possible that Jewish dietary laws and sabbath observance are more likely to dissuade Jews from remaining Jewish than to encourage them. Cohen asks, but doesn't specifically answer, "how far the burden of the yoke of the law can be reduced if it is still to be retained."

But why should the yoke be retained in the first place? Here we come to the paradox at the heart of Cohen's vision of Judaism. If Judaism is a religion of reason, then Israel is no more than a metaphor for humanity; but it is nevertheless incumbent on Jews to serve as the bearers and witnesses of that religion. Like creation and revelation, this Jewish mission is a continual process, one that will last as long as humanity itself, because morality is an infinite task. And Jews can find proof of their divine mission precisely in the suffering that being Jewish has always entailed. *Religion of Reason* offers several encomiums to the nobility and meaning of Jewish suffering: "The messianic people suffers vicariously for mankind," Cohen writes. "Israel is the historic people of suffering," and "suffering has become its vital force."

It could not be clearer why Cohen was so strongly opposed to Zionism, which was gaining strength across the Jewish world in the last two decades of his life. To him, Zionism meant trying to turn back the clock of Jewish history. Judaism had once been confined to a particular piece of territory, but it transcended that identity in order to become a world religion with a message for all humanity. This transcendence involved terrible suffering and continued to expose the

Jews to persecution, but suffering was itself a religious duty, a burden that the Jews had to continue to bear on behalf of God and the world.

Zionism, however, wanted to turn the Jews into just another nationality. For Cohen, this would be to forfeit the Jews' special mission: "Isolation in a separate state would be in contradiction to the messianic task of the Jews," he writes. In an age of nationalist violence, Jews would be hurting the cause of peace everywhere, and the status of their own coreligionists in particular, if they were to constitute Judaism as a rival nation, rather than a religion whose members could be at home everywhere.

But worst of all, to Cohen, was the idea that Zionism would lead the Jews to forfeit their role on the front line of suffering. Franz Rosenzweig, a younger Jewish philosopher who was a close collaborator of Martin Buber's, once attempted to convince Cohen of the value of Zionism, only to have Cohen respond dismissively: "Those fools want to be happy!" The anecdote has become famous because it so pithily captures Cohen's disdain for what he thought of as the shallowness of the Zionist ideal. To this austere religious moralist, it was far better to suffer for mankind than to succumb to the desire for normality. Of course, had Cohen known just what was in store for the Jews of Europe in the twentieth century, he might have had to rethink his idealization of Jewish suffering.

Judaism as a Civilization
by Mordecai Kaplan

WHILE BUBER AND COHEN WERE RESPONDING TO the pressures and opportunities of Judaism in Europe, Mordecai Kaplan was reckoning with the very different conditions of American life. Born in Lithuania in 1881, Kaplan came to America with his family at the age of nine, early in the great wave of Jewish immigration, and lived until 1983. The son of a rabbi, he was educated in a yeshiva and received rabbinic ordination himself. At the same time, he studied philosophy at City College—thus living out the dream that David Levinsky never achieved—and Columbia University. He began his career as the rabbi of one of New York City's leading Orthodox congregations, and was a leader in the Young Israel movement, which pioneered an American form of modern Orthodoxy.

But Kaplan became convinced that Orthodoxy did not offer a plausible future for American Judaism. In time he left the Orthodox movement and became a professor at the Conservative movement's Jewish Theological Seminary in New York. But even there he remained a controversial outlier, as he moved toward an ever more radical redefinition of Judaism. In 1922, Kaplan founded a new kind of synagogue, the Society for the Advancement of Judaism, where he signaled his innovative approach by officiating at the first bat mitzvah ever celebrated in America, that of his daughter Judith.

This was an unmistakable statement against patriarchal tradition and in favor of gender equality, which shocked many traditionalist Jews. But Judaism, Kaplan believed, could no longer be defined as it had been for twenty centuries, as a religion based on divinely revealed laws that were interpreted and enforced by a rabbinic elite. His own experience as an educator and community leader told him that in the twentieth century, most American Jews had abandoned that kind of observance. It would be a struggle to convince them to keep any attachment to Judaism at all.

Yet Kaplan was convinced that it was crucial for American Jews to remain Jews. The question was how Judaism would have to evolve to make that an attractive prospect—to convince Jews that being Jewish was a gift and a mission, rather than an accident and a burden. Kaplan offered an answer in his 1935 book *Judaism as a Civilization*, still one of the most insightful analyses of American Judaism. Much has changed in the Jewish world since Kaplan wrote, but the fundamental question he grappled with—how do you convince Jews to remain Jewish when they have stopped believing in Judaism?— remains central to this day.

"Before the beginning of the nineteenth century all Jews regarded Judaism as a privilege; since then most Jews have come to regard it as a burden," Kaplan states at the beginning of the book, and this disaffection of Jews with their Jewishness is the biggest threat facing the Jewish future. To explain it, he offers a wide-angle sketch of Jewish sociology and theology. For most of history, he argues, Jews inhabited a world in which people of all faiths believed that the purpose of earthly life was to achieve salvation in the hereafter. Rabbinic Judaism, no less than Christianity and Islam, taught that this world was—in the words of the classic rabbinic text *Pirkei Avot*—a "vestibule to the World to Come." A Jew's purpose in life is to obey God in order to be rewarded after death, and the Torah, given by God to Moses on Mount Sinai, offers detailed instructions about what God expects.

But the rise of what Kaplan calls "the modern ideology" has destroyed this kind of supernatural belief, for Jews as well as for many followers of other religions. Kaplan uses the term "ideology" without critical intention: for him it means something like "worldview," and he makes clear that he shares the basic convictions of modern rationalism. It is not science per se, he believes, that poses an insoluble challenge to Judaism. Philo and Maimonides had long ago figured out ways to harmonize the Torah with an Aristotelian picture of the cosmos, simply by reading the Torah's text allegorically. A modern Jew could do the same thing with Darwinism or modern physics, if he wanted to.

The problem is that he doesn't want to, because he no longer believes that the Torah is a divine revelation. The credibility of this belief has been destroyed by "the objective study of history," which shows that every culture develops parallel religious concepts. Judaism is just one among many examples of a people giving expression to its spiritual aspirations. Coupled with the modern reluctance to believe in miracles such as the parting of the Red Sea, which were once taken as proof of God's unique relationship with Israel, comparative religion deals a deadly blow to the belief that the Jews are a chosen people.

And if there is no divine mandate to be or remain Jewish, why would anyone take on the burden that Jewishness represents in the modern age? Belief in Jewish chosenness presents a social and political problem, since it conflicts with Jews' status as equal citizens of the various countries where they live. During the nineteenth century, the Jews gained legal rights in most Western states. But emancipation was granted on the condition that Jews stop thinking of themselves as a separate nation or people, and assume a new identity as Frenchmen, Germans, Americans, and so forth. Most Jews, Kaplan writes, were happy to pay this price, since the appeal of belonging to a modern secular state is greater than the appeal of belonging to an oppressed religious minority. For this reason, the emancipation of the Jews has been "as severe a blow to Judaism as the destruction of the Jewish commonwealth" by the Romans in the first century CE.

"Had the Jews been accorded not merely political but also social and economic equality, they would long ago have disappeared as a distinct group," Kaplan writes with striking pessimism. But from the vantage point of the early 1930s, it is clear that emancipation and assimilation have turned out not to offer a real escape route from anti-Jewish hatred. With Nazism in power in Germany and anti-Semitism on the rise throughout Europe—and still formidable in the United States—Jews were in a sense even worse off in the twentieth century than they had been in the Middle Ages. Then, they could take shelter from Christian and Muslim hostility in their belief that they were a divinely elected nation; if pushed to the extreme, it was at least possible to escape Jewishness by conversion. Modern racist anti-Semitism, however, considers the Jew a biological alien as well as an economic rival. There is no way of pacifying its hatred short of expulsion or extermination. Twentieth-century Jews are thus suspended between two ways of life: they no longer belong to the Jewish nation and they don't yet belong to the nations of the world. No wonder that, as Kaplan writes, "the Jew is maladjusted morally and spiritually."

This is not to say that Judaism hasn't tried to adjust to the new conditions. On the contrary, modern Judaism's three denominations—Reform, Conservative, and Orthodox—each had its own prescription for how to sustain Judaism in adverse conditions. In *Judaism as a Civilization*, Kaplan canvasses these three movements, examining their institutional achievements and the writings of their leading exponents to assess their strengths and weaknesses. And in each case, he finds, the weaknesses predominate.

Reform—or as Kaplan calls it, "Reformist"—Judaism had been predominant in the United States before 1880. At that time the American Jewish population was mostly made up of immigrants from Germany, where the Reform movement was born. As a result, in Kaplan's time Reform was the favored denomination of wealthier and more assimilated Jews, who kept a wary distance from the new waves of Eastern European immigrants. This fact plays a part in Kaplan's assessment that Reform Judaism is socially respectable but spiritually feeble. It is not really a durable form of religious belief, he argues, but a halfway house between Jewishness and assimilation, in which Jews who still felt some loyalty to their ancestral faith could tarry for a generation or two.

Kaplan credits Reform Judaism with honestly acknowledging the objections to supernatural belief. It accepted modernity's "shifting of the center of gravity from interest in the hereafter to interest in transforming the world we live in, and the substitution of the authority of reason for the authority of tradition." Reform dispensed with two of the central principles of historic Judaism—belief in the Torah as the revealed word of God, and the concept of Israel as a nation. Instead, it stakes everything on the third central principle: faith in God, though a God who had been rendered highly abstract and metaphorical. In Kaplan's view, however, this belief alone provides no good reason why a Jew should remain Jewish. If what Judaism teaches is a universal ethical code, there is no reason why it requires solidarity with other Jews or fidelity to Jewish traditions. In short, Reform offers no logical or emotional basis for "the insistence that merely because one is born to Jewish parents he is duty-bound to remain a Jew"; and without that insistence, Judaism is unable to reproduce itself.

At the opposite extreme is what Kaplan calls "Neo-Orthodox" Judaism, the denomination in which he himself was educated. Kaplan points out that Neo-Orthodoxy, or what today would be called modern Orthodoxy, is not simply a continuation of age-old practices and beliefs. It is "neo" because, just as much as Reform, it is a self-conscious response to the challenge of modernity. The key battleground on which it fights is Torah: for Neo-Orthodoxy, there is no compromising on the belief that Torah is the divinely revealed law of God. "Whenever any of our views is in conflict with a teaching of the Torah, it is that view which must yield and not the teaching of the Torah," as Kaplan puts it.

Such a faith has an obvious appeal to "certain types of mind" who cannot tolerate skepticism or ambiguity in matters of religion. Orthodoxy provides the Jew with firm ground to stand on. But to Kaplan, this confidence is bought at too high a price. Orthodoxy constitutes "a kind of self-hypnosis that derives its assurance from a deliberate evasion of certain facts." These facts are not just those of objective history and comparative religion, but also moral facts; for the Torah often conflicts with our modern intuitions about right and wrong.

How, Kaplan asks, can one believe in the God of the Torah who ordered the extermination of the Midianites?

By contradicting the moral and intellectual instincts of twentieth-century Jews, Orthodoxy condemns itself. In Kaplan's view, "it is no longer possible to have any ordinance obeyed merely on the ground that it is commanded by God." As for Conservative Judaism, Kaplan dismisses it as incoherent. In attempting to combine the progressive spirit of Reformism with the traditional practice of Orthodoxy, it loses what is best in each.

After arguing that none of the existing varieties of American Judaism is satisfactory, Kaplan is ready to introduce his own idea, which is that Judaism should not be considered only, or even primarily, a religion. Such a definition fails the modern Jew on two grounds: it entails supernatural beliefs that he cannot assent to, and it implies that Judaism is primarily a relationship between man and God, rather than what it has historically also been, a relationship between Jews themselves. Instead, as Kaplan's title says, we should think of Judaism as a civilization—a creation of human beings that shapes their individual and collective lives in countless ways. A civilization is something much broader than a creed: it includes "history, literature, language, social organization, folk sanctions, standards of conduct, social and spiritual ideals, esthetic values."

The implications of this shift are profound. As Kaplan himself says, it is a "Copernican revolution" in the way we think about Judaism, "based on the proposition that the Jewish religion existed for the Jewish people and not the Jewish people for the Jewish religion." It follows that in making decisions about the future of Judaism, Jews should not be primarily concerned with pleasing God or sustaining tradition. Rather, he urges in a pragmatic spirit, Jews should ask what elements actually work to enhance their collective life. If a practice or belief gives the Jewish community greater strength and unity, if it heightens the moral refinement and social commitment of the individual Jew, then it should be kept—or, if need be, invented. If, on the other hand, it induces skepticism, resistance, or resentment, it should be modified or abandoned without guilt.

The argument that Jews need a Jewish civilization in order to flourish might seem to lead directly to an embrace of Zionism. At the time Kaplan was writing, the Jewish settlement in Palestine was small but growing rapidly, and he looked forward to it emerging as a world Jewish center; he estimated that the Land of Israel could one day accommodate as many as three million people. (This proved to be too modest—today, Israel's population is close to nine million.) Kaplan is very enthusiastic about the role that a Jewish national home could play in reviving Jewish culture, and he half acknowledges that the logical conclusion of his argument would be to urge all Jews to make *aliyah*. But Kaplan is above all a realist. Just as it is unreasonable to expect most modern American Jews to embrace Orthodoxy, so it is unlikely that the five million Jews who had found a home in the United States would be so committed to living in a Jewish civilization that they would leave for Palestine. The real problem is how to enrich Jewish life in the Diaspora.

To begin with, Kaplan acknowledges that American Jews will always live primarily in American civilization. Speaking English and going to public schools will automatically give them entry to the dominant culture; their Jewish civilization will be secondary, something they must consciously decide to cultivate. But Kaplan does not see this as a source of division. On the contrary, he embraces the idea of being a "hyphenate," a Jewish-American. Indeed, he sees such a complex identity as a model for societies of the future. "What is needed is to normalize their status in the state, to have the cultural hyphenism of minority groups accepted as legitimate," he writes. By demonstrating the possibilities of pluralism, Jews will teach the world to avoid militant nationalism of the kind that was taking over Europe as he wrote.

To make Jewish civilization worth the effort, however, Kaplan believes it must be "reconstructed"—an idea that gave rise to the Reconstructionist movement in American Judaism, which he founded in 1955. This involves both concrete institution-building and the more nebulous realm of ideas and emotions. When it comes to the former, Kaplan's proposals are relatively modest. American

Jews should learn Hebrew, the language of both the religious past and the Zionist future. Synagogues and temples should give way to community centers where social, athletic, and educational activities can bring Jews together. Jews should foster arts such as music, literature, and dance in order to enrich their cultural heritage.

More ambitiously, Kaplan wants American Jews to restore some form of the *kehillah*, the communal organization that governed Jews in the past. He hopes the *kehillah* will assume some civil responsibilities, including arbitrating disputes and recording marriages. But it should not reproduce the class and denominational divisions that already split American Jews: "The *kehillah* should embrace all classes of Jews, men and women, rich and poor, Orthodox, Reformists, Conservatives and radicals." Such an institution would make plain that being a good Jew doesn't mean subscribing to a particular religious doctrine, but accepting one's responsibilities in the Jewish community.

Yet the problem of religion is not so easily laid to rest, and much of *Judaism as a Civilization* is devoted to puzzling out just how to integrate religious practice into Kaplan's reconstructed Judaism. On the one hand, he does not want to follow Reform in its renunciation of everything that makes Judaism Jewish—Hebrew, liturgy, sabbaths and festivals, dietary laws. These practices have value for Kaplan as what he calls "folkways," instilling color and specificity into Jewish life and creating bonds among fellow Jews. They should be maintained, he writes, but "only whenever they do not involve an unreasonable amount of time, effort and expense." For instance, Kaplan sees nothing wrong with Jews keeping kosher in their own homes while eating non-kosher food in restaurants or at the homes of non-Jewish friends.

This selective approach to Jewish observance takes for granted that what earlier generations regarded as *mitzvot*, commandments from God, are actually human inventions, which can be altered as Jews see fit. (Indeed, Kaplan prefers to replace the word *mitzva* with another term, *minhag*, meaning "custom.") That is because God, in Kaplan's understanding, is not a supernatural being who gives orders to mankind. "It is imperative that men break away from the habit of identifying the spiritual with the supernatural," he writes.

Rather, Kaplan defines God as "the life of the universe, immanent insofar as each part acts upon every other, and transcendental insofar as the whole acts upon each part." A little later, he tries again: "The God-idea is not an idea but the reaction of the entire organism to life." These elusive and abstract definitions do not become much clearer after lengthy explanation. What is clear is that Kaplan associates religious faith with the highest elements in human nature as he understands it. Religion should offer "a glimpse into life's unity, creativity and worthwhileness"; it should "enable the individual to effect affirmative and creative adjustments in his living relationships with reality."

But Judaism must not rely on fictions that are unacceptable to the modern mind. If this means that the traditional understanding of God as creator and redeemer is no longer available, that is not necessarily a loss, since Kaplan believes that no Jew can any longer affirm such ideas about God with a good conscience. By subtracting traditional religious belief from Judaism, Kaplan believes he can leave it in a more defensible position. In fact, what he is really doing is to substitute Judaism itself for God as the object of devotion and the source of value. In this sense, *Judaism as a Civilization* is the perfect expression of an American Judaism whose primary concern is its own survival.

Halakhic Man
by Joseph Soloveitchik

B Y 1944, A DECADE AFTER KAPLAN OFFERED HIS PRE-
scription for the survival of Judaism, the Jewish people had been
pushed to the brink of extinction in Europe. Kaplan wrote in full
awareness of the danger of Nazism. Yet even when he wrote that
modern anti-Semitism was worse than medieval anti-Judaism, he
could hardly have imagined that it would result in genocide. With
European Jewry decimated, the future of American Jewry became all
the more urgent. If Judaism was to flourish anywhere, it now seemed,
it would have to be in the United States.

One of the most remarkable things about *Halakhic Man*, the book
published by Joseph Soloveitchik in 1944, is that it makes no explicit
reference to either the European catastrophe or the challenges facing
American Judaism, even though Soloveitchik's experiences had put
him in close touch with both. Born in Poland in 1903 to a dynasty of
famous and influential rabbis, he received a traditional Jewish education and was ordained as a rabbi himself. But unusually for Jews of
his background, he also attended secular universities in Poland and
Germany, studying philosophy and theology and writing his PhD
dissertation on the thought of Hermann Cohen.

By the time he emigrated to America in 1932, Soloveitchik was
uniquely positioned to serve as a bridge—between religion and philosophy, Orthodoxy and modernism, Europe and America. In this
sense, he occupied a position akin to that of Kaplan, another rabbi
who combined traditional and modern training. But where Kaplan

moved away from Orthodoxy and resolved to create a new Judaism
free from supernatural beliefs, Soloveitchik remained firmly within
Orthodoxy. Indeed, he became its most important leader, known in
the modern Orthodox community simply as "the Rav," *the* rabbi.

Halakhic Man shows that Kaplan was right to refer to modern
Orthodoxy as "neo," for Soloveitchik's religious thought is fully
informed by modernity and responds to its challenges. The book
was written in Hebrew, like the classic works of rabbinics, but in a
modern, intellectual Hebrew, the language of the seminar more than
the synagogue. Soloveitchik's frame of reference includes great rabbis and commentators—including some of his own ancestors—but
also Western philosophers from Plato to Nietzsche, as well as modern Christian thinkers like Kierkegaard and Karl Barth. By demonstrating that these frames of reference can coexist in the same mind,
Soloveitchik implicitly refutes both liberal and ultra-Orthodox Jews,
who converge in their belief that modernism and Jewish tradition are
irreconcilable. It is possible, he shows, to make use of secular thought
without giving way to it.

In one crucial way, however, Soloveitchik refuses to engage with
modernity's challenge to Jewish belief: he will not debate the existence of God or the idea that God gave the Torah to the Jewish people. For an Orthodox believer, these are axioms that must be accepted
before any discussion becomes possible. Soloveitchik of course knew
all the findings of biblical criticism and comparative religion, which
convinced Kaplan that the traditional understanding of Judaism
could not be sustained. But he does not address them in *Halakhic
Man*, even to refute them. "When halakhic man approaches reality, he comes with his Torah, given to him from Sinai, in hand," he
writes, and that is that.

Yet the whole form and argument of *Halakhic Man* are, in sub-
tle ways, at odds with this straightforward declaration. Traditional
works of Jewish wisdom focus on law and ethics—they are about
what Jews should do. But Soloveitchik's interest is primarily psychological and even aesthetic: he is writing about what it feels like to

live according to *halakha*, Jewish law. As his title suggests, his focus is not on the law itself but on a human type, in which he finds both grandeur and beauty. "From the very midst of the laws," he writes, "there arises a cosmos more splendid and beautiful than all the works of Leonardo da Vinci and Michelangelo."

In other words, Soloveitchik is not arguing that Judaism is true, but that it is good and beautiful. By writing the book in Hebrew, he was addressing this argument not to the world at large but to committed modern Orthodox Jews, who would have been the only readers both interested and capable of understanding it. (The book was not translated into English until 1983.) If *Halakhic Man* is a work of Jewish apologetics, whose intention is "to defend the honor of the Halakhah and halakhic men," then these are the Jews it was meant to hearten, rather than the disaffected Jews Kaplan had in mind.

The reason why the honor of Jewish law needs defending is that modern Jews live in an intellectual climate dominated by post-Christian ways of thinking about religion. In this climate, Soloveitchik suggests, two attitudes toward religion are possible. One is to reject faith in the name of reason and science. "When theoretical and scientific man peers into the cosmos," he writes, "he is filled with one exceedingly powerful yearning, which is to search for clarity and understanding, for solutions and resolutions." This human type, which Soloveitchik calls "cognitive man," has no use for anything that cannot be rationally explained. When he encounters a mystery, his impulse is either to reduce it to "necessity and lawfulness" or else to dismiss it as a fallacy, as "nonbeing and nothingness."

Cognitive man has great authority in the modern world, since his approach to the universe has given humanity knowledge and power that earlier generations never dreamed of. But there is also a way of being religious that has its own prestige in the twentieth century. This is the way of what Soloveitchik calls *homo religiosus*, "religious man," for whom the miraculous and mysterious are a source of deep fascination. *Homo religiosus* is defined by his contempt for ordinary reality: he "is dissatisfied, unhappy with this world. He searches for an existence that is above empirical reality." Such longing is typical of mystics and Platonists, for whom "this world is a pale image of another world."

Cognitive man and *homo religiosus* divide the universe between them. The former is master of this world, the latter is devoted to the beyond. Both have their justification, since they are each responding to valid dimensions of human experience. Yet for Soloveitchik, this seemingly natural division completely misses what is distinctive about Jewish spirituality. Of course, *homo religiosus* can be found in all faiths, including Judaism, which has a robust mystical tradition. But the fascination with supernatural forces and other worlds that is characteristic of kabbalism and Hasidism is contrary to the spirit of *halakha*. As a halakhist—someone who lives according to Jewish law and devotes his life to its study—Soloveitchik represents a spiritual third way, one which is equally foreign to Jewish and Christian mysticism, as well as to modern philosophy.

Halakhic man has more in common with cognitive man than with *homo religiosus*. Like his secular counterpart, halakhic man has no use for the mystical and the mysterious, and he recoils from formless emotionalism. He is devoted to rational thought and to the clear organization of reality. "Both the halakhist and the mathematician live in an ideal realm," Soloveitchik writes, since both interpret the physical world through the lens of orderly, abstract categories.

But while the mathematician and the physicist derive their categories directly from their study of this world, the halakhist's have a different origin: Torah. For Jewish tradition, Torah in this sense encompasses not just the Five Books of Moses but also the Oral Law, the vast collection of statutes compiled in the Talmud. Because *halakha* touches on so many areas of life—from clearly religious matters like prayers and holidays to seemingly mundane subjects like torts, marriage, and dietary rules—there is effectively no aspect of Jewish experience that is not mediated by Torah. For Soloveitchik, *halakha* provides the lens through which the observant Jew views nature itself: "When halakhic man chances upon mighty mountains, he utilizes the measurements which determine a private domain, a sloping mound that attains a height of ten handbreadths within a distance of four cubits."

To an outsider, this might seem like an impoverished view of the world. *Homo religiosus*, certainly, would prefer to revel in the mysterious essence of being. And Soloveitchik acknowledges that "halakhic man's approach to reality is, at the outset, devoid of any element of transcendence." But the transcendence that seems to be missing actually returns to halakhic man by another route: through the law itself. Because the law is divinely ordained, it becomes the instrument through which the world makes contact with God. There is no world above, where God is more present than he is here below; on the contrary, by giving his Torah to human beings, God shows that what we do in this world is his chief concern. "*Homo religiosus* proclaims: The lower yearns for the higher. But halakhic man, with his unique mode of understanding, declares: The higher longs and pines for the lower."

Halakhic man knows no estrangement from ordinary reality, because it is only in daily life that he can carry out the commandments, the *mitzvot*. Equally, he is never mired in uncertainty or doubt about how he is supposed to live, because *halakhah*—which comes from the Hebrew root meaning "to go"—makes his path clear. As a result, halakhic man knows none of the angst that became a central concept in modern theology and philosophy. Jewish spirituality is objective, rooted in action and performance, rather than subjective, a matter of emotion and mood. Indeed, Soloveitchik rather looks down on religious feeling, seeing it as a trivial, unreliable basis for faith: "A subjective religiosity comprised of spiritual moods, of emotions and affections, of outlooks and desires, will never be blessed with success."

The objectivity of Judaism shapes the soul of halakhic man, creating a distinctive human type. Soloveitchik forthrightly acknowledges that this type has limitations as well as strengths. Because halakhic man serves God through cognition of the law, intellectual pride has been a feature of Jewish sages since Talmudic times. "Neither humility nor modesty characterizes the image of halakhic man," Soloveitchik writes. "He hates intellectual compromises or fence straddling, intellectual flabbiness, and any type of wavering in matters of law and judgment." It is not hard to see how the habits of mind cultivated by many generations of halakhists could be transferred, in the modern world, into the realms of ideology and politics.

Soloveitchik also perceives that death presents a difficult challenge for halakhic man. If this world is the only place where God can be served, then death must be an alien and terrifying prospect. "Judaism abhors death, organic decay, and dissolution," he observes, thinking of the ritual taboos against coming into contact with diseased bodies and corpses. No wonder "halakhic man is afraid of death." But it is better, Soloveitchik believes, to be afraid of death than to be fascinated by it, in the unwholesome fashion of the mystic.

Many of the duties of halakhic man are ritual and formal. He must pray at the right time in the right way, he must eat this food and not that, he must refrain from work on sabbaths and holidays. But in Judaism, there is no separation between ritual duties and ethical duties. For Soloveitchik as for Cohen, the heart of the law is always justice, and it is above all in the pursuit of justice that halakhic man serves God. Indeed, he does so with such wholeheartedness that he is immune to temptation and sin: "Halakhic man does not struggle with his evil impulses," because he has fully internalized God's commandments until they become his own will. For Soloveitchik, desire is no more tempting than mysticism; both must give way before the stern conscientiousness of the observant Jew.

Still, halakhic man may be tempted in other ways—for instance, by the renown and influence that come with intellectual preeminence. That is why Soloveitchik echoes an ancient tradition of rabbinic wisdom that counsels against personal ambition: "Neither ritual decisions nor political leadership constitute the main task of halakhic man." Rather, he should cultivate justice in society as he does in his own soul. "The actualization of the ideals of justice and righteousness is the pillar of fire which halakhic man follows," Soloveitchik writes, alluding to the sign that guided the Israelites during their wandering in the desert. And justice, for the modern Jew as for the prophets, means social justice—in "the marketplace, the street, the factory," not just in the synagogue.

For Soloveitchik, doing justice is not only an ethical obligation; it is closely connected to the metaphysical truth at the core of Judaism, which has to do with human freedom. Freedom is the focus of the final section of the book, which describes the creativity of halakhic man. This may sound like a paradox, since Soloveitchik has spent the first half of the book dwelling on attributes that seem to be at odds with creativity. We expect the creative person to be emotional, intuitive, and rebellious, while halakhic man is intellectual, law-abiding, and austere. The observant Jew is all superego and no id, to use Freudian terms (which Soloveitchik avoids). How does creativity enter into this picture?

Soloveitchik's answer is that living according to God's law is the ultimate demonstration of creativity, because it depends on human freedom. Here he sounds like Kant, who believed that true freedom was obedience to the law that we make for ourselves. Of course, the individual Jew is not the source of *halakha*, God is; but God has given human beings the ability to choose to obey the law, as well as the ability to interpret it. For this reason, Soloveitchik writes, the Jew "lives a free, autonomous, individual and unique existence." His behavior is not determined by physical or social forces, as modern ideologues believe; he is not merely the representative of a race or class. Rather, the individual always has the power to decide how to act, which is why he is responsible for his own actions. "Choice forms the base of creation," as Soloveitchik puts it.

Inevitably, even halakhic man will sometimes choose wrongly—in religious terms, he will sin. But in his understanding of sin, halakhic man once again differs sharply from *homo religiosus*—in just the same way, Soloveitchik implies, that Judaism differs from Christianity. For the latter, human beings are unable to overcome sin without God's grace. But Judaism believes in the ability of the individual to change his ways through repentance. "Halakhic man is engaged in self-creation, in creating a new 'I,' " Soloveitchik writes, whenever he decides that the future will be different from the past. In this sense every Jew is a partner of the Creator, since by choosing bring about God's will on earth, each individual "creates an ideal world, renews his own being and transforms himself into a man of God."

Perhaps the most remarkable thing about the vision of Judaism that Soloveitchik advances in *Halakhic Man* is its refusal to allow Jewishness to be defined by a sense of crisis. For Kaplan, writing *Judaism as a Civilization* ten years earlier, it was essential to think about Judaism in terms of tangible results—its ability to maintain the adherence of Jews, to better their lives, and to reproduce itself into the future. But none of these concerns enters into Soloveitchik's purview, not even as the Jewish people was being literally destroyed, because for him the essence of Judaism has nothing to do with historical contingency. It is possible to be a halakhic man in the twentieth century, just as it was for the sages of the Talmud in the second century. How many people pursue that path is not what matters; indeed, Soloveitchik's vision is in some ways frankly elitist. What matters is that the observant Jew, the halakhic man, is able to serve God confidently and proudly.

God in Search of Man by Abraham Joshua Heschel

WHEN JOSEPH SOLOVEITCHIK WAS STUDYING FOR HIS doctorate at the University of Berlin in the 1920s, one of his fellow students was Abraham Joshua Heschel. Heschel, born in Poland in 1907, would go on to succeed Martin Buber as the head of the most important Jewish adult education program in Germany. In 1940, he fled Nazism at the last possible moment and came to America, where he eventually joined the faculty of the Jewish Theological Seminary, becoming a colleague of Mordecai Kaplan. Heschel spent his life among Jewish thinkers who tried to reconcile the traditions of Judaism with the demands of modernity. In America, he would become the most prominent of them all, thanks largely to his political activism and his efforts to promote interfaith dialogue. A famous photo shows Heschel marching arm in arm with Martin Luther King Jr. and other civil rights movement leaders in Selma, Alabama, in 1965.

But Heschel's best-known book is far from political in nature. What has made *God in Search of Man* one of the most popular works of American Jewish spirituality, ever since it first appeared in 1955, is its emphasis on the emotional and intuitive elements of faith—what Heschel calls "depth-theology," a reference to the theory of depth psychology made famous by Freud. For Freud, the term suggested that much of the mind's activity took place below the threshold of rational consciousness, in what he called the unconscious. It was a mistake to reduce human beings to what they know about themselves, since the most important elements of our minds are buried, and they require careful excavation in order to be seen.

Heschel does not exactly endorse Freud's view of the mind, and certainly not his views on religion (the founder of psychoanalysis was a militant atheist). But he does share the conviction that what counts most in human experience is pre-rational, not easily amenable to explanation in words and concepts. In particular, Heschel takes issue with "the widely preached equation of Judaism and rationalism," which he sees as "an intellectual evasion of the profound difficulties and paradoxes of Jewish faith, belief, and observance." It is not enough to be Jewish because Judaism makes sense, Heschel believes. Rather, he wants to wrestle with exactly those elements that do not make sense, that remain unprovable and impractical.

To this end, Heschel employs a literary style that is a hybrid of rational argument and emotional exhortation. A descendant of one of the greatest Hasidic rabbis, Dov Baer of Mezritch, he draws on the emotional and mystical strands of Hasidic tradition. Yet he is also learned in modern philosophy, and he knows that he is living in an age predisposed to accept scientific judgments over religious ones. The tacit premise of *God in Search of Man* is that to be a faithful Jew in the mid-twentieth century is to court skepticism, even from one's own rational mind.

Heschel faces this challenge much more directly than Soloveitchik in *Halakhic Man*. For Soloveitchik, the historical truth of the Torah is axiomatic. Heschel, on the other hand, takes seriously the modern mind's reservations about the very first steps of Jewish belief. But he doesn't believe that Jews can be argued into believing in God or practicing Judaism. Rather, the core of his teaching is that the existence of God is something that every person must experience in order to know it. We don't come to know that God exists in the way we know that two plus two equals four, through irrefutable logical argument. Rather, we know it in the way we know that we are happy or sad or in love: God is something that happens to us. In particular, God comes to us when we experience what Heschel calls "wonder or radical amazement," an overwhelming sense of the mystery and majesty of being. But for this to happen, we have to remain open to it. That is the message of Heschel's title: it is not we who are looking for an absent God, but God who is looking for his absent people, ready to enter our lives if we are willing to let him.

But how can a Jew begin to hear God's call? Heschel explains that there are "three trails that lead to Him," which he calls worship, learning, and action. "The first is the way of sensing the presence of God in the world, in things," Heschel writes; "the second is the way of sensing His presence in the Bible; the third is the way of sensing His presence in sacred deeds," that is, in Jewish observance. This three-part division provides the key to the plan of *God in Search of Man*, which is what Heschel's subtitle calls "a philosophy of Judaism." But this is not philosophy in the sense that Cohen practiced it, a matter of rigorous conceptual analysis. Rather, in keeping with his understanding of religion as experience, Heschel aims to encourage the reader's exploration of Judaism and remove the obstacles in his path.

The first step in this journey is to humble the unjustified arrogance of reason. The beginning of wisdom is the recognition that our understanding is sharply limited: there is much more to being and the universe than we know, or can know. "Being is mysterious," Heschel writes, quoting Ecclesiastes: "That which is, is far off and deep, exceedingly deep." Science can tell us a great deal about the way things act, but it can't solve the mystery of why anything exists in the first place. That is a religious question, and religious belief is born in those moments when the mystery of being becomes unignorable.

That is why the primary religious experience, for Heschel, is awe, which he defines as "a way of being in rapport with the mystery of all reality." We may not be able to explain why we know that God is present in moments of awe, but we are still certain that he is. Nor can one person convince another of the truth of this experience; rather, "every man has to find it himself." In this way, Heschel removes the question of the existence of God from the realm of rational debate, where skeptics have the advantage, and makes it a subjective or existential matter, something that can only be known from the inside. For those who cannot find God, Heschel has a kind of contemptuous pity, but he denies that their lack of insight constitutes any kind of proof.

Awe is susceptible of different interpretations. Contemplating the mystery of the universe might well lead some people to pantheism, the belief that the world itself is divine. But Judaism teaches that God is transcendent, above and beyond the world he created. For awe to turn into Jewish faith, it must recognize that our love and gratitude is due to the Creator, who is not just a force of nature but a being with a mysterious kind of life. As Heschel puts it, God is not a "concept" but a "concern."

The great problem for faith is that our sense of the nearness of God is transient. How can the Jew sustain his certainty in moments when God feels far away? For Heschel, precisely this is the purpose of Judaism: "The essence of Jewish religious thinking does not lie in entertaining a concept of God but in the ability to articulate a memory of moments of illumination by His presence." What is true in the life of the individual believer is also true of the history of the Jewish people. God is no longer immediately present to us, but there was a time in the past when he did appear, and the Bible is the record of those appearances. For Heschel, the fact of revelation underscores that the God of Judaism is not, like the gods of polytheism or pantheism, identifiable with natural processes, which are always the same. As opposed to "process," the Jewish God manifests himself in "event"—distinctive moments when he intervenes in the course of history to make himself known.

To put it another way, he is a God not of space but of time. Just as the Jews are a chosen people, Heschel writes, the Torah documents a "chosen time" when God was present in the world, as when he parted the Red Sea or spoke to Moses on Sinai. That is why studying Torah allows the Jew to make contact with the divine and bring it into his own life. "The Jew is never alone in the face of God," Heschel declares, because "the Torah is always with him." This is Heschel's rebuttal to those who would claim that in the twentieth century, Jewish law is obsolete. On the contrary, he says, "a Jew without the Torah is obsolete," since it is the Torah that maintains the Jew's connection with God.

But how do we know that the Torah actually is the record of a divine encounter, rather than a work of human imagination? Doesn't modern science tell us that miracles such as the ones recounted there are impossible, and doesn't modern scholarship analyze the Bible as the work of human beings? Believing in God because of the experience of awe is already a challenge, but believing in Judaism because of the testimony of an ancient text is even more difficult.

To face this difficulty, Heschel appeals once again to the limits of reason. There are many things about the universe that we don't understand, and we can't rule out a priori the possibility that God might speak directly to human beings. As to the claim that he spoke to the Jewish prophets, Heschel falls back on an appeal to the authority of tradition. Surely the prophets themselves believed that God was speaking to them, and who are we to contradict such venerable figures? The wisdom and sublimity of the Bible, in Heschel's view, are themselves proof of its divine spirit, since it would be impossible for human beings to write or even imagine a greater text. When it comes to weighing thousands of years of Jewish belief against the doubts of a modern individual, belief must prevail.

Yet Heschel leaves open the possibility that the Bible can be read allegorically or symbolically. Idolatry of the text has never been a Jewish value: on the contrary, Judaism grows out of the millennia of interpretation that wove the divine text into human lives. We are, in a sense, partners with God in creating the Bible's meaning. But this is only possible if we approach the text in the right spirit of openness and humility. Just as Heschel believes we must experience God in order to know that he exists, so "we must accept the Bible in order to know the Bible."

Accepting the Bible means believing in the truth of the historical events it relates. But it also means heeding what the Bible tells us about God's will for the Jewish people. This is the third of Heschel's three ways of coming to know God, through "sacred deeds" or *mitzvot*; and it is here that he faces his most difficult task as a persuader.

It is comparatively easy to say that you believe in God and even that you accept the Bible, especially if there is some leeway in interpreting it. But Judaism demands more than statements of faith. It is a religion of actions, requiring the Jew to structure his entire life in accordance with the law.

This includes universal ethical principles—do not murder, do not steal—but also particular ritual observances, which modern Jews have widely abandoned. This mass defection from Jewish practice forms the background to modern Jewish theology, which is largely concerned with restoring some kind of authority to a religion that has lost it. For Kaplan, this involved heavily moderating Judaism's demands. For Soloveitchik, by contrast, the failure of most Jews to follow *halakha* can do nothing to impair its authority and majesty.

Heschel is loath to see sacred Jewish traditions that have endured for thousands of years abandoned in his own time. The passion of *God in Search of Man* is partly owed to Heschel's sense that the survival of Judaism itself is at stake in his generation. "We are either the last, the dying, Jews or else we are those who will give new life to our tradition," he writes. Part of this urgency comes from the Holocaust, which for many Jews is evidence against the existence of God, or at least against the idea of God's particular care for his chosen people. Heschel, however, draws the opposite conclusion from the Holocaust. Though it never becomes a central theme of the book, he invokes the Holocaust as support for the idea that man cannot live without belief in God. That God does not intervene to prevent human beings from committing evil is a truth long accepted by the faithful, and need not pose a novel challenge to belief. What is new about the Holocaust is that it destroyed the pretensions of secular modernity, which had claimed to be building a better future by discarding the religious beliefs of the past. Now that progress has issued in catastrophic evil, that claim must be reassessed. A world in which the Holocaust is possible needs God, and Judaism, more urgently than ever.

For just this reason, however, Heschel argues that Judaism must meet the modern Jew halfway. "Vast numbers of Jews loyal to Jewish

law now feel that many of the halakhic restrictions tend to impede
rather than to inspire greater joy and love of God," he acknowledges.
And if the purpose of Judaism is to bring human beings close to
God, then laws that fail to serve this purpose should be reinterpreted.
In a daring theological argument, Heschel proposes that not all of
the Torah is equally applicable at all times in Jewish history. Only a
few *mitzvot* were known to Abraham, who lived long before Moses
received the Torah, yet Abraham was able to serve God. Perhaps
"each word and each deed of the law has its own time in which it can
and must be kept." Delicately, Heschel suggests that the twentieth
century might be another time in which the law must be modified in
order to serve its true purpose.

But this is far from the main thrust of Heschel's argument. The
best way to get Jews to perform *mitzvot*, he believes, is not to make
them fewer or easier, but to restore the meaning they have lost. Here
Heschel employs the same kind of existential argument he made
concerning God and revelation. Jewish observance is not something whose rewards can be logically demonstrated to a nonbeliever;
rather, it is an experience whose holiness is disclosed only to those
who participate in it.

The meaning of Judaism is not found in simply carrying out the
laws. To achieve its true purpose, *halakhah* must be supplemented
by two other key terms. *Kavanah*, usually translated as "intention,"
is for Heschel a form of "attentiveness to God": it is the quality of
deliberate piety without which sacred deeds lose their sacredness. It
is not simply the words of a prayer that matter, as if it were a magic
formula; rather, prayer comes alive when it is spoken with the proper
kavanah. Likewise, Heschel writes that *halakhah* must be supplemented by *agada*, the term used for the non-legal sections of the
Talmud devoted to wisdom, legend, and lore. *Agada*, for Heschel,
stands for "the immeasurable, inward aspect of living," the spirit that
animates the body of the law. Clearly, his own spirit is drawn toward
these passionate, imaginative elements of Judaism.

Yet it would be a mistake, Heschel believes, to seek *agada* and
kavanah without *halakha*, the spirit of the law without its body. The

need to contain feelings in actions and to enliven actions with feelings is what makes Jewish observance beautiful and dramatic. Properly understood, *mitzvot* are not burdensome because they are not dead traditions; they are expressions of living spirit. "Judaism is a reminder that joy is a way to God," Heschel declares, in what could stand as his theological motto. "There is joy in being a Jew, in belonging to Israel, to God, in being able to taste heaven in a sacred deed." The central purpose of *God in Search of Man* is to show the reader that Judaism, even in the twentieth century, can be the medium of such spiritual delight. Neither intellectual skepticism nor the inertia of indifference should prevent the Jew from claiming this heritage. That is the ultimate reason why Jews should remain Jews, even in an era when, as Heschel acknowledges, "there is a high cost of living to be paid by a Jew"—a cost measured in doubt, dread, and, for millions, violent death.

To Mend the World
by Emil Fackenheim

T HE HOLOCAUST WAS AN EVENT OF SUCH TERRIFYING
magnitude that it took American Jewry a generation to begin
to come to terms with it. Soloveitchik, writing in the midst of the
Holocaust, does not directly mention it. Heschel, writing ten years
after the event, takes account of it but does not make it central to his
vision of Judaism. Most historians agree that it was not until the Six-
Day War, fought by Israel in 1967, that the Holocaust moved to the
center of American Jewish thought and identity, where it remains to
this day. The prospect of Israel's defeat leading to a second genocide,
followed by the pride and elation of the Israeli victory, seems to have
allowed Jews to think about the death of the six million in new ways.

One of the intellectual landmarks in this process came in the
spring of 1967, shortly before the Six-Day War, when the philosopher Emil Fackenheim delivered an address in which he introduced
the idea of "the 614th commandment." Traditionally, Judaism enu-
merates 613 *mitzvot* in the Torah. But the Holocaust, Fackenheim
argued, had given Jews a moral imperative so urgent as to qualify
as a new *mitzva*: "Thou shalt not give Hitler posthumous victories."
This formula is open to multiple interpretations, but for Fackenheim
it meant above all that Jews must ensure the continued existence of
Judaism and the Jewish people.

Fackenheim himself was a refugee from Nazism. Born in Germany
in 1916, he was held in a concentration camp after Kristallnacht, but
was able to escape to England and then Canada, where he completed

his education and spent most of his subsequent academic career. A Reform rabbi as well as a professor, he recognized that a more Orthodox theologian would never claim to be able to add to the number of God's commandments revealed to Moses on Sinai. "What commandment can be ranked with Sinai and Revelation, however 'liberally' the two are understood?" he writes. "Yet to stay with the 613 now proved impossible . . . To deny Hitler the posthumous victory of destroying this faith was a moral-religious commandment."

For Fackenheim, this was more than hyperbole. It was a way of recognizing that the Holocaust was one of the most important events in Jewish history, comparable in its theological implications to Sinai itself. If Sinai marked the beginning of the covenant between God and Israel, the Holocaust might well look like the annulment of that covenant. This makes it fundamentally different from the many other persecutions and massacres that the Jewish people has endured over its long history. "For Judaism," Fackenheim writes, "the Holocaust is a destruction without adequate precedent. It is new."

Fackenheim explored the implications of that unprecedented newness in his 1982 book *To Mend the World: Foundations of Post-Holocaust Jewish Thought*, one of the most important works of what has become known as Holocaust theology. The title alludes to the concept of *tikkun olam*, the repair of the world, which has a long history as a legal, mystical, and political idea in Judaism. *Tikkun*, repair, and *teshuva*, return, are fundamental terms in Fackenheim's thought, pointing the way toward a potential recovery of Jewish faith after the Holocaust. But it is not until the end of the book that they come into focus. That is because Fackenheim believes it is wrong to try to hurry past the "rupture" of the Holocaust in order to begin the work of overcoming it. Indeed, such overcoming is, strictly speaking, impossible. Only by fully thinking through the magnitude of the rupture, and incorporating it into the future of Jewish belief, might it be possible to fulfill the 614th commandment.

The Holocaust may not mean the end of Judaism, but Fackenheim begins from the premise that it is the end of a major phase in Jewish history—what he calls Exile Judaism, which until the twentieth cen-

tury seemed like the only possible Judaism. This is the faith formu-
lated by the rabbinic sages following the destruction of the Temple
in the year 70 CE, and the ensuing expulsion of the Jews from Judea
by the Roman emperor Hadrian in the year 135. Those events might
well have spelled the end of Judaism altogether, since they removed
from Jewish life two things that had always defined it: a territorial
homeland and a center of divine worship.

In order to survive, Exile Judaism had to address these absences.
Pragmatically, this involved shifting the basis of Jewish devotion
from pilgrimage and sacrifice to prayer and legal study. Theologically, Fackenheim writes, it meant embracing three central convictions. First, the exile was a justified punishment for the sins of the
Jewish people. Second, this punishment did not mean that God had
abandoned his relationship with Israel; he continued to dwell with
them even in exile from the Holy Land. And third, the exile would
not last forever. Jews maintained a messianic hope that at the end of
days, they would be redeemed and return to their land.

For Fackenheim, these beliefs meant that Exile Judaism was theologically unaffected by the actual experiences of the Jewish people
as they moved from place to place through the ages. "The normative
thought of rabbinic Judaism," he writes, holds that "nothing decisive
has occurred, or can occur, between Sinai and the Messianic Days."
Torments like the expulsion from Spain in 1492 or the Chmielnicki
massacres of the seventeenth century demonstrated the misery of
exile in especially acute ways, but they did not change the way Jews
thought about their relationship to God. When Jews died violently
at the hands of their enemies, they did so as martyrs, for the purpose
of *kiddush hashem*, sanctification of the name of God.

For many Jews, the principles of Exile Judaism are still in force
today, even despite the Holocaust. That explains why, as Fackenheim points out, "Jewish thinkers of unquestionable Jewish authenticity such as Martin Buber and Abraham Joshua Heschel said little
about the Holocaust—and that little with great reluctance." However
deeply the Holocaust damaged the Jewish people, for these thinkers
it did not fundamentally change Judaism. Rather, they believed that

the important task after the Holocaust was to "nurture" Jewish tradition, "to bring to life its wisdom, its faith, its God."

But for Fackenheim this is a kind of evasion, because he believes
that Exile Judaism is no longer possible. It died exactly eighteen hundred years after it began, in 1935, the year that the Nazis promulgated
the Nuremberg Laws. These laws, which deprived Jews of German
citizenship, were the first step on the path that led to the Holocaust.
And the Holocaust cannot be compared with earlier examples of
Jewish suffering in exile because it is unique, not just in Jewish but
in world history. Its evil must permanently change the way we think
about both humanity and God.

Fackenheim knew that not everyone saw the Holocaust in such
absolute terms. After all, the history of the world is filled with murder, war, and even genocide: just look at the African slave trade, the
extermination of the Native Americans, or Pol Pot's murder of some
three million Cambodians just a few years before the publication of
To Mend the World. Why is the Holocaust what Fackenheim calls,
using a Latin term, a *novum*, a "new thing"?

For Judaism, he argues, the Holocaust is new because it cannot be
understood according to the traditional vocabulary of Jewish martyrdom. The six million Jews killed by the Nazis and their helpers did
not choose to die for the sake of God or Jewishness, because nothing
they could have done would have saved their lives. To choose death
over conversion is a *kiddush hashem*, but the Nazis' racialized anti-
Semitism made it impossible for a Jew ever to stop being a Jew. In
this sense, Fackenheim writes, "Hitler murdered not only Jews but
Jewish martyrdom." The Holocaust took away the possibility of giving Jewish death meaning.

In a wider historical and moral perspective, too, Fackenheim
believes that the Holocaust is a *novum*. It goes beyond other cases of
mass murder in its goal—total extermination of the Jewish people,
without a single survivor anywhere—and in its achievement—one-
third of the world's Jewish population murdered, including almost
all of the most traditionally pious, whom Fackenheim calls "the most
Jewish of Jews." It was unique in its combination of irrationality—

the Nazis placed killing Jews above all other goals, even their own survival—and rationality—the genocide was not a spontaneous orgy of violence by sadists, but the work of a systematic bureaucracy manned by fairly ordinary officials, as Hannah Arendt had argued in *Eichmann in Jerusalem.*

Finally, the Holocaust was unique because of what Fackenheim calls the "anti-world" created in Auschwitz, a place where all human logic and moral value was turned upside down. For him, the prisoners that Primo Levi and others referred to as *"musselmen"*—the living dead, unable to think or feel—disprove the traditional philosophical idea that there is an inviolable core of human dignity. Modern, progressive thinkers believed that human beings were "infinitely perfectible," capable of becoming better and better as society improved. But the unthinkable cruelty of the perpetrators and the unimaginable suffering of the victims of Auschwitz show that humanity also has an "infinite malleability for evil" which could not have been imagined in advance.

In this sense, the Holocaust challenges not only Exile Judaism but also the Western philosophical tradition. Much of *To Mend the World* is devoted to a close analysis of the thought of philosophers whose ideas about religion, history, and ethics must be reassessed in the light of the Holocaust. Fackenheim points, for example, to the sublime moral philosophy of Kant, whose categorical imperative held that all human beings are of infinite worth, and so they must be treated as ends in themselves, not means to an end. "Kant, in short, *believes* in humanity," Fackenheim writes. *"But is that belief warranted?"* In Kant's own age, the late eighteenth century, the idea of the inextinguishable dignity and worth of humankind "could not be verified," but it was at least possible to have faith in it. "Not until the advent of the Holocaust world," however, "was this belief *refuted.*"

Unlike some other Holocaust theologians, however, Fackenheim does not finally embrace nihilism. His 614th commandment expresses his belief that Judaism can and must survive. Yet this cannot be the same Judaism that sustained the Jewish people for two millennia of exile. For one thing, the prospect of messianic redemption, once a cornerstone of Jewish faith, has become permanently problematic. "A Messiah that can come yet at Auschwitz did not come is himself inaccessible," Fackenheim writes. Indeed, the Jew can no longer fully believe that the existence of the world is good, as God himself declared after the sixth day of Creation. Today, the Jew must always ask, "Why does anything—Man, World, God—still exist?"

Throughout *To Mend the World*, Fackenheim insists that an authentic reckoning with the Holocaust allows no retreat to comfortable certainties. Even to speak of overcoming the Holocaust is blasphemous: "Where the Holocaust is there is no overcoming, and where there is an overcoming the Holocaust is not." How, then, can the Jew reconcile the fathomless evil of the world with the need to keep living? To put the question in its most basic terms, how do Jews continue to bear children in a world where Auschwitz happened, and therefore could happen again?

Fackenheim's answer is radically simple. The only way we know that *tikkun*, repair, is still possible is because the victims of the Holocaust themselves practiced it. The abstract resources of philosophy and theology cannot help us; rather, we must attend to the stories of the ordinary people who, in the midst of the worst torture and suffering, somehow managed to maintain their commitment to life and to Judaism. Such victims are not martyrs in the traditional sense. What was possible for them was not *kiddush hashem*, sanctification of God's name, but rather what one rabbi in the Warsaw Ghetto called *kiddush hachayim*, sanctification of life. Simply attempting to live was itself a holy deed in the face of the Nazis' determination to annihilate Jewish lives.

In his chapter on "The Spectrum of Resistance During the Holocaust," Fackenheim gives several examples of such sanctification. In Buchenwald, a group of Hasidim once exchanged four rations of bread—an amount that could make the difference between survival and starvation—for a pair of *tefillin* that a Ukrainian guard had found. Some women in Auschwitz gave birth to children, even managing to hide them and raise them. These small, individual acts are not what we ordinarily think of as resistance to Nazism, but for

Fackenheim they belong on the same "spectrum of resistance" as the mighty Allied armies that succeeded in destroying the Third Reich. All of them were ways of resisting Hitler, refusing to give him the victories that he wanted: the conquest of Europe, the destruction of the Jews, the annihilation of the human spirit.

Here, then, is Fackenheim's answer to the problem of how Jews can observe the 614th commandment. As he puts it, "a *Tikkun* here and now is mandatory because a *Tikkun* there and then was possible." But this repair can only ever be "fragmentary," because we cannot return, after the Holocaust, to the tenets of Exile Judaism— neither its messianic faith nor its accommodation to the condition of exile and powerlessness.

What does this mean in concrete terms? For Fackenheim, a large part of the answer has to do with the State of Israel. In *To Mend the World*, we see at work the transformation of Israel into one of the pillars of late twentieth-century Judaism—a theologization of the state that Herzl and the early political Zionists could not have imagined. "Israel," as Fackenheim puts it, is "an orienting reality for all Jewish and indeed all post-Holocaust thought."

That is because the Jewish state is the ultimate example of the 614th commandment in action. The ability of the Jewish people to create a country of their own just three years after the Holocaust, and to sustain it against steep odds through a series of wars, refutes the Hitlerian wish for the Jews to disappear. While Fackenheim never actually calls the state miraculous, he comes close in describing it as "an ontological near-impossibility": the sheer unlikeliness of its existence creates a claim on the Jewish people. He even paraphrases Voltaire's famous quip that if God did not exist, it would be necessary to invent him: "If in our time there were no State of Israel, it would be religious necessity, with or without the help of God, to create it."

It follows that in a post-Holocaust world, anti-Zionism is no longer a legitimate political position for Jews (or, for that matter, for Christians). Whereas Hermann Cohen, early in the twentieth century, could maintain that Judaism's ethical mission required that Jews live in Diaspora, the Holocaust had rendered this idea shameful, at least in Fackenheim's view. The most basic requirement of Judaism is that Jews continue to survive, and the Holocaust has proved that they cannot rely on the gentile world to guarantee their survival. This marks another break with Exile Judaism, which believed that, despite all its ordeals, a "holy remnant" of the Jewish people would always survive. The Holocaust showed that this cannot be taken on trust. If Judaism is to live at all, it has to live by its own strength, and only in Israel has Jewish strength become actual. The *tikkun* represented by the State of Israel is, Fackenheim acknowledges, "fragmentary" and full of risk; but it remains the Jews' best prospect for mending a broken world.

Standing Again at Sinai
by Judith Plaskow

T HOUGH THE CHALLENGE OF MODERNITY FORCED
these Jewish theologians to think about Judaism in radical new
ways, one thing about them was utterly traditional: they were all
men. Indeed, from the beginning of Judaism until the mid-twentieth
century, virtually every figure of authority in Jewish thought was
male. There were rare exceptions, like Bruriah, the wife of the Talmudic authority Rabbi Meir, who is described as holding her own in
the legal debates of the rabbinic sages. But for the most part, Jewish
women were not given access to the languages and texts of Jewish
law, philosophy, and theology.

In the last part of the twentieth century, thanks to the transformation of American society by the feminist movement, Reform and
Conservative synagogues began to welcome women as clergy. The
first Jewish woman to occupy a congregational pulpit anywhere in
the world was Sally Pricsand, an American, who was ordained by
the Reform seminary Hebrew Union College in 1972. And while
Orthodox women can't be ordained as rabbis, some modern Orthodox communities offer women opportunities for religious study and
communal leadership that would have been unimaginable for most
of Jewish history.

In her 1990 book *Standing Again at Sinai*, however, the feminist
theologian Judith Plaskow proposes that the transformation of Judaism must go further. To take feminism seriously, Plaskow argues in
this landmark work, means more than simply admitting women

to leadership roles in a tradition that had always been patriarchal. "The need for a feminist Judaism," she writes, "begins with hearing silence"—the missing voices of the Jewish women who, since biblical times, had not been allowed to participate in defining what Judaism is. What would Judaism look like, Plaskow wonders, if women had played an equal role with men in shaping its beliefs, values, and practices?

Plaskow's simple innovation is to define "the Jewish people," for whom the Jewish religion exists, as *all* the people—women as well as men. This was a revolutionary idea, since the normative Jew addressed by Jewish text and law has always been a man. God, in the Bible and in Jewish prayers, is always referred to by male pronouns and titles such as "father" and "king." Men are the bearers of most of the *mitzvot*, since Jewish law exempts women from having to fulfill time-bound positive commandments, on the theory that their duties in the home make regular prayer, for instance, impossible. (It is for this reason that Jewish men traditionally recited a daily prayer thanking God that they were not created as women.) In Orthodox Judaism, women cannot read publicly from the Torah, be counted in a minyan (the quorum of ten required for prayer), or sit among men in the synagogue.

It is true that women are the subjects of important areas of Jewish law having to do with marriage, divorce, and sexuality. But as Plaskow points out, in the Mishnah, the central compendium of Jewish law, these are mostly found in the division called *Nashim*, "Women"—a title which implies that all the rest of the laws have to do with men. "If the Mishnah is accepted as normative and perceived simply as 'Torah,' then its definition of women as Other is incorporated into Jewish life, and its patriarchal perspective is assumed to reflect the divine will," Plaskow argues.

But "no verse in the Torah is more disturbing to the feminist," Plaskow writes, than Exodus 19:15. This chapter relates the most important event in Jewish history: the appearance of God on Mount Sinai and the institution of the covenant between Him and the Jewish people. "You shall be unto me a kingdom of priests and a holy nation," God promises, and the people respond, "All that the Lord has spoken we will do." Yet as Moses instructs the Israelites how to purify themselves for God's appearance, he says: "Be ready for the third day; do not go near a woman." All of the people are present at Sinai, yet the words of Moses and God seem to be addressed only to the men.

It is against this implication that Plaskow sets her title, *Standing Again at Sinai*. If the patriarchal bias in Judaism begins at the beginning, then a feminist Judaism must return to that beginning and change it. Of course, Jews only have the freedom to reshape Torah if it is a human document, rather than the literal word of God. For Plaskow, as for Kaplan and other modern theologians, the Bible is not a true record but a sacred myth that expresses the moral insights and spiritual yearnings of the ancient Israelites—what she calls their "Godwrestling," their attempt to come to terms with the divine. As such, it speaks in the vocabulary of its own time, which was deeply sexist.

As Plaskow points out, Judaism has already evolved in profound ways from the days of the patriarchs. After the destruction of the Temple, it changed from a national faith based on cult and sacrifice to a diasporic religion based on prayer and law. Modernity has changed the Jewish people just as profoundly as exile once did; so why should we not take the opportunity, and the responsibility, to create a new, post-rabbinic Judaism, one that will incorporate feminist thinking into its core concepts? In this way, Plaskow arrives by a very different route at the same destination as Fackenheim, who believed that Exile Judaism had come to an end in his time.

Jewish philosophers have long dismissed the notion that a transcendent God could have a body or a gender. But the idea persists in the language Jews use every day, and as Plaskow notes, proposals to change that language often meet with fierce opposition. If God is genderless and all descriptions of God are necessarily metaphorical, there seems to be no good reason why God couldn't be addressed as "she," "mother," or "queen." Yet Cynthia Ozick, in an essay Plaskow quotes, saw such a proposal as a deep betrayal of Jewish monothe-

ism: "Millennia after the cleansing purity of Abraham's vision of the
One Creator, a return to Astarte, Hera, Juno, Venus, and all their
proliferating sisterhood?" Ozick demands incredulously.

Plaskow is undeterred by such objections. It is true, she writes, that
biblical Judaism was born out of a struggle against paganism and
nature-worship. The prophets repeatedly chastise the Israelites for
backsliding into worship of the Canaanite god Baal, erecting private
altars and praying in sacred groves, even consorting with sacred prostitutes and sacrificing their children to Moloch. But, Plaskow asks,
are we so certain that the victory of the Jewish God over his pagan
competitors was a good thing? After all, the victory of monotheism
over polytheism was also a victory of a male deity over female dei-
ties. Perhaps we need to reclaim polytheism as part of the heritage of
Jewish women: this might be a way of seeing "a larger Torah behind
the Torah," rather than simply rejecting polytheism as "utterly foreign and other."

From the point of view of normative Judaism, such a line of thinking is entirely heretical. But Plaskow begins from the premise that
normative Judaism must be rejected, because it is a religion shaped
exclusively by men. Indeed, her critique of Judaism goes much deeper
than its treatment of women—or, rather, its treatment of women
serves as a key to unlock the basic error in its worldview, which is its
embrace of dominance and hierarchy. Judaism is deeply concerned
with distinctions: it distinguishes between the Jewish people and the
nations of the world, between the sabbath and the days of the week,
between the Land of Israel and the rest of the globe, between ritual
purity and impurity, between kosher and forbidden food. In each of
these binaries, one is sacred and the other profane or taboo.

But what if this kind of thinking—what Plaskow calls "the suspicion and ranking of difference"—is the source of Judaism's elevation
of men and masculinity and its denigration of women and femininity?
If so, then Jewish feminism has an enormous task of reconstruction
to perform: "Jewish feminists cannot transform the place of women's
difference within the people of Israel without addressing the larger
system of separations in which it is embedded." And the cornerstone

of that system is the idea of Jewish chosenness—a concept that lay at the heart of Jewish identity until modern times, when emancipation and assimilation made it seem dubious, even dangerous. For Plaskow, chosenness must be rejected in favor of a more modest conception of Jewish "distinctness," a way of thinking about difference that rejects ideas of superiority and inferiority.

If the goal of Jewish feminism is to abolish domination, however, it cannot avoid a reckoning with the greatest dominator of all: the Jewish God. Doing away with gendered pronouns for God is only the first step in a process that must ultimately confront the inherently masculinist idea of God as a "dominating Other," whose relationship with human beings is "profoundly asymmetrical." "God's maleness connotes power," Plaskow observes, "and God's power is an extension of his maleness." If so, then eliminating his maleness means eliminating his power, at least if that is understood as "power over"—the kind wielded by a patriarch or a king.

In place of such a God, Plaskow writes, Jewish feminists have already begun to experiment with other divine metaphors. Some of these are drawn from pagan goddess-worship, others from pantheistic nature-worship; crucially, they affirm "that the earth is holy and that all parts of creation have intrinsic value." Here Plaskow is directly opposed to Cohen, who saw monotheism as the particular enemy of pantheism, crediting Judaism with the key insight that God is above the world, not within it. For her, on the contrary, God should be understood not as the ruler of the universe but as a "lover, friend, companion, cocreator."

Such a transformation in the Jewish notion of God also requires, and facilitates, a transformation in the way Jews think about sexuality. Plaskow observes that rabbinic Judaism speaks about sexuality in paradoxical ways. The Talmud details women's right to sexual pleasure and makes sex between husband and wife a positive duty. Chastity is contrary to God's first commandment, "Be fruitful and multiply." At the same time, Jewish tradition is highly suspicious of any kind of sexuality that deviates from the married, heterosexual norm. Even within marriage, sex is limited by the ritual impurity that attaches to women during their menstrual period. There is no shortage of rabbinic sources that speak of women as temptations and snares for men, encouraging separation of the sexes as much as possible. For Plaskow, this puritanism is a key part of Judaism's oppressive legacy toward women. She calls for its replacement by a sex-positive ethic that sees eroticism as a key part of both individual and communal life.

Judaism without chosenness, God without majesty, sacredness without hierarchy, sex without taboo: Plaskow's feminist theology creates what is practically a new religion, in which many of the beliefs and certainties of earlier Jewish thinkers are turned upside down. In doing so, she demonstrates a commitment to justice for women that is also a profoundly American commitment to freedom and equality. For some feminists, she knows, such a difficult reconstruction of Judaism might seem like a waste of time. It might be easier to simply reject it as a patriarchal throwback and start over with a new faith, or do without faith altogether. Yet as *Standing Again at Sinai* shows on every page, Plaskow remains committed to the task of rehabilitating Judaism: "I affirm my own Jewishness as a central part of my identity," she writes. Indeed, it is because she belongs to Judaism and it belongs to her that it is possible, and necessary, for her to give it a new form and content—a conviction she shares with most of the great Jewish writers of the twentieth century.

SELECT BIBLIOGRAPHY

EUROPE: THE FUTURE DISAPPEARS

Babel, Isaac. *Red Cavalry and Other Stories*. Translated by David McDuff. London: Penguin Classics, 2005.

Frank, Anne. *The Diary of a Young Girl: The Definitive Edition*. Edited by Otto Frank and Mirjam Pressler. Translated by Susan Massotty. New York: Bantam, 1997.

Franklin, Ruth. *A Thousand Darknesses: Lies and Truth in Holocaust Fiction*. New York: Oxford University Press, 2010.

Hilberg, Raul. *The Destruction of the European Jews*. One-volume edition. New York: Holmes and Meier, 1985.

Kafka, Franz. *The Trial*. Translated by Breon Mitchell. New York: Schocken, 1998.

Klemperer, Victor. *I Will Bear Witness: A Diary of the Nazi Years, 1933–1941*. Translated by Martin Chalmers. New York: Modern Library, 1998.

———. *I Will Bear Witness: A Diary of the Nazi Years, 1942–1945*. Translated by Martin Chalmers. New York: Modern Library, 2001.

Levi, Primo. *Survival in Auschwitz*. Translated by Stuart Woolf. New York: Touchstone, 1996.

Sachar, Howard M. *Dreamland: Europeans and Jews in the Aftermath of the Great War*. New York: Alfred A. Knopf, 2002.

Schnitzler, Arthur. *The Road to the Open*. Translated by Horace Samuel. London: Howard Latimer, 1913.

Singer, Isaac Bashevis. *Satan in Goray*. Translated by Jacob Sloan. New York: Farrar, Straus and Giroux, 1996.

Wiesel, Elie. *Night*. Translated by Marion Wiesel. New York: Hill and Wang, 2006.

AMERICA: AT HOME IN EXILE

Bellow, Saul. *The Adventures of Augie March*. New York: Penguin Classics, 2006.

———. *The Victim*. Penguin Classics, 2010.

Cahan, Abraham. *The Rise of David Levinsky*. New York: Penguin Classics, 1993.

Howe, Irving. *World of Our Fathers*. New York: Galahad Books, 1994.

Kazin, Alfred. *A Walker in the City*. New York: Harcourt Brace Jovanovich, 1969.

Kushner, Tony. *Angels in America: Revised and Complete Edition*. New York: Theatre Communications Group, 2013.

Malamud, Bernard. *The Complete Stories*. New York: Farrar, Straus and Giroux, 1997.

Ozick, Cynthia. *Collected Stories*. London: Phoenix, 2007.

———. *Art and Ardor*. New York: Alfred A. Knopf, 1983.

Roth, Philip. *Goodbye, Columbus*. New York: Vintage, 1993.

———. *Portnoy's Complaint*. New York: Vintage, 1994.

Sarna, Jonathan. *American Judaism: A History*. New Haven, CT: Yale University Press, 2004.

Schwartz, Delmore. *In Dreams Begin Responsibilities and Other Stories*. New York: New Directions, 1978.

Yezierska, Anzia. *Bread Givers*. New York: Persea Books, 2003.

ISRAEL: LIFE IN A DREAM

Agnon, S. Y. *Only Yesterday*. Translated by Barbara Harshav. Princeton, NJ: Princeton University Press, 2000.

Amichai, Yehuda. *The Poetry of Yehuda Amichai*. Edited by Robert Alter. New York: Farrar, Straus and Giroux, 2015.

Castel-Bloom, Orly. *Dolly City*. Translated by Dalya Bilu. Champaign, IL: Dalkey Archive Press, 2010.

Elon, Amos. *The Israelis: Founders and Sons*. New York: Holt, Rinehart and Winston, 1971.

Grossman, David. *See Under: Love*. Translated by Betsy Rosenberg. New York: Farrar, Straus and Giroux, 1989.

Hertzberg, Arthur, ed. *The Zionist Idea: A Historical Analysis and Reader*. 2nd ed. Philadelphia: Jewish Publication Society, 1997.

Morris, Benny. *1948: The First Arab-Israeli War*. New Haven, CT: Yale University Press, 2008.

Oz, Amos. *A Tale of Love and Darkness*. Translated by Nicholas de Lange. New York: Harvest, 2005.

———. *Where the Jackals Howl and Other Stories*. Translated by Nicholas de Lange and Philip Simpson. New York: Harcourt Brace Jovanovich, 1981.

Segev, Tom. *The Seventh Million: The Israelis and the Holocaust*. Translated by Haim Watzman. New York: Hill and Wang, 1993.

Shapira, Anita. *Israel: A History*. Translated by Anthony Berris. Waltham, MA: Brandeis University Press, 2012.

Yehoshua, A. B. *Mr. Mani*. Translated by Hillel Halkin. New York: Harvest, 1992.

Yizhar, S. *Khirbet Khizeh*. Translated by Nicholas de Lange and Yaacob Dweck. New York: Farrar, Straus and Giroux, 2014.

MAKING JUDAISM MODERN

Buber, Martin, *On Judaism*. Edited by Nahum N. Glatzer. New York: Schocken, 1996.

Cohen, Hermann. *Religion of Reason out of the Sources of Judaism*. Translated by Simon Kaplan. Atlanta, GA: Scholars' Press, 1995.

Fackenheim, Emil. *To Mend the World: Foundations of Post-Holocaust Jewish Thought*. Bloomington: Indiana University Press, 1994.

Heschel, Abraham Joshua. *God in Search of Man: A Philosophy of Judaism*. New York: Farrar, Straus and Giroux, 1976.

Kaplan, Mordecai M. *Judaism as a Civilization*. New York: Reconstructionist Press, 1957.

Mendes-Flohr, Paul, and Reinharz, Jehuda, eds. *The Jew in the Modern World: A Documentary History.* 2nd ed. New York: Oxford University Press, 1995.

Plaskow, Judith. *Standing Again at Sinai: Judaism from a Feminist Perspective.* New York: HarperOne, 1991.

Soloveitchik, Joseph B. *Halakhic Man.* Translated by Lawrence Kaplan. Philadelphia: Jewish Publication Society, 1983.

INDEX